A
DIFFERENT
KIND OF
DAUGHTER

*The Girl Who Hid From
the Taliban in Plain Sight*

MARIA TOORPAKAI

with Katharine Holstein

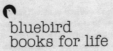
bluebird
books for life

First published in the UK 2016 by Bluebird

This paperback edition published 2017 by Bluebird
an imprint of Pan Macmillan
20 New Wharf Road, London N1 9RR
Associated companies throughout the world
www.panmacmillan.com

ISBN 978-1-5098-0081-0

1 3 5 7 9 8 6 4 2

A CIP catalogue record for this book is available from the British Library.

Typeset by Ellipsis Digital Limited, Glasgow
Printed and bound by CPI Group (UK) Ltd, Croydon

Visit www.panmacmillan.com to read more about all our books
and to buy them. You will also find features, author interviews and
news of any author events, and you can sign up for e-newsletters
so that you're always first to hear about our new releases.

For every woman and child of war and oppression
the world over, struggling to play and learn in peace.
May these pages help to light your dark paths to freedom.

Contents

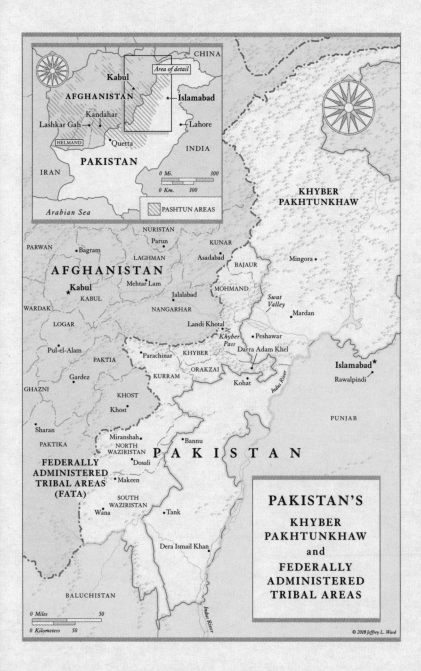

CHINA

Area of detail

Kabul

AFGHANISTAN

★ **Islamabad**

Kandahar

Lashkar Gah

● Lahore

HELMAND

● Quetta

INDIA

PAKISTAN

IRAN

0 Mi.   300

0 Km.   300

Arabian Sea

▨ PASHTUN AREAS

KHYBER
PAKHTUNKHAW

NURISTAN

PARWAN   Parun   KUNAR

● Bagram   LAGHMAN   Asadabad ●   Mingora ●

AFGHANISTAN   BAJAUR

Kabul ★   Mehtar Lam   MOHMAND   *Swat
Valley*   Mardan ●

KABUL   Jalalabad ●

WARDAK   NANGARHAR   Landi Khotal ●

LOGAR   *Khyber
Pass*   ● Peshawar

Pul-el-Alam ●   Parachinar ●   Darra Adam Khel

PAKTIA   KHYBER   **Islamabad** ★

Gardez ●   ORAKZAI   Rawalpindi ●

KURRAM   Kohat ●

GHAZNI   KHOST   *Indus River*

Khost ●   PUNJAB

Sharan ●   ● Bannu

PAKTIKA   Miranshah ●   P A K I S T A N

NORTH
WAZIRISTAN

FEDERALLY   Dosali ●
ADMINISTERED
TRIBAL AREAS   ● Makeen
(FATA)   SOUTH
WAZIRISTAN

Wana ●   ● Tank

Dera Ismail Khan ●

PAKISTAN'S

**KHYBER
PAKHTUNKHAW**
and
**FEDERALLY
ADMINISTERED
TRIBAL AREAS**

BALUCHISTAN

0 Miles   50

0 Kilometers   50   *Indus River*

© 2016 Jeffrey L. Ward

Prologue: A Prophecy

They send girls like me to the crazy house—or simply stone us to death. Lucky girls might get married off to a rival clan, in the hope of tainting the tribe's blood. I am the product of one of those punitive tribal marriages. In a sentence meant to damn them both, my maverick mother married my renegade father having never laid eyes on him until their wedding. The tribal elders did not foresee the instant love match or the combined force of my parents' courage and shared ideals. They certainly did not foresee me. And they could not stop our brazen family of Pashtun rebels from multiplying.

Even among my own, I was considered a different kind of daughter. I hated dolls, was miserable wearing fancy dresses, and rejected anything remotely feminine. My ambition would never come to life in a kitchen, or flourish within the four walls of our home. Just to stay sane, I needed to be outside, under the open sky and running free—the very thing that tribal law forbade.

When I was still very little, my father borrowed an old Zenith television set and VCR and came home from the local bazaar with a used video about the hunting tactics of lions. Buried in that video, as in everything my father showed us, whether on television screens or in old books, was a life lesson that we had to search to find. Sitting on the cool clay floor of our living room, we watched a lion in the heart of the hot African plains stalk a herd of gazelles. The lion is actually a very slow predator, yet it hunts some of the fastest creatures on earth. From the outset, the lion was physically outmatched. Still, hungry as he was, he lounged like a lazy king in swaying grasses, casually surveying his surroundings. Every now and then he got up, stretched, and inched closer to his prey. As the gazelles looked over, he simply stared back with a devil-may-care attitude, betraying nothing of his intent. The gazelles' placid confidence came from the fact that they could so easily outrun the lion, but that false faith in their ability would be their undoing. The lion possessed two game-changing talents—a cut-throat patience and a phenomenal ability to conceal itself. I remember well how the graceful beast leapt out from the grass and dug its teeth and claws into the exposed neck of a stunned gazelle that had been unaware of him sitting there all the while. *How stupid the gazelle was*, I thought, *and how cunning the cat*.

*

Just before my fifth birthday, I complained to my father that I could not suffer another suffocating dress and would prefer to wear loose clothes like the boys I'd watched playing outside in the dirt. He laughed and then told me not to worry. It might have been the yellow T-shirt and shorts he bought for me at the bazaar that set everything in motion. I didn't heed his warning to wear them only within the high walls of our property. And in my part of the world, for a girl to venture out uncovered was *haram*— forbidden, a sin against God.

On the day I wore my yellow outfit, the panorama of peaks and valleys past our front iron gates lured me. It was the first time I'd been alone outside the house, ready to run out under the open sky. With my clean dark hair all coiled and done up in a rainbow of ribbons, I slipped into the blaze of noon, the shirt already sticking to my back, braids and skin dripping sweat. The sun heating my limbs, I stopped for a moment in the courtyard, held out my arms, and experienced a great rush of freedom. I looked down at my legs, seeing the smooth landscape of my own limber form, so often concealed and already going pink. Then I pulled back the latch, pushed open the heavy gate, and bolted. Coming back unobserved, I never told a soul what I'd done.

On a sweltering afternoon, I sat kneeling by a low windowsill, chin cupped in my hand, staring out over the wide river plain behind our house. My mother had put me in a new dress, constellations of beads and silk threads embroidered all over the heavy fabric. It confined me head to toe like a coffin. From outside, I could hear rippling laughter as a group of boys played, running and kicking up clouds of dry dirt that blotted out my view of the serrated horizon. I heard the constant thud of feet kicking a ball, and I felt, as I watched and listened, a sudden fist of intense heat punch at my gut. There were ten of them at least, all dressed in loose clothes, kicking a soccer ball around between the low projections of rock. The ball zigzagged between their nimble feet and I panicked as I sat in the house, suddenly understanding my own fate as though reading my future in a book—embalmed for life in pretty clothes, doomed to either go to school or stay home. In that moment, my heart went to stone. There was no in-between for girls like me who wanted to run outside and play games and sports in the open air. Suddenly I was aware that, despite all my liberal father's efforts, his myths and big maps of the continents, and everything about the wider world he'd tried to teach me, I would never truly be free. In our culture girls remained indoors, quiet and veiled for life.

I didn't think about what I did next. I simply got up, backed away from the sill into cool shadow, tearing off the dress, ripping at the seams, clawing at the arms. Then, in a quiet rampage through the house, I pulled every one of my dresses out of the closets and into the garden. One by one. They were so heavy, it took an entire hour.

The cooking pit under the tree outside was shallow, just four bricks and a few sticks of wood set under a grill, but I knew where my mother kept the kerosene and matches. In a cabinet on a shelf in the kitchen. I moved fast, before I could change my mind, knowing full well that if I allowed myself to think too much, I would stop. Hauling down the full can of kerosene, I dragged it with both hands slowly across the floor without spilling so much as a drop, then out the back door, cutting a long track in the dirt leading straight to the pit. I had already stacked the dresses in a pile—one atop the other—over the cooking bricks, their ornaments reflecting facets of sunlight, fabrics almost leaden. Even when the wind gusted through the garden, the garments remained as still as corpses. Staring at the heap, I hesitated for only a second: it was a shame to incinerate that beauty, and yet to ignore what I knew was to seal my own death sentence. I soaked the clothes in kerosene clear as water and I struck a match. Standing back, I watched the flame fly at my command like a small shooting star.

In a sudden burst, all the air around me raced up, rushing through my hair and stealing my breath, and the stack of dresses suddenly disappeared before me, behind a wall of flames. All those beads and crystals sparked, destroyed in an explosion of hot red embers rising straight into the blue sky, billowing with black smoke. All that bright silken color disintegrated within minutes into browns and blacks. I ran into the house and found my brother's shirt and pants, an outfit we called a *shalwar kameez*, and slipped them on. Then I went to the kitchen and found a sharp knife. In a moment, I was hacking away big chunks of my black hair, tossing the clumps into the flames, which turned them instantly to ash.

My father stood there a long while, watching, though I hadn't seen him, his gaze going from his wild, dancing child to the lifeless heap of dresses. I learned much later that on that hot afternoon, he'd seen another girl in me—the sister he'd failed to save so many years before. From an upstairs window, he'd glimpsed her figure hauling a pair of heavy galvanized buckets full of water across the family courtyard. Then she stopped suddenly and stood strangely still. He saw the first bucket drop, then the second. Spilled river water streamed over the hot stones as the buckets rolled past her feet, the hem of her dress dripping. He heard his sister gasp just once in pain and watched her body fall as though a bolt of lightning had struck her.

By the time he got to her, she was on the ground, the clear sky reflected in the domes of her wide open eyes. She was dead.

People in the village said she'd had damaged arteries or some other defect that made her heart stop beating. My father believed she'd died from nothing more than the great weight of her many sorrows. His sister had been just like me—strong, androgynous and hot-tempered. A tomboy simply could not survive in the cage our culture expected girls to live in.

By the time my father was a man, he'd seen many girls die of their own hand to escape—cousins who poisoned themselves to avoid arranged marriages, others who simply stopped eating until they perished from hunger. Often girls doused themselves in kerosene before lighting a match. Once he'd watched a girl in the village go up like a human torch. When it was over, he'd seen what was left of her charred body. Other girls had done the same, though more often it was done to them, in bride burnings over dowry disputes or as a sentence meted out for some unpardonable sin.

"My sister, was just like you, Maria—strong and different, born of the lion—and they would not let her be."

Then my father approached the burning pit and stepped up to me, laughing. He ran his fingers all through my massacred hair.

"My new son must have a name befitting a great warrior and the battle just won without blood. We will call you Genghis Khan."

Then he leaned down and repeated the name into my left ear—and into my right, he recited the holy *azan*. And Maria was gone.

1. Between the Mountains

Breathtaking mountain chains framed my childhood home, a boundless vista known only as "the Abode of God." They were massive daggers of rock, full of light the color of fire. Nestled between the peaks, hidden in soft pockets, flowed rivers edged with villages made of mud and stone. And above it all, a big blue dome of clear sky stretched out with no end. Across the valleys, where corn grew and sheep grazed, there was sometimes no human in sight. No sound. A person could walk for days across the plains and not see a soul and yet feel God's touch everywhere.

For me, that quiet and beautiful land is heaven. Still, when the world thinks of my home, they envision an outpost of hell. South Waziristan is one of the Federally Administered Tribal Areas of northwest Pakistan, but in reality it governs itself through an ancient system of tyrannical tribal laws. Ax-shaped, its 2,500 square miles of territory cut into the lawless and blood-soaked border of Afghanistan, and it is the present-day head-quarters of the Taliban. My native land is considered the most dangerous place on earth, but it lives in my mind as the tribal home I would go back to without a second thought if I could —if no one there wanted me dead.

In the afternoons of my childhood, a steady breeze blew and the dancing gusts shifted from warm to cool and back again. But as the weather changed, before a storm or as the seasons slid one into the next, a new wind would steal over the mountains, rushing through the peaks with long strips of cloud and wrapping the ranges as though in thick reams of gauze. The nameless foreign scents and, as I imagined, whole invisible worlds carried on that sweet wind dared my mind to roam far beyond our quiet place between the mountains.

That same breeze blew on the day I was born, November 22, 1990, in a village like all the others, quiet and small, an insignificant speck nestled in a wide green valley. My mother, Yasrab, was twenty-six years old and had no help in giving birth to me—not a hospital or a doctor, and no medication of any kind. Neighboring women came and went with cups of cool water, quick whispers, and strips of clean cloth. Men left to pray at the mosque, eat mangoes picked from the wild groves, suck on sugar cubes, and stayed well away. The birthing room was kept dark and no one could hear a sound through the locked door. When it was over, it would not really matter to the clan whether my first cries were hearty or whimpering, or if I was born alive or dead. I came into this world like my sister, Ayesha Gulalai, four years before me—a girl, a blemish on the face of our tribe.

My father, Shams Qayyum Wazir, not yet thirty himself, was a liberated man of noble blood, which meant that he was a renegade among Pashtun men. Shams never once made my sister and me feel inferior to our brother, Taimur Khan, who was born five years before me, or to the twin boys, Sangeen Khan and Babrak Khan, who came as a double blessing when I was four. Unlike in other Pashtun families, where the females were subservient to the males, we all lived within our large mud-brick home as carefree equals. Together, we adhered to our Muslim faith, observing feasts and fasts and praying five times each day, but my father taught us that people the world over found many ways to reach God. My family were freethinkers, and it was that quality that would eventually make us outcasts within our conservative tribe, at the same time as it liberated us.

*

Every inhabitant of Waziristan, North and South, is known as a Wazir; but Wazir is also a name that refers to a sprawling Pashtun tribe among the many that exist in our region, connected by the same Pashto tongue and governed by our Pashtunwali code of honor, the ancestral laws that settle our many blood feuds and rivalries. Though the Wazir are splintered into clans, we come together as one at the hint of a foreign threat. No outside power, however mighty, whatever their modern weaponry, has ever succeeded in subduing the Wazir, or even occupied our ancient territory for a single day. British imperialists, with their experience in conquering and colonizing, unleashed legions of soldiers in uniform over the heart of Waziristan, only to encounter fearless Wazir warriors who forced them back, massacring four hundred British soldiers in a single afternoon, as my father once told me with great smiling pride. To a guest in their home, Pashtuns will offer up their every precious possession, but insult them once and they'll have your severed head in a sack before you so much as blink.

During my childhood, I saw no people but those of my blood, whom I could recognize from just a glance. Even if they could get there, tourists never visited my small thicketed-away portion of the world. Foreigners wouldn't manage a step onto our land before catching every dark Wazir eye. Wazir people are heavyset and tall, with strong limbs and powerful wide hands. In protecting their own, Wazir women are fearless, and their voices thunder up and shake from deep inside their bodies. They used to say that when a Wazir woman spoke, you had better listen. According to one legend, our people are descendants of a famous Pashtun leader called Suleiman and his son, Wazir. From their progeny, many tribes flourished and spread out in vast human tributaries, consuming masses of land where they settled.

On a map, Waziristan appears like a patch sewn to the tattered edges of Pakistan and straddling the Afghan frontier across the Preghal mountain range. Shared bloodlines and an interwoven past, which began in the ancient valleys of Afghanistan, spill across the border straight through the Khyber Pass, part of the Silk Road. No boundary carved into stony ground by any man with the muzzle of a rifle, or painted onto paper with the blood of thousands, could ever cut deep enough to tear apart the tapestry of our common lineage. Everywhere I went, my land, my people, my father reminded me that I was a full-blooded Wazir. I am Wazir before all else.

Every memory I have of our first house, with its mud-covered *pucca* bricks, begins the same way: a slow film opening in the silent morning, warm sunshine thick over everything. In my home there seemed to be a magic in the way the day was born, though it was always the same routine, like a family anthem of activity playing out in every home and in every village. All Pashtun mothers woke very early, before the first crow of the rooster. A tribal mother required no alarm or even much forethought to go about her day. Her duty—to set in motion the rhythm of the family—was as sacred and inborn a task as the beating of her heart, and its momentum pried open her eyes, however tired she might have been from the tedious domestic labor of the previous day. In everything a Wazir mother did, she followed in the long, rutted path of the mothers and grandmothers and great-grandmothers who came before her. She was permitted no other way. She had no access to television or newspapers or magazines, and even radios were scarce. Knowledge itself was a stranger, not to be trusted—or even invited in.

I grew up with the accepted practice that a Pashtun woman remained in the home and only ventured out enveloped in head-to-toe garments called *abayas* or *burqas*, or big shawls called *chadors* and with a male—even just a young boy—watching at her side. To confine a woman in such a way—duty-bound between four walls and hidden away inside her clothes—was known as having her live in purdah, the conservative Muslim custom of secluding women so that they may not be seen by men. This practice was never questioned, in the same way a person would never question the direction of the wind or the rising and setting of the sun. To outsiders, such a tradition seemed like imprisonment, but to me, at least at that time, the women never seemed unhappy dressed that way. There was a simple harmony in knowing what we were all meant to do, where we all belonged. And we did belong—to our station in the home and to our family's position within the tribe. I believed this until I stopped belonging.

I always imagined my mother's waking imbued a living spirit into everyone who woke after her—my father, my sister, my brothers, even me. Before she rose to face her day, there was nothing at all but an infinite void: no sky, no ground, no river, no spooned-out mountain valley to see. My mother's rising seemed to set the sun alight, just as she piled up wood and lit the fires for cooking and fanned the smoke.

All through our mud house my family stirred in their dark, cool rooms that smelled of earth, waking one after the other. For the good of the home, which often contained several multigenerational families, Wazir mothers all rose first and, like a gentle echo, the children next. Men, like long-slumbering beasts, were always last to rouse. The younger men looked after the older ones, shaving their leathery, time-creased faces and tending to their clothes and hair. In Waziristan, many people lived in huge houses, walled-in compounds with extended families all living together under a single roof—aunts and uncles, cousins and grandparents, and, of course, the children. The family always built the house together, and everyone had a position in its hierarchy—the elders at the top—as though the family were a machine, each person a moving part.

Even the birds, which we revered, had a special place among us. We removed a single *pucca* brick from the wall of our front porch so that a pigeon could make its nest there, and one always came and perched, finding its place among us by some instinct that I never understood. Someone always had the duty to break up the hard leftover bread into tiny pieces and feed it to the bird so that it would stay.

In my village, every child had a simple task to complete. The girls always looked after the youngest children before they themselves could eat breakfast. Some walked with big buckets fully half their height to the stream that wandered in a silver thread, bubbling with cool water, past the village. I sometimes ran with my metal bucket, banging it with a broken stick, dry dust from the hot ground swarming around my sandal-clad feet. In the high white sun of summer afternoons, we went to the mountain stream in small, chattering groups and jumped into the rippling water. Lotus-like flowers adorned the surface, floating like delicate teacups.

By the time I came back to our house with the full bucket, heavy and spilling over, my mother would already have finished preparing a breakfast yogurt drink, made from churning fresh milk inside a barrel. There was the smell of fresh naan bread, chopped mint, steaming pots of black tea. As soon as the last men arose, the entire family assembled, the children all happy and loud. The fathers sat quietly on silk mats against the walls. The women moved among the group, slipping between sitting bodies like the stream into whose cold current I'd just lowered my bucket, serving fresh, simple food, such as small bowls of sliced fruit—all of us in the big warm kitchen that was the heart of our house.

But the thing I loved best of all about morning in Waziristan was a quiet ceremony that unfolded the moment I handed over the fresh water, having played my part, which I think of now almost as a sacred duty. With this water, my mother would dampen the earthen floor of our home, dunking her hands in the bucket and letting big silver drops rain down with quick flicks of her fingertips. Once the ground drank in the cool mountain water and it softened, she would sweep and tamp it down, releasing a sweet, clean fragrance from the moist clay. The soft perfume rose and traveled through our house, its invisible beauty telling everyone that the long day had begun.

But before I was old enough to know that anything existed beyond our idyll, we would have to leave it. My family moved out of that sprawling house with its big airy rooms, far away from the hard-minded certainty of our customs and the lofty position that we held within our tribe, all of which my father relinquished by standing up for his ideals and allowing his wife and daughters to live in relative freedom. He wanted us all to receive a good education and knew we would have to flee the confines of our small village to ever even dare to dream. Our small family were also unapologetic in their radical ambitions, every last one of us: when she was only six, my sister, Ayesha, was already participating in debating competitions all over the region and writing speeches about women's rights, democracy, child labor and the environment; at the age of four, I was permitted to dress in boys' clothes and run amok with a slingshot through the village; my mother, whom we called *Aami*, pursued university degrees; and my father, our *Baba*, who also had given his wife permission to stop wearing her *burqa*, stood at the center of it all like a ringmaster, breaking ancient rules with the relentless daring of a hot-blooded Wazir.

None of these details mattered to me at the time, not really, but they were serious offenses to the elders of our village. Offenses to the tribe. Offenses to God. The elders had locked my father up for his liberal ideas twice before. The pursuit of enlightenment carried penalties—imprisonment and, in the worst cases, death. If we were all going to get an education, we had no choice but to leave, and for good. Yet even in that environment, fear never existed, even as an afterthought. That was the great thing about being Wazir and about being my father's daughter. We feared nothing. We simply moved on and kept living.

And we would move many times in the coming years, each new town drawing me in to a story full of adventure and strange characters, both heroes and villains, all of them shaping the woman I would become. Even now, one of those journeys across the valleys stands out as the place and time in which I learned that my world was a cauldron of dangers, not just for me personally, but for everyone who lived in it. This was a startling discovery, whose raw horror, despite everything that happened to me before and after, has never left my battered psyche. Often when I think back to my childhood in Pakistan, I think back to the moment I lost what it meant to be a child for good.

I was seven years old and already living as a boy. My father took a job teaching at the college in Miranshah, a modern town spreading out in a dense mass of concrete across a valley bordered by the rough peaks of the Hindu Kush. Every new journey always began the same way. My father and mother loaded up a cart with necessities like cooking pots, mattresses filled with dead leaves, my father's dusty textbooks, and a pair of loudmouthed chickens, and we set off. We were heading toward North Waziristan, and the journey was bumpy and long, with our crude vehicle ferrying our family through mountains that loomed over the dry dirt road. I remember the trip as a trance of passing scenery as we moved slowly through villages, stopping to buy mangoes and apricots from ramshackle stalls. The roads were rocky and narrow, and the sky above was a wall of light and heat. It must have taken us a long time to pass from South Waziristan into the northern region.

*

At first, my life in Miranshah was no less free or happy than it had been in the unspoiled valleys of South Waziristan, or anywhere else we'd lived. I napped in the soft pool-like shade of acacia trees and skipped across the flat rooftops. I swam as a boy in the swift river and ran along its muddy banks, and in quiet moments I'd stop and let my gaze linger far across the long, populated valley toward the treacherous and fabled foothills of the Kush. I paid little attention to the fact that, materially, we had less—less food, fewer clothes, and we were all crammed into a small concrete house inside the college colony.

When my father gave me money to run to the market for food, I had no idea that that small handful of soiled rupees was so hard to come by. Poor was a word I never learned until we left home for good. To get to the local market—or anywhere in town —I had to scale a concrete wall and navigate alleyways, the coins jingling like tiny bells in the frayed pockets of my shirt and pants. It was the ninth month of the lunar Islamic calendar, and a crescent moon showed like a thin fingernail through the cloudless wash of the late morning sky, signaling the holy month of Ramadan. I had a satchel full of pine nuts gathered from the forest, to trade for cups of white rice or a bag of fruit. My mother surely sent me with a warning not to linger. I left my family at home, fasting as they would from sunrise to sunset for the entire month, and walked out the front door. I recall the silence at that time. You could feel our part of the world folded into itself in heavy prayer. I sprinted to the cement wall, swung myself over and down into the narrow, shadowed alleyway. Along its full length, I saw no one. I always walked with my body slightly bent, feeling my size—so tall for a girl, so big—hands jammed into my pockets. I looked like a young boy, determined and fast, who knew where he was going. I'd taken that walk, been sent on that same errand, many times. When I got to the end of the alley, I heard the revving of an engine rise and fall, then cut out. The air carried the hot stench of gasoline. I saw a man dressed in a bright, clean *shalwar kameez* step toward the open door of the market store and slip into the interior darkness. The window on the far side of the small wooden market framed a picture of another empty street behind it. A short counter stood at one end, where an old man sat, half-asleep, against the wall.

I walked to the other end, along a table holding baskets of produce.

Two more men entered the market behind me. The sourness of male sweat overpowered the scent of coriander and cardamom that always hovered in the air of the shop. I went to the fruit baskets tucked into a shadowed corner, eyed a ripe pomegranate, tapped it with my finger, and picked it up.

The men stood around the store. I heard whispering and the shuffling of feet.

Outside, in the street behind the shop, a car engine started up again. I saw the car approach, the side windows slowly opening. Datsun. Even then, I knew cars. My father had taken a new job teaching a class in auto mechanics and machinery at the local college. His classroom—where I'd spend whole afternoons playing around—was a huge garage crammed with half-gutted vehicles; greasy engine parts always sat on tables, like mechanical specimens, waiting for the next lesson.

Behind me, the men in the shop went silent. The old man at

the counter stood up and looked over, just as the car came to a stop right below the window. The car doors flung open. Several figures spilled out. Then, as though in one long, sweeping motion, they climbed through the shop window and stood inside. The air in the room pulsed. No one moved for several seconds. I could hear my own breath, feel my own heartbeat, as they quickened. Then one of the intruders drew a pistol. I would learn later that it was a Tokarev, Russian-made, a relic of the Soviet invasion of Afghanistan and the weapon of choice in that part of the world. In the coming years, I'd see the same gun, iconic to our region, many times over. He loaded the chamber, lunged forward, and fired three fast rounds into the head of the man who'd entered the shop before me. I could not move a muscle. I had no instinct for what to do. Confusion and terror swallowed me whole. I heard a gasp and something heavy hit the floor. My eyes searched for anything else but what I knew lay before me—the peeling paint on the ceiling, a broken strap on my sandal, the quick shadow of a bird cutting past the open window. But I had to look over at the wounded man. I remember feeling bad about his shirt for some reason and I focused on it hard—such a clean garment had been soiled beyond redemption.

A second man fired right into the neck of another. Now two figures were on the floor, bleeding. The one shot in the neck had his fingers at the bullet hole, trying to plug it, I think; but he could not. The wound let out strange wet sounds, like an infant suckling. For an instant, I thought of my twin brothers, Sangeen and Babrak, at home, napping in their shared crib. I wanted to cry out. *It's not real*, I told myself again and again. *It's not real*. Then something left the man, some invisible weight, and he stopped moving, hands dropping in dull thumps to the floor. His eyes shifted quickly in their sockets and went still.

The third man was harder to kill, though he'd already been shot several times in the back. He was flailing on the ground, legs kicking. He grabbed at things—the dead man's shoe, table legs, a length of electrical cord; then he just reached up and grasped with wide-open hands at the hot gunpowdered air. His blood smeared the floor in a wing pattern as he arched across it, half-crawling on his side. Then, he slowed. He was bleeding from the mouth and lay there jerking, as though the cord had sent a current through his body. The shooters all watched without saying a word, standing over him, following his slow journey across the floorboards and looking down until he stopped and there was no doubt he was dead. Two men squatted and grabbed at the spent body, hoisted it up and carried it to the window and tossed it out. Then they all climbed out, one after the other.

No one so much as looked in my direction as I remained frozen between the long tables of ripe fruit. The car revved as they dumped the body, lifeless and dripping, into the trunk. I stood with the old man, both of us staring. Then the car sped off. As the sound of the engine died away, my entire body began to shake. The smell in the place was sweet and metallic, like wet coins. There was a loud ringing in my ears and nothing else. In that moment, a strange splitting of my childhood took place, like a canvas torn in half, and I knew that a part of me was gone. A long silent scream rose from my throat. I stood there awhile, mouth open, the pomegranate still in my hand, fresh blood at my feet.

I didn't say a word to anyone about it when I got home. I don't know why. No one asked me about the stains on my shoes. Life had changed. We were living in a different world—it was as simple and as terrifying as that. If I could ask Allah to erase a single memory, it would be those brief minutes of carnage in which I learned that men could kill other men without mercy, and with a child standing as witness. I told my father the pomegranate was all I could get, handed it to him, and knelt down to pray.

2. *The Mullah*

I was born with three names. Most Pashtun girls receive only one. One week after my birth, my father shot up from sleep. Years later, he told me that he often woke that way, startled and lost, sure that a sudden voice calling out had summoned him. He reached for my mother, felt heartbeats knock between the rising and falling wings of her shoulder blades, and then he gently pulled his hand from the comfort of her skin. All quiet, still he could not sleep again. His infant daughter slumbered in a hammock near their bed, no bigger than a loaf of bread, swaddled in tight reams of white cloth—Pashtun babies always slept bound neck to feet to prevent their limbs from flailing. Getting up, my father did not dare touch me, but lowered his cheek to mine and let my newborn breath warm his face. Feeling his way along the rough mortared walls in the darkness, he found clothes on hooks, his boots on a polished stone shelf by the door. Before slipping out, he would have attended to his prayers, kissed the jeweled silks of his sacred mat, and bowed east, where the still-unseen sun was slowly making its way from the other side of the world.

My father told me that outside, on the cracked dirt road, his feet found the right path through the dark, as though an invisible string tied around his body had pulled him. The first faint threads of dawn spread over the ground that led him higher into rocky hills over which the last shadows of night receded like deep bruises fading from the earth. He made his way past hibernating mango groves and the two dead acacias positioned as skeletal guards by the stream at the far end of our village. Walking through that acacia gateway, Shams tapped a weak trunk, as everyone did as they passed by there, to hear the soft, hollow sounds echo. Then he jumped stone by stone across the flickering stream and went out into the valley.

All his life, my father could walk for miles and miles over terrain and end up nowhere in particular, but come home with whole worlds full of wisdom. He taught me that Earth itself was but one place, and if you left from one end and walked for eternity, you'd end up right where you started. It was November, and the thin air was laced with ice, eagles were circling, the lazy sun still hiding. The elements, however cruel, could not deter my father from his walks, or from his thoughts, which always had a definite purpose. Circumstances and discomfort have never deterred me either; I received all of my resilience from him. Even now, while apart from my father, I often walk the foreign land I live in, thinking of him, out there wandering, half a world away.

He told me he hiked for hours that morning to clear his head, tracing the basin edge like the rim of a great bowl. I was his second daughter, but one week old, born helpless into a pinprick on the surface of a boundless earth, where I could be sentenced to death for pursuing any ambition beyond the roles of dutiful wife and daughter, for nothing more than daring to dream. All the physical beauty surrounding my father, every miracle laid out before him from soil to sky, could not alter that hard truth. From the sound of my first howling cry, purdah awaited his sinless infant girl.

Not a soul had come to see his new daughter when she was born. No one left coins. Rifles remained silent, propped against walls like forgotten walking sticks. No feast. Only foreboding—his own and my mother's. My father stared along the tumbling wall of hills and ridges, the just-visible sun like a jewel on the serrated peaks. On that morning, I reached my seventh day, a holy event to our people, and my father thought out loud: "If she has breathed one week in Waziristan, she might as well go on doing so forever."

"*Maria!*" he suddenly shouted, with all the air in his lungs.

His voice catapulted across the wide-open basin. Seconds later, the echo of my first name came back to him again and again, boomeranging off the blue vault and swooping down shadowed ridges along which Alexander and Solomon had marched whole armies. Every living thing heard the reverberations of my name and the next two that followed. The very air of Waziristan knew who I was before I did. *Maria. Gulgatai. Toorpakai.* Then my father took up his wool cloak and wrapped his shoulders against the pounding wind. He squinted into the sunshine, and he made his way back down to earth.

My mother could hear her husband approaching when he passed through the dead-acacia gate. His voice came forth, singing in wild Pashto couplets and calling out. Despite the hours spent hiking the frostbitten passes, he ran to her. The tips of his black mustache were white with snow, as though he'd dipped his face into a sugar bowl, and she told him that, laughing as she warmed his grinning face between her palms.

Opening her drowsy eyes to the first whispers of dawn, my mother had felt the empty space beside her, and she knew. She knew my father, still half dreaming, was out searching the surface of the sky for those three names, precious gifts to bestow upon their newborn daughter. He'd done the very same thing for my sister, Ayesha.

Panting, my father slipped off his wet boots and found me staring up in a basket by the kitchen. I lay as still as when he'd left me within my soft cocoon of cloths. The kitchen overflowed with perfumed heat—the scent of scattered cumin, pounded coriander seed—and he was happy to find his infant so contented. My father leaned down close to my face. Then he smiled, winter frost still on him and his brown eyes somehow blue, as if within those clear domes he'd trapped bits of sky. A hand on my heart, he whispered his gifts to me.

First into to my right ear and breathed the *azan*, our Muslim call to prayers, as was the custom in our part of the world. Then he moved to my other ear.

"Your given name is Maria, for purity, because the cruelty of our world has yet to alter you. *Inshallah*, it will never succeed. Second, I give you Gulgatai, as your pink face even now is pinched tight and betrays only the innocent promise of a rose-bud. We have yet to know the great beauty that lies hidden within you. Lastly, you'll be known as Toorpakai, a girl with black hair that is the envy of the darkest night. Maria, you have three names, but one life. Live well and with meaning. Never be afraid, because you are my daughter. Above all else, in your blood, you are a Wazir."

At that moment, I became who I am. Shams slipped a single gold coin into a fold of my blanket. To this day, I keep that very coin with me, often concealing it in the well of my palm until the metal grows hot. I've never shown the coin to a soul, and never will. When I hold it up to even the faintest light, it shines like the winter sun that greeted my father. I know that if I were to find that place on the rim of our valley, even decades from now, I would hear the still-living echo of his voice dancing along the tumbling Suleiman Mountains.

Years later when I would ask Shams a simple question about life, he'd always weave me a whole tapestry of words.

"Where did I come from, Baba?"

"Well now, Maria, I caught you with a fishing net from a bend in the mighty Indus."

I never doubted that myth for a moment.

Then my father told me God sent a great lion to Tibet and made its ferocious mouth the guardian source of the mighty, life-giving river Indus. From then on, every tribal child came to be, dropped like shooting stars into the moving folds of the estuary and floated as carelessly as fallen leaves toward home.

"But you, Maria, were not like the others, simply born without a care into a moving current. Somehow you came into this world straight from the legendary lion's ferocious mouth. This is why you are so strong. When I caught you, your flailing fists tore through my net, and it took ten men to haul you in."

*

Our land, too far from the nourishing Indus, was arid, rainfall a rarity. Monsoons and oceans were but beautiful rumors, biblical tales told by old men, patches of blue on a map. Shams' river myth suited me. Perhaps I was born with a fire in my soul that needed putting out, because I would have given half my life to jump just once into the ocean—to know the beauty of curling waves and feel their pounding thunder eclipse the beating of my heart. I imagined whole days of rain, big drops like a deluge of diamonds falling from the sky; how strange and beautiful it would be to see the world glazed and polished with wet—everything clean.

My father kept buckets full of water lined up in a row along one side of the house. When he found them drained, he'd send a boy from the village out to the stream to fill them again. The water remained cold a long while in the wall shade, bits of leaves or insects landing on the clear surface. I could dip my whole arm in, and watched mesmerized as goose bumps stippled my skin right up to the elbow. Sometimes I simply put my lips to the cool surface and took a long drink. Even in summer, the water always tasted of ice.

Every June, cold water became precious, but we had a plentiful supply from the river running near our house. In the summer, South Waziristan raged with a heat that slapped the air around, making it shimmer. Gathering clouds of dust blew on mid-afternoon wind like hard spit cursing across the valley bowl. Grains infiltrated everything—hair and eyes, nostrils and lungs. I found grit in the tiny wells of my ears, coating my skin like sandpaper. It encrusted lashes, roughened my tongue; it turned the sun blood red.

During those hot spells, I poured buckets of water hauled from the river over myself, sometimes four times each day. Sometimes more. The weight of the full buckets overwhelmed my arms, and so I would drag them by the thin wire handle, water spilling over the lip and leaving a wet trail that vanished instantly to steam or seeped into the hard, pounded clay of our courtyard. I never once needed an excuse to bathe; it was an obsession my father encouraged.

"Cleanliness, Maria, is half of faith."

"Then I have more faith than any Pashtun."

Sometimes Shams called me Tahara, which, like Maria, is the Arabic word for purity. Before prayers, custom demanded that a supplicant bow before God, a state of *taharah*, free from all forms of filth, both of the mind and the flesh. Because I was always playing outside in our courtyard with those buckets full of river water, no one ever called me in before prayer for *wudu*, the ritual washing. I lived in a state of perpetual *wudu*. Every week, Shams brought me bars of white soap from the market, wrapped like small gifts in wax paper and smelling of sandalwood and fragrant oils I could not identify. I would squat on the ground outside, slippery bar in my hands, and my father would lift the metal bucket high, pouring clean water over me, rinsing away the film of dust from my body.

When no one was looking, I often ate bits of soap the way other children sneaked spoonfuls of raw honey or handfuls of sugar cubes. The white soap from the market stall was always sweetest, and I'd take small bites of it like bird pecks, careful to smooth out my teeth marks using a wet thumb. I'd never consume so much at a time that anyone would notice, as it was a private pleasure that I knew full well was peculiar to me. Once, my mother caught me nibbling, crouched low by the big metal laundry basin, and I heard her gasp as I licked my lips. Looking up, I swallowed very slowly and dropped the bitten-up brick. In parts of the world like America, she told me, mothers rinsed their children's mouths out with soap and water as a punishment when they used bad language. It occurred to me that I didn't know what she meant by "bad language," as I'd never heard a mean thing spoken in my home. I couldn't imagine such a strange practice as forcing a child to eat as a penance what I thought of as a secret delicacy. Sucking on my fingertips, I laughed and said the soap there must not be as good as ours.

"I don't think there is an angel in heaven, Maria, who is as pure as you are. God willing, the world never sullies you."

*

When I was just four and too young to venture out alone, as soon as the heat had abated and the world came alive again—mostly with living sounds; birdsong, chattering schoolboys, a holy man calling the pious to pray—I would spend most of the day on our roof, feet dangling over the edge. After weeks of hauling full, clanking buckets of water from the compound wall and across the courtyard, my arms swelled with new strength till I could no longer slip them easily into my dresses, which to me was a blessing. I liked to sit, sleeves rolled way up to the shoulder, and curl my fists, watching in fascination the rise and fall of hard ridges of stretched skin where there had been nothing before. Sometimes I thought I could feel myself growing, though I was still very small.

I'd woken up that morning, bathed in the courtyard, and sat on a stool in the kitchen as my mother oiled and plaited my long, straight *toorpakai* hair, reciting dates and historical events like mantras that had no meaning to me whatsoever. She'd been up half the night studying for midterm exams in Middle Eastern history and religion, cramming facts into her brain that would vanish in a day, replaced by another series, for another test. I could feel her fingers dancing along my scalp, pulling apart tangles, my long tresses a torment to us both; but for some reason, to shear it was out of the question. I never understood why. Sometimes I thought it was because of my name—if I cut off my black hair, I'd have to give up Toorpakai and one-third of myself.

Later that morning, the house was empty. I checked the front-facing windows and tore off my red-and-orange dress, leaving it in a pile like a bit of sunset left melting to a puddle on the floor. With no other comfortable garments to wear—everything in my cupboard was adorned with heavy beads and ribbons—I left on my thin white slip. Walking out to the side of the house, I climbed an old rusted drainpipe, the hem of my slip catching several times on nails, to our roof. At the top, I hoisted myself up and I tiptoed the perimeter ledge like an acrobat, considering how to fill the empty free hours ahead. In those days, with everyone at school, time was my own canvas to paint. Every now and then, a neighbor would stop in to check on me, but most of the time I was left alone in the house. Sunlight so soft, after a while I dozed face-up on an old straw mat positioned on the floor like a raft. A steady stream of lazy daydreams colored in a full hour. I was lost at sea. The sole survivor of a shipwreck. An explorer in search of new land. A lonely cloud drifting. An eagle. Anything at all.

Later, I took my lunch on the roof—a cup of yogurt, bowls of lentils and nuts. I went back down to wash in the buckets and climbed back up again; that's when I heard the gleeful voices of the men, eruptions of clapping like rain. I had no idea why they shouted so, but I was drawn to the sound, the way it rose up in unison and fell again like music, knowing that the very rhythm had a special purpose I could not name.

I closed my eyes, tuned in again to the high-pitched chattering beyond. I squinted into the distance, saw nothing. Canopies of leaves grew a richer green as the light dipped deeper into gold that I could barely see past. Then a small white ball suddenly emerged from the treetops and rose high. It seemed to hover, spinning a moment as though suspended in the air, then it dropped down again. Someone let out a booming shout and the ball was back, rising even higher as though pushed by the force of the erupting cheers below. This time, before it vanished again to earth I was on my feet.

I ran fast without shoes. It was not hard to find my way. The only road outside our home curved in one direction and led me past several clusters of village dwellings, along the stream and out into open space. I continued on, moving off the road to a rut cutting between trees toward a park of soft meadowland, a few blue pines here and there, which I'd only ever seen from a great distance. Now I could hear the men clear as day, and I walked toward them, finding myself on a hill looking down to a long, flat field. A tall willow stood nearby, full branches over the slope, and I stepped within its green umbrella, resting my hands on the twisted trunk. I leaned forward and looked through the curtain of branches into the field below. Down there, some fifty feet away, a large group of men stood dressed all in white against the vivid emerald green of the freshly cut lawn. I thought that, in all their pristine brightness, they must be holy men. I saw one holding the clean white ball between his hands. Many other men sat on benches or stood along the perimeter, watching the activity in the field.

A long net with holes far too big for catching fish cut the field into a perfect half, and on either side stood a formation of men in two rows three across, one extra player positioned at the back. The player with the ball stretched and took his position on the rear line. Face set with concentration, he tossed the ball way up into the air. No one made a sound. I held my breath. Within a beat, his other arm went up and he slapped the ball open-palmed and hard so that it shot straight over the net. A man on the other side pounded it back before it hit the ground, and a breathtaking back-and-forth volley ensued. Mesmerized, I didn't dare blink. When at last it hit the grass on one side, half the men in the crowd shouted out with jubilant approval, while the other half jeered. The sounds rose high and fell away again, and I suddenly understood that I was watching a game in which only one side could win.

From my hideaway under the willow, I followed the quick movements of the ball and felt each powerful hit with a strange all-consuming excitement that stole my breath. Later, I would learn the game the men played down in the village field was called shooting volleyball. It was one the most popular games in the country, second only to squash. At barely four years old, crouching under the willow tree and spying on the game, I knew that every dream I'd ever had was eclipsed—I was hooked.

After a little study, I understood the basics of the game and mimicked the players from my hiding spot, jumping and slapping an invisible white ball down over an imaginary net with my small open hand. The day was fading slowly into a long twilight, and I felt my skin growing hot from the wild exertions of my play. Then I heard a hard slap, and as if by some miracle, the round white ball flew in my direction. Arching in a shallow curve, it hit the ground barely two feet from the willow and rolled to a sudden halt. For a moment I didn't move. I'd never held a ball of any kind. Never played a sport in my life. Without thinking, I crawled out from the curtain of branches, my skin hot, my heart racing. I could feel my braids coming apart as I ran and bent down to retrieve the ball. Sweat dripped down my heavy hair to my hot back, where the fabric of the white dress slip stuck to my skin like a sheet of paper. I held the ball; it was smooth and made of soft leather. The men below all stared up the slope and called loudly in my direction. Still cradling the ball, I peered back at them down the hill to the playing field, where they stood watching me. Two men from the crowd were already approaching. They called out. Propelled by their shouting, I took a breath and tossed the ball high to the heavens and watched it spin. In tandem, my other arm and hand rose, and I jumped in my bare feet, slapping the ball open-palmed with everything in me. The moment my small hand made contact, the volleyball soared. Barely arching, it landed in the green field full of men. Voices exploded at once, and some of the white figures came running up the slope after me, their mouths hanging open in shock. I could feel my hand burn and stared down at my palm, seeing the red mark like a branding. My fate had suddenly changed—I could feel it. So I stood there grinning and waited for the men to come to me.

The first man from the approaching group crossed into a pool of tree shade. His bleached *shalwar kameez* suddenly darkened as he stopped before me, staring, saying nothing. I recognized him as the cousin of a mullah from one village over. Not more than a week before, he'd celebrated marriage to a girl who'd gone to school briefly with my sister, Ayesha. I looked away from him. I realized just then that he'd also been the player who'd served the ball toward me.

The men who followed were all tall and clad in unblemished whites. They were not holy men. I recognized a few as my father's colleagues from the neighboring college, where he sometimes gave guest lectures on varying subjects, from modern poetry to physics. My father had spent a lifetime reading textbooks, memorizing facts and formulas, theories and verses, as though they were all on a conveyor belt feeding straight into his brain. More than one of those men had been regular visitors to our home, where they sat on rugs in the living room, eating slices of fruit from white plates, always engaged in discourses that sounded to me like a foreign language. World affairs. Politics. Sometimes they prayed together on silk mats in a special room near the front door of our house. Then I noticed the mullah from our mosque; he approached twisting the coils of his thick graying beard in his fingers. He stared down at me and pulled a red ribbon from my hair like a vein from my head.

"I would like to play," I said, half-smiling, no idea at all how wrong I was about that.

"Is that what you think is going to happen?" he said. In the cool shade, his face showed barely a feature, like the dark side of the moon.

"No, not yet. I am asking." I felt a rivulet of sweat run down my spine.

"Asking who—Allah? Me?"

"I'll beat everyone. You saw me hit the ball." I dug my bare heels into the raw ground.

Something sinister entered the mullah's eyes. I didn't know enough yet about the state of things outside our compound to know that I had said the wrong thing.

After considering me for a moment, the small tears along the hem of my dress, my bare feet and arms, the mullah placed his hands on either side of my head. He seemed to study my shape, squeezing my skull. I could feel his pulse tap at my temples. A man behind him laughed.

"*Inshallah*," I whispered, minding my manners.

The mullah kept one hand on my cheek, holding it hard. Then I saw his right arm rise straight up, open-handed, and the setting sunlight flickered faintly between his fingertips.

The slap to my face came so hard and fast that it sounded like a gunshot. The air in my lungs rushed out and I stumbled backward in my slip dress. The skin along my jaw pulsed with a pain that I'd never known. My mind raced with a fear that was new to me. It threatened to stop my heart—part of me wished it would. Instantly, the inside of my mouth was warm and slippery with blood.

If I thought he was done, I was wrong. He hit me twice more, all the while keeping a hand hooked to my shoulder to keep me from falling back.

When he let go of me at last, I fell to my knees in the dirt. I wanted to call out to my father, to the mighty Indus to come carry me to the Arabian Sea; but I said nothing, blinking eyes fixed dead to the ground before me. I could not breathe; it felt as though all the air had left the world.

The mullah leaned down at the waist, wiped a trail of blood from my face, and then smeared it like the juice from a crushed berry on a strip of white cloth pulled from his pocket. When I saw his casual cruelty in that single act, I thought that in his cool anger the man might kill me. I could not feel my own skin. I floated, and yet I was still there on my knees, afraid to move.

Instead, he cupped my chin in his hand and forced me to meet his gaze.

"A girl like you is dirty," the mullah said, and he spat into my wide-open eyes. "Go back home to your father, dirty girl."

Every man in the group after him walked past me and spat before going back down the hill to resume their game.

As soon as I heard the jubilant shouting again, I ran.

When I got home, no one was there, and I stepped out of my thin, ruined garment, which had sour spit and my blood spattered all over it. I went to the side of the house and found the buckets all full and wished hard for my Baba to come home, as though if I concentrated hard enough, that urgency might take flight and find him. Kneeling before the water, I saw on the surface the reflected ugliness of my pummeled cheek. The pain astonished me. As I stared down into the bucket, my sufferings coupled into a great sorrow that I knew would have no end. I had a new knowledge that, however I tried, I could never erase.

Bending over the water, I dunked my entire head into the

bucket, the sudden rush of cold taming my bruises. While under the surface, in that pure dark silence, I released a single long wail.

An hour later, when my parents found me, I was lying on my side next to the upended buckets, all the river water gone. My father carried me into the house and wrapped my body in white sheets. Then he placed me shivering and whimpering into the warmth between himself and my mother. Bringing his face close to my right ear, he whispered my three names over and over again until I fell asleep. "Maria. Gulgatai. Toorpakai." But all I heard was "Dirty Girl."

3. An Unlikely Bride

If my mother hadn't married my father, she'd be dead. It was my father who would save her, but when my mother first met him— on their wedding day—she feared him. Waking for the last time in her father's large house, she opened her tear-swollen eyelids to the caramel-colored walls of her bedroom, limbs stretched across the bed on which she was born and she slowly let her lungs fill and held her breath. At barely twenty, and the daughter of an affluent elder, she was already an old maid. But she couldn't outwit a thousand years of tribal code any longer. From the moment of her swaddling, when women gathered around her hammock and tore up bits of white cloth in which to bind her small limbs, destiny stalked her.

Turning in her hot sheets to see the morning star through thin curtains, Aami cursed the star and the earth. The scent of lamb's blood still sweetened the air after three days of feasting in preparation for the wedding, and my mother often said that she thought, then, it might as well have been her own throat they'd slit and drained over the hot stones in the yard. There were stories of girls who doused themselves in kerosene and lit a match. The ones who ran away didn't get very far and, once caught, wouldn't live very long. My mother murmured the name of her betrothed—a young man whose bloodlines could be traced back to ancient kings—rolling the sound around in her mouth like a stone. *Shams*. Sight unseen, she told me, she hated him.

In a corner of her room, Aami's bridal slippers sat side by side; clusters of beads adorned the tips like frozen flowers sewn onto cream satin. Sometimes, to show me, my mother pulled out those shoes, wrapped in reams of tissue, from a battered leather trunk in her room where she tucked her precious things. How useless I found her pretty mementos, until I crossed oceans and needed my own: my gold birth coin, a lock of my sister's hair, my baby brother's handprint captured in faded blue ink, a smooth pebble plucked from the village stream minutes before we left our tribal home. Every now and then, my mother liked to spread her touchable memories out over the floor: photographs, gold bangles, a silk bag embroidered with orchids, tarnished silver coins, a sack full of rings, smooth river stones collected from her father's house, an old jean jacket patched at the elbows, and the bridal slippers. How tiny those slippers were; I could barely fit a hand inside.

On her wedding day, after the morning meal, my mother's blue-blooded future in-laws would arrive with her *jora*, the traditional bridal dress—a beautiful thing, heavy with pink pearls, bright swirls of embroidery, and a Milky Way of crystals embedded into thick layers of ironed silks. Even bodiless, the dress could almost stand up like another woman. Covered head to toe, my mother would hide all day within the garment's chamber as though she wasn't there at all, as though none of it was actually happening. From her bed, she could see the row of metal hooks where they planned to hang the dress. She'd held the tools and watched her father hammer in each hook.

She hadn't slept long, and when she did fall asleep, she slipped out of consciousness as though falling through floors to the center of the earth; when she woke, breathless, she set to memorizing every blemish on the walls that had greeted her for her entire childhood and would be a memory by next sundown. Alone with her thoughts, a quiet state that within hours would be a lost luxury, my mother calculated any number of ways to escape what she already knew she could not.

I have asked my mother many times why she never ran.

"Maria, I had no one to catch me at the bottom of that cliff. Besides, it wasn't written that way. Allah had other plans. One of them was you."

From the open window, Aami could hear rifle shots signal from a neighboring village miles away. *His* village, she was certain. *Naksha Wishtal*—the ritual target shooting that set every tribal wedding day in motion was about to take place. She knew that her father would start out with the bow and arrow handed down to the firstborn son of each generation; his great-great-grandfather had used it to kill, one by one, whole ranks of British invaders from the caves of Tora Bora.

The night before my grandfather had prepared his ceremonial weapon while my mother watched silently from the kitchen threshold. Sitting on a silk mat, he pulled an imaginary arrow from his quiver, held it tight between his fingers, and steadied himself. My mother stepped in closer as he drew back the cord, closed her eyes. It could all be over in a millisecond. No pain. How she wished he had a quiver full of sharpened arrows at the ready, though she knew he'd require but one. Catching sight of his daughter, her father set aside his weapon, leaned an elbow against his knee, and they exchanged a long, peculiar glance. The moment contained a whole continent of unspoken things, as though they were passing a sealed letter between them. Theirs was a bottomless sadness that neither dared speak of—in a day, according to their own laws, he wouldn't be her father any longer.

Jirga meetings held between elders from both clans had set out the parameters of my parents' blind betrothal: how much the groom's family would have to pay in *walwar* as compensation for the provision of household goods she'd bring to her new home, to repay the bride's father for the misfortune of having to clothe and feed a female from her birth to her marriage. In Waziristan, the greater the wealth and status of the girl's family, the higher the *walwar*, or "bride price" she garners. The more money the groom's family pays for the acquisition of a bride the higher their esteem for her, and the better she is likely to be treated. Once the *walwar* is given and the marriage takes place, the girl becomes the full possession of her husband and his family. However they treat her, she forfeits the right to complain or to seek protection from her father ever again. Local *jirgas* took place outdoors in a flat-terraced field behind the village, where the men assembled in a semicircle under the canopy of a white tent. My mother had watched from her father's window as a group of young men erected the tent, spreading the tarpaulin over a huge skeleton of poles. Aami saw dozens of men, as quiet and sober as pallbearers, enter single file through a slit in the side. Then a young boy discharged a single round from his rifle and scrambled down the hill toward his home.

The first day, many hours passed without a break. Sometimes the women would hear shouting and make out a few words here and there like flares, and then the cacophony died down again. A gunshot signaled the opening, closing, and recesses of each meeting, and several times each day, the men would all come down the hill to eat and pray. "It will be over soon, Yasrab, you will see," they told her—but it wasn't. One week passed, then another, and still the men shouted back and forth like barking dogs.

Intermarriages between tribes were uncommon, and my mother was not a common bride of South Waziristan. Most Pashtun girls married cousins—first, second, or third—or at least a known man from the village, if there were any suitable grooms to be had. Most Pashtun brides were also younger than twenty. Barely one in ten thousand women had earned what she had—an official high school diploma—walking miles through mud-tracts and maize fields to school, and taking classes by mail. Her gold-crested certificate, with its swirls of black calligraphy, sat in a frame for all to see as they entered the house. My mother knew from her studies that she'd lived as few Wazir girls had: in the top 10 percent of her gender simply by virtue of being born into a household that encouraged her to attend school at all; the top 3 percent the moment she learned to spell her name; one in a million the day her father said, "Keep going, see what you learn next." What happened next was Shams, my father.

When at last the *jirga* came to an end, the elders rose and the gathering poured from the tent opening in an avalanche of excitement, arms entwined like brothers, rifles booming, drumbeats shaking the earth beneath my mother's feet. Ten days—that's what it took to bind two foreign fates together for eternity. Already my mother heard their two names uttered together as though they were one, and she knew she'd lost part of herself.

Her betrothed was from a powerful family, and my mother believed that their union was part of a complicated agreement that would settle a long-running blood feud. For this alone, she supposed the elders expected her to show gratitude. The peace brokered using my mother and father as its instruments was not drawn in ink but with blood, her father explained to her. There might have been horrific violence of some kind; perhaps some brothers had killed the brothers of others, as sometimes happened. Such savagery, once provoked, she knew, could unleash endless waves of vengeance, until every stream ran red. Aami was never told the finer details, but those details mattered little. For all intents and purposes, she had been sold.

As far as my mother knew from history books, treaties were flimsy things that fluttered away as paper to the winds. It was a treaty that ended the First World War and simultaneously sowed the seeds of the Second. In 1893, by agreement with Abdur Rahman Khan, the "Iron Emir" of Afghanistan, the British drew the Durand Line along the Hindu Kush, spanning the mountains that tumbled between Afghanistan and Waziristan, as a way to establish their dominion, only to find themselves facing the wrath of Pashtun warlords and the poison-tipped arrowheads of Aami's great-great-grandfather. In spite of that agreement, for over a century the local tribes had swung freely back and forth over the boundary like a pendulum—Taliban leader Mullah Omar tiptoed right across it when the British returned to Afghanistan with their American allies after 9/11.

My mother had no idea why they'd chosen her of all the village maidens. They say that one afternoon a local mullah spotted her veiled form stepping off a local bus and walking the long rutted mile the rest of the way to her school. Even though the traditional Pashtun covering obscured her face, he knew exactly who she was—the only girl from her village going to school. As he stood back watching, she crossed a cornfield with a satchel hoisted over one shoulder while reading out loud in a soft clear voice from the Quran; and he saw in her intelligent grace the perfect pawn. He also saw a threat. Before she knew it, my mother became a sacrificial lamb offered to the rival clan, in a peace offering called *swara* when girls, some of them very young, are given to right a wrong.

And the opposing clan chose Shams, my father, a scion of an influential tribe, as an offering in kind. In marrying the two, the tribal leaders stitched a tight seam between the clans, one that would span generations. Pashtun elders always planned the future as though it was a slow game of chess started long before and continuing well past their own life spans, seeing themselves as extensions of the ancients, carving a path of dominion over their kin. All this meant but one thing to my mother—a sudden end to her education, all her university applications shredded into scrap to light the cooking pit out back, her plan to study for a degree in Lahore disintegrating in the curls of black smoke. Once the marital agreement was secure, it could not be undone.

But neither clan knew that each faction chose the bride and groom with great care and in secret, not as an offering of peace but as a curse and a sentence. My father, though a scion from the bloodline of Pashtun kings, had twice found himself locked up in an insane asylum for wildly disrupting *jirgas* with speeches about the rights of women to seek an education, receive medical care, inherit or buy property, or to simply own and drive a car. When the elders banned him from the meetings, he simply took to the streets, spray-painting Pashto couplets demanding freedom in big, bleeding letters across mud walls, spattering them over huge valley stones.

For her part, my mother had gone too far with her schooling. She simply knew more than was prudent, her quiet intelligence growing like an abscess on the face of the tribe. Ignorance secured a woman to the home, but my flighty Aami was rarely even indoors; several men had seen her hiding between rows of trees in the mango groves, a book open between her hands—not always the Quran. Many thought it wouldn't be long before she ran off with her romantic ideals and sealed a fate worse than death. So rather than sentence the two heretics to stoning or crazy houses, they simply sentenced them to each other.

The morning of the wedding, neither my mother's father nor his future son-in-law would allow the other to lose at their target competition, and so the game took many more turns than was customary. In that cool blue morning hour, the men found in their quiet, jovial game a genuine and unexpected kinship. Later, the bride and groom would agree that it was a sign from Allah, and that the wise mullahs, who stood nearby watching, should have taken heed.

Only when a shooter struck the bull's-eye could the message go back to Aami's tribe that the wedlock ceremonies should begin. Women were already assembled in my mother's sitting room, surrounding her. Her cousins had adorned her hands and arms with henna, patterns of flowering vines and soaring birds. They placed gemstone rings on her slender, trembling fingers. Already she had slipped into the cocoon of her *jora*, her face and the full length of her body obscured right down to her slippers. Through the milkiness of her veil she would see only what she chose to see, which was nothing at all. Forms moved about like specters in the cloudy light. Entombed in so many satiny layers, she could feel her own trapped breath, the perfume from the oils on her skin and in her plaited hair overcoming her like a drug.

The woman from her village with the most sons—seven in all—had braided her hair, threading ribbon through the thick strands. It seemed to my mother that as the morning hours passed, the women did not cease arriving to adorn her. She thought: *How they try to disguise with beauty such an ugly thing*. When my mother saw her bare self again, it would no longer be her own. Every inch of her, including her mind, would belong to her husband. In Aami's foreboding, she had to resist the urge to simply rip the dress away and run.

When word came that my father and my maternal grand-father had both hit the target dead center in an unprecedented

tie, the gathered women looked from one to the other in astonishment. Someone said it was an auspicious sign—but of what,
no one said. Then Aami heard a deep roll of drumbeats, the
crackle of gunfire pulsing from the heavens, and she knew the
men—in the grand procession known as *janj*—were coming like
a storm of music to gather her up in her silks and take her. She
felt the ground beneath her dainty slippers fall away, and they
placed her on a cot garlanded with flowers.

At the mosque, my mother saw his face at last. Standing
before him, with the *pesh imam* murmuring holy passages, my
mother peered at my father through the slit in her veil. Somehow
reading her smallest movements, her groom looked over, and for
a second their eyes held one another's. His eyes seemed bottomless to her and so clear. He grinned—but she feared him. She
looked past his face to the big square hands hanging at his sides,
and she listened to his voice repeating the mullah's prayers. His
hard jawline might as well have been cut with a hunting knife.
Then her turn came to speak. Breathless, Aami recited the name
of her bridegroom's father three times as her wedlock father. In
turn, he promised to care for her as an equal to the other females
in his household. With those pronouncements they fulfilled
their marriage contract called *Nikah*, and a change took place in
the very air my mother breathed. She was married. It was done.

At dusk, they traveled as husband and wife in a lone car
decorated with flowers and bells. Rifles boomed. The hum of
song and beating of drums. My mother was veilless now. A full
moon illuminated the world with a silver light, and as they set
out into it, my father never spoke to my mother, not a word. The
roar of the engine was all she heard. Night fell quickly, the hills
went black, and she could see hordes of insects swarming like
smoke in the glare of headlights. I asked my mother many times
about that hour-long drive on the winding, muddy roads between
the mountains.

"I had no idea whether he was a devil or a god, but he held
my very life in the palm of his big hand."

They crossed the border into my father's village and veered

past the mosque and onto a narrow side road. Around a bend, my mother saw her new home, the one in which I would be born, emerge from the night. High up on a hill crowned with blue firs, the house stood out like a fortress. My father had to stop the car to pry open the tall front gates, and my mother—still draped in her heavy *jora*—got out to help him. Together they pulled the iron bars back, and the rusty metal groaned. She saw a heavy padlock hooked to the gate, noticed that her husband kept a large ring of many keys in his pocket, and wondered if the locks were to keep people out—or in.

The compound was very dark; only a few lamps lit the hallways as my father led his bride up a staircase. Her silken footfalls whispered over the pounded-clay floor. Still they said nothing, exchanged no pleasantry, even as she tripped once on a step. My mother pulled her *hijab* over her face. She told me that she concentrated hard on every movement, so as not to think too much, because, she said, to think too far ahead was to fall into panic. To panic was to flee, and to flee was to sentence my grandfather to lifelong shame and to face certain death.

In a corner of the house, my father stopped at a set of doors and then led my mother over the threshold into their marital wing of the house. She realized from the furniture that she was in a living room and accepted the chair silently offered to her. When she sat down, her cumbersome *jora* crinkled and cracked as she pulled at it. How she wished to take off the fabric sarcophagus; and how she loathed the idea all at once. The old women had told her that it was her sacred duty to perform whatever act was requested. She noted a book lying open on a table, and it stopped her thoughts. Many others stood in tall stacks on the floor. She squinted through her garb at the spine and said quietly: "*Moby-Dick*." Somehow, my father heard that murmur, and he stopped and turned to stare at her. A large box in his hand, he approached his terrified bride and knelt before her.

"I think you must have come here to test my wisdom, Yasrab. I can see from your eyes that you worship the sun, and from your grace that you are a queen."

My mother even now recalls the shock that reverberated through her in that strange moment. She felt his fingers pull at her *hijab* to reveal the fullness of her face. He was gentle, and never once touched her skin. Body damp from fear, she was sure he could smell it on her. Even in middle age, my mother would tell us that if she closed her eyes, she could still hear every word of their first conversation; the sound of her own young voice in that moment, and all the horror it held, still chilled her.

"I am no Queen of Sheba, and you are no King Solomon."

My mother told me that my father laughed so hard, tears flooded his dark eyes, and he shook his head so many times, she thought it might rattle. Then he reached deep into a box and opened it. Pulling out a blue garment, he stood up and unfolded a denim jacket, the silver buttons shining like coins before her. Draping it across her lap, he pulled her *hijab* way down over her shoulders, letting out her shining braids and all the heat trapped in there.

"Then I will make you one."

In those few seconds of absurdity, my mother guessed instantly that the elders had sentenced her to marry a madman. She held up the stiff garment.

"What do you expect me to do with this, Shams? Wear it over my *burqa* or on my head?"

"That is a jean jacket, Yasrab. Levi's, from America. My wedding gift to you. And I expect you to wear nothing on your head unless you choose to. Inside these walls, and with me, you are the queen of the house."

On their wedding night, my parents stood together before a mirror, both dressed in denim; she in her deep blue jacket and he in boot-cut jeans laughing, looking at themselves again and again, seeing a whole world of possibility unfold in their shared reflection—awed as though they'd discovered an entire continent in a single day.

"The first time he spoke to me, Maria, your father's words struck my heart and made it chime. It was a miracle. In one week, I was back at school."

*

Two weeks later, a sixteen-year-old girl from their village fled with a boy her own age in a battered horse-drawn cart for the city of Peshawar. The young couple explained that they wished only to marry, but it made no difference to the posse that came after them. Their physical coupling was attested to by several witnesses, and both the girl and boy were sentenced to death long before they were caught. The boy's family would have to pay blood money to the girl's father to make amends for the shame their sinful acts placed upon the family. Once the money was paid, the offending boy was shot—one bullet to the nape of his neck— as no punishment could undo what had been done. The girl's family had already promised her to a man from her village who had recently lost his wife in childbirth. It also made no difference that they prayed five times each day in a perfect state of *wudu*. Shame descended upon their families like a swarm of locusts, and the village grew still as the *jirga* tent went up. The girl was a small-boned thing with blue eyes so unusual that some thought it was a sign of impurity.

From the flat roof of my father's family home, my mother had a perfect vantage of the rocky gulley where executions took place. She made herself watch what she could have been, had fate written a different story for her. On the day of the execution, the men approached in a solemn group, all clustered around the girl, who was already draped in the brown robe and veil that she would die in. A heavy rope tied about her waist was used to pull her along as though she were a goat.

Several men came forward and took the girl by her shoulders, then held her face so that she stood erect and stared straight ahead. A bearded man stepped up to face the girl and read aloud the lengthy punishment. My mother could see the girl shifting about within the heavy draping, her head nodding slowly several times. A man asked that before they kill her, she agree with the sentence, and Aami wondered why. Still does. She wanted to shout out—*no*. Instead, up there hiding in the shaded sanctuary of the roof, she only whispered it over and over to the careless wind. The girl's eyes darted back and forth, back and forth, from the shallow pit before her to a sullen man with a red *kaffiyeh*. The whites of her eyes shone; even from where she crouched, my mother could see them. Beseeching. The girl still held some hope of mercy and held out her hands to the man who was likely her father, though aloud she asked for mercy only of God. Now the man in the *kaffiyeh* stepped closer to the bearded one, hands clasped over his protruding belly. Aami strained to hear them; as they spoke, she committed every word like a sacrament to memory.

"Is there anything you'd like to say to your daughter now?"

"No."

"Ask him to forgive me before God does. Please."

"Every girl asks this of her father at the moment of her stoning. It is common. And I will tell you what we say to every man in your position. Surely, Allah will reward you for forgiving your daughter such a thing as your shame."

"No, it is not in me to forgive her. It would not be in any man's heart."

"Baba, forgive me, forgive me."

"No. Do not call me that. You are no longer my daughter and I am no longer your father."

"All right. You are not her father; but, as she has asked, you must forgive. She was compelled to do this thing by a man, and she must serve as a warning to other women who come across such men."

"Forgive me. Forgive. Forgive . . ."

"Just do it, as much as it makes you ill. In minutes, Allah will forgive her anyway."

"Baba, forgive me."

"Do not call me that. I told you. Fine, I forgive you. Now will you be quiet?"

"Good, that's it. Take her to the pit and tie her feet."

Leading her quivering form, his hands tight around the rope at her waist, the father stopped twice to straighten the crude robe as her feet tripped against the dragging hem. He seemed rushed, and glared at his daughter in annoyance. She didn't see him; already her eyes were elsewhere. Carefully, as the others stood around examining rocks, he pushed her with one hand down into the pit. Instinctively, though she had closed her eyes, the girl crouched to her knees. The bearded man nodded in approval and told her to say a prayer. She did so; but her words were barely more than air and it was impossible for Aami to hear her. Then the father jumped in after his daughter and tied her feet so that she could not run. A woman who escaped a stoning with her life was often allowed to live.

"Hold my hand, father. Hold my hand a moment."

My mother heard her utter those words several times, and clenched her own fists. She could feel the girl's cold hands slip into her own.

"No."

"Hold my hand."

"My hand cannot go from yours to the stone that will kill you."

The girl laid her head down on the loose sand surrounding her and waited, all the while uttering a staccato of whispered prayers. The first and second rocks made her cry out loud enough to echo, and she jerked to one side in her bindings. Every man took a turn, each rock falling in a direct blow to her head, and after many she grew quieter and still. My mother looked away and hated herself for that moment of cowardice. She gathered up all her breath and held it in. Where just minutes before she'd seen a pale, blue-eyed face, already there was only a wash of blood. My mother told me that she forced herself to give her eyes fully to the scene, fixing them unblinking on the body, slumped and still twitching in the pit. At last, the bearded man whistled and approached and kicked the girl once to find her still moving. Then he motioned to another man, who stepped forward and presented the shamed father with the salvation of the largest death-blow stone. Without a flicker of hesitation, the girl's father took the boulder and raised it way up with tremendous force, a torrent of rage twisting through him. Standing no more than five feet from his half-dead child, he hurled the heavy rock like a catapult into her already ruined face. And she was gone.

After my mother witnessed the execution of the young girl named Adeela, she'd scoured the Quran again and again. Finding not a single word about what she sought, she asked my father to ask a holy man what he had to say about the ritual. My father returned home with a pomegranate in his hand. He held it out to her like an offering and told her what he'd learned at morning prayer.

"The woman must be buried in the earth up to her chest, her feet and hands tied in case she attempts to flee. The chosen stones must not be large enough to kill her with one or two strikes. Or small enough to be called pebbles."

As my father spoke, he descended as though he were sinking into the floor and held his new wife's slippered feet, unable to let go:

"Forgive me, Yasrab."

"Why?"

"You came here to test my wisdom, and I failed you already. I have no answers."

"But you just told me what I asked for."

"Forgive me. Just say you do."

My mother always said that it was in that moment, my father's damp face looking up at her, beseeching between her cumin-scented palms, that she felt their marriage was consecrated. She knew that she was safe.

"All right, Solomon, I forgive you. Get up from the ground now, and take hold of my hand."

4. Genghis Khan

I gave Maria up when I was four and a half in the Valley of God—*Dera Ismail Khan*—west of the Indus, four miles inland from the wide, muddy banks. There I saw the river that birthed me, *Abasin*, for the first time that I could remember, threading its lazy silver water along a vast green plain, when our family moved out of South Waziristan to the Khyber Paktunkhwa province in Pakistan proper. We crossed into the level ground of the pleasant town of Khan at noon in a white pick-up truck, our belongings trussed in huge bundles to the roof; two squawking chickens in a cage; bottles of water; several oranges rolling around; a record player; and my mother's heavy textbooks tied up in stacks at our feet.

This was not an exile but an exodus, one of many to come. We'd travelled more than two hundred miles away from our tribal home, on a thin road running the southern extension of the Khyber Pass. In the high heat of early summer, driving from my father's village to the city, our old truck barreled through the carbon haze of Daraban Road. We were moving to a region known as a cradle of higher learning, full of colleges and universities, all accepting female students. And within months, my mother would be among them, taking courses for four years until she received a bachelor's degree in history.

My father's first wedding gift to my mother was a midnight-blue pair of Levi's; the second, which came years later, was the continuation of her education. No more correspondence courses or long journeys back and forth between the mountains to attend lectures. When my father told the village elders he wanted to move his family, they believed his tale about returning to the polytechnic college where he'd taken a position teaching classes in engineering. He left out the part about my mother's acceptance letter to the Government Degree College, the one she kept folded in her pocket, to pull out and read again and again.

A thin mud wall spanned the perimeter of Dera Ismail Khan, and the entry gate looked to me like a secret archway into a pleasant, bustling citadel. Those first glimpses of the town left me spellbound: tree-lined boulevards as wide as flooded rivers; buses and big trucks; zigzagging mopeds; swarms of bicycles, spinning wheels and blurs of limbs cutting through traffic. And so many people everywhere, strolling up and down the lanes or lingering in chattering groups: Muslims moved among Hindus, Sikhs, Punjabis, Baluchis, Jats, and Pashtuns, rich or poor, all them known collectively as *Derawals*.

Our truck sped down University Road toward my father's college, stirring up dust, the chickens protesting and my laughing mother holding me in the soft spoon of her arm. She was pregnant, and her belly swelled tight as a drum and so round; I rubbed it many times as though she were a Buddha. My eight-year-old sister, Ayesha, who would be starting first grade at the local girls' school, was nestled on the other side of her. Taimur was up front with my father, a map held out between his hands. We entered the neighborhood where college employees lived, and everything slowed and quieted. It was full of short, meandering streets that ended in cul-de-sacs, where professors lived, every house stuccoed white. Behind the neighborhood, a huge valley sloped down to a long, flashing thread of river, with mountains far off in the distance.

Within a month of moving into our university house, my mother left in the dead of night and disappeared for several days. I know now she was at the city hospital maternity ward, giving birth for a fourth time, but for the first time in a bright, sanitary room.

When my father led my mother slowly up the front walk a

few days later, both of them grinning ear to ear and each cradling a small swaddled bundle, I simply assumed they'd been away fishing for babies in the Indus. How lucky my father had a big net—they'd caught two.

My parents named the first boy Sangeen Khan, and on the seventh day following the ritual naming, proffering a polished gold coin, my father knelt down before me with the second twin.

"This one is for you, Maria. The current swept him into my net just as I was about to hoist up Sangeen. Then I noticed two small cuts at his temples—see there? And I knew he was yours."

"What are the marks?"

"Those are from the front teeth of the Great Lion, Maria. He marked your temples the very same way. Here, take your brother and give him his name—Babrak Khan."

And so I held out my short arms and took hold of the sleeping infant. Crouching, I felt his newborn breaths flutter against my cheek, and I brought my lips close to his tiny seashell ear.

"Babrak Khan. Never be afraid, because you are my boy. I will look after you." And then into his right ear, with all the love I thought existed in the world entire, I breathed the *azan*, our Muslim call to prayer.

*

Every morning, all the members of my family except the twins and me would set out from the front gate like travelers, bags slung over their shoulders, lunches packed, into the dense sunlit streets of Dera Ismail Khan, on their way to classrooms and lecture halls. My father would walk Ayesha and Taimur to the local elementary school before making his way to the college where he lectured, while my mother rode the public bus to her own classes. Even when he had to travel far or was in a rush, he always went around town on foot. When my father walked, people paid attention as his tall noble figure passed by. To this day, they say that Shams Wazir walks like a general.

Hours spent alone were routine to me, my solitude second nature; but now, two wailing infants populated the quiet stillness of my world. Rather than go to school, I had to stay home to learn to be a mother—fast. And somehow, I did. Ayesha had already shown that she was academically gifted; she read simple textbooks and was rapidly learning to speak English. Still so young, I showed very little interest in books and a great deal in my twin brothers. Not yet five years old and I already felt like an adult, as many Pashtun children do; we grow up quickly in the tribe. We have no choice.

My mother had started school part-time and was gone several afternoons each week. On days when she was home, she would often take what time she had to give me lessons in spelling and arithmetic. In the early evening, when both my parents returned, satchels full of papers, eyelids swollen from reading, they sat down to rest in the lamplight of our small living room. I brought them steaming green tea in little cups and then handed over a howling Sangeen. Babrak, however, was all mine, and he stayed with me as much as possible—my parents had known exactly what they were doing.

Often, before leaving for her university lectures my mother oiled and braided my hair, slipping long, shiny lengths of ribbon along each braid. She dressed me up to look just like the dolls I regularly tossed around or defaced with pens. She took great pleasure in these rituals, but I did not. Every now and then, an old man came to our door with a huge pile of folded dresses tied up in a white sheet and carried in a bundle balanced on his head. His wife was a seamstress, and he made a living peddling her ornate creations door-to-door. It took my mother weeks of selling washed-out tin cans at the metal depot to save enough rupees in her big collection jar to make a purchase. Sometimes she bought two or three garments at a time, each one more lavish than the last. And every one of them was my torment.

*

When the twins were six months old, my mother started taking more classes and was often gone for whole days. She always left a small bottle of goat's milk, which I'd learned to heat over our single electrical element in a shallow pan of hot water, testing the temperature with a drop on my wrist. I liked to lick it off, so sweet and as white as a pearl against my skin. After the twins started on solid food, I took great pleasure in concocting their meals. I peeled mangoes and mashed them with a fork, and I soon figured out that I could pulverize anything into baby food: naan bread soaked in broth, white rice boiled with lentils, a tangerine; all together in strange soupy concoctions the twins accepted, smacking their smooth, wet gums as though I was offering them nothing but God-made manna. Kneeling on the cool clay floor, I scooped small morsels of food from a bowl with my fingertips and fed the babies, who were only just sitting up, by dropping little bits into their open, toothless mouths.

Once the twins were satisfied, their tiny hands sticky with mango juice and clutching at my braids, I carried them out into our garden out back. I wandered about in the sunlight, reciting verses from the Quran called *ayahs* and swaying until my arms strained and I put my brothers down on a carpet of blankets spread out in pools of shade, always watching as they rolled about grabbing at the air, grabbing at anything with their tiny fists. Once, I caught Sangeen with a stone in his mouth, and I learned my lesson. Eventually they would tire, and I would watch for a few minutes as they slumbered there together, to be sure their sleep was sound, trying to guess at what they saw behind those small, twitching lids. Gently I wrapped their small, warm bodies with cloth, as though they were packages, and slipped each into his hammock like a seed into a pod. They made soft sounds as they slept, like birds.

While the twins napped, I thought nothing of leaving them in their hanging beds while I put on my sandals and slipped out into the neighborhood. One day, I promised myself, I would run all the way to the Indus, so that I could see it gleaming along the edge of the field and give my greeting, at last, to *Abasin*. Until then, though, I restricted myself to the quiet little cul-de-sac just outside our front door, and usually just sat on the low curb by the gate. A Saraiki woman across the way, in a house that was the mirror image of ours, often came out to check on me or, more likely, my baby brothers. Sometimes she offered a cup of fresh yogurt, or I brought her buttermilk with which she made us mounds of dough for naan bread. Her fair Indo-Aryan skin held bold features so perfect in their symmetry they might have been painted, and her long locks of tar-black hair gleamed when she moved. Cloistered within my Pashtun tribe, I'd seen only Wazir faces like my own, and at first her exotic grace startled me. I'd never seen eyes so big, and her many beautiful children, who always swarmed at her waist, all looked just like her.

Our Saraiki neighbors often admired me in turn for my embroidered dresses and long, intricate braids, marveling at the juxtaposition of delicate adornments against my hard tribal posture. The muscles on my arms were as big as avocados from carting babies around. You could see when I walked tall and proud—always my father's daughter—that I came from a long line of Wazir warriors.

Often at dusk the cul-de-sac would transform into a vibrant stage, a lone streetlight illuminating a pair of drummers assembled underneath the wooden lamp post. At the first loud beat of the *dhol*—a double-headed drum decked in pompoms—every able-bodied Punjabi from the neighborhood converged on the street and started to move in a wild dance of rolling bodies called the *Bhangra*, rocking their hips, sweeping their arms and feet— what locals called the "happy way." The music reverberated in my chest, and I sat and watched them in awe.

*

Not long before my fifth birthday, I became keenly aware that I wasn't a typical tribal daughter—I wasn't a typical girl at all. Given the choice, I would much rather have played out in the mud plains with Taimur, tossing a ball or shooting marbles, than sit around playing dolls with my dainty sister, Ayesha. Finally, I told my father in a long, impassioned tirade that I wanted to wear clothes like my brother's. He listened, hoisting me up into his lap, and nodded his head, laughing out loud. Everyone in the family had already noticed that I was far more masculine than I was feminine. Not long afterward, my generous Baba came home from the bazaar with a pair of yellow shorts and a matching T-shirt for me to wear around the house. I don't think he ever dreamed that I would go out into the street in those clothes, which I did, always unobserved. Sometimes I look back and believe that that bright, boyish outfit actually changed my whole life.

One day, I strolled along in my sports clothes, following the thin white wake of a passing plane and reciting *suras*—short chapters of the Quran—to the blue heavens. The high, panicked whinny of a horse and the sudden pounding of a wild canter startled me. I saw the white-haired man sitting high on his horse cart, red *kaffiyeh* and AK-47 at his side, hanging from a decorated strap, coming toward me. He moved like a strange vision from an ancient time, threading in and out of tree shade, and I had to stop to watch him. The horse and cart gradually slowed as the man pulled on the reins with gloved hands, and they veered off the pathway. In a moment, the tall rider and horse faced me head-on. I searched the pockets of my shorts for sugar cubes, which I often stashed like candy.

I could feel the intensity of the heat coming off the animal's skin and hear the rough, wet breaths. Its massive belly bulged and its big long neck shone almost silver as I reached out to touch the horse. The man made a sound and the horse stepped forward several paces and I ran my hands along its side as it moved past me. Then I felt the hard tip of a boot tap at my shoulder, and I looked way up at the man's face silhouetted in black shadow against a bright backdrop of summer sky.

"I see the ribbons in your hair, girl, and the devil on your filthy skin."

I brought a hand to my face, felt a silky ribbon slide down my wet back. I should have known by then to run. He loomed above me dark and wheezing, and the horse grunted and looked back. The man fingered his gun strap and nodded as he looked me over from head to toe. Then a riding whip came down through the air with the hiss of a spitting cobra, slicing down my cheek. I shrieked. Loud and hard. I cursed not just the man sitting stunned in his saddle but the dark mountains from which I was sure he had traveled to find me. Before he could hit me again, I ran, back to our neighborhood, up our walkway, and into the pounded-clay rooms of our home.

Within days I allowed my mother to dress me without any grievance, saying nothing, blank-faced as she dropped a heavy, embroidered garment over my head, the weight of the dress nearly equal to my own. While twisting silk ribbons into my hair, fingertips sweetly scented with oil, she looked at me and pointed to the thin red line emblazoned like a burn across my cheek. I shrugged, holding back a torrent of anger. In a day it would be gone, I told her.

That afternoon, from an open window, I watched the boys from our village play in the dry dirt field some distance from my house. I sat there leaning against the mud sill, observing their free movements and feeling my skin grow hot. The gleeful shouting and the back-and-forth dance of the rubber ball between the boys' quick bare feet tormented me. Every now and then, a boy would glance over in my direction and we'd look at each other. I didn't put much emotion into what I did next. A strange new rush of adrenaline and raw instinct propelled me into the fateful act that would define my entire future.

When I lit the pile of silken, kerosene-soaked dresses in the pit, they went up in a wall of flames that made loud cracking sounds like the gunshots fired in celebration of the birth of a new tribal son. The many ribbon adornments came loose and fluttered up with the sudden rush of air and embers. The burning heap of dresses themselves looked like small female bodies stacked lifeless on a pyre after the passing of a fatal judgment. I left everything to burn and put on my brother Taimur's shirt and pants, rolled up the sleeves and cuffs. In another minute, I took a knife to my long hair, tossing the thick, tangled clumps into the fire. Then I ran as though possessed around the flames raging under the tree.

My father entered the garden as the last tongues of smoke

raced up to the bright sky, bits of fabric disintegrating into the hot blue air. For a while, he simply watched me. When I finally turned and caught sight of him standing there, I could see that he was stunned but not angry; I saw in his face a recognition of the very thing he always hoped I would harness—pure Wazir courage. Then he stepped up to me and the two of us stood together in the softly descending ashes, watching the smoke travel toward the horizon like a prophecy. He laughed as he bade farewell to his second daughter and welcomed into his arms his new son.

After I burned my dresses and cut off my hair, my mother and father allowed me to dress and live as I pleased—as Genghis Khan. There was simply no other choice for a child like me, who was living less than half a life as a girl. I had made up my mind already, and it was safer to help me be myself.

And life as a boy was beautiful—without silk ribbons or beaded dresses or long, black braids. It was a bold and rugged beauty, free to run under blue skies. It was sweat-soaked T-shirts and my brother's cast-off shorts. Running shoes and flying kites on the wide-open plain. On one of my first days as a boy, I went out back and crossed into the valley. I joined the group of boys assembled around a huge projection of rock that I knew from my window-watching was their regular meeting spot. Stepping over the blackened pit of an extinguished campfire, I kicked the soot off my new white shoes, eyes never leaving the soccer ball dancing between pairs of moving feet.

The group had names for everything. They called the ball "Magic," the field itself "Ocean," the wealthiest among them "Dubai," the poorest "Uthana", which is Pashto for penny. The fastest was a lean Punjabi called Boomerang. Fists pinned to my sides, hair shorn down to the scalp—my name, I told them, was Genghis Khan.

Deliberately, I walked up to the ball and kicked it. Hard. I heard the taut rubber smack against my shoe and felt a sharp sting. Up it went, as though commanded, into a short, powerful arc. Everything stopped. We watched it spin, black and white blurring to gray, until the ball dropped again to the earth, sending up thin plumes of dust, and all the boys ran out shouting into the sunshine after it. One sure kick was all it took to let them know I would keep up in their group. Dubai and I stood together alone; and he grinned, tapped the glass on his gold watch. He was impressed. I already knew they were short a player.

"Just on time, Genghis Khan. Welcome."

Every afternoon that my mother was home to look after the twins, I met the boys at the base of the rock and we poured across the flat plain, zigzagging around boulders and clusters of tall grasses, playing soccer, firing slingshots, running for no reason at all and stirring up huge sandy clouds. I sprinted among them until my shirt was soaked down the front and back and my temples dripped. When I'd had enough exertion, I'd kneel on the hot-plate ground. Strong, unashamed, hardened from head to toe, I was always first. The youngest by far, I excelled at every physical match. No opponent could beat me; within a week they didn't dare try.

It was strange to think that while they had just met Genghis Khan, I'd known them all for months, watching from the shadows of an upstairs room. I'd seen them sitting on the dry terrain in a semicircle, legs crossed, peeling mangoes, the juice making their fingers glisten as they gnawed on huge pits. Sometimes one or two would brawl, voices cracking, fists flailing, stopping only when someone decided there was too much blood. One of the boys occasionally brought a handmade bow, and they'd wander around whittling away at thin branches with their pocket knives, fashioning arrows to shoot into the hearts of sand-filled sacks. Later, they'd disappear into the summer shimmer as they moved toward the Indus on long afternoon hunts for something live to kill: rabbits or gazelles. For a long time I'd hated those boys; now we were one and the same.

Other afternoons, I'd hike alone along the long, battered farm road running out of town straight into a mile-wide collar of sugarcane fields. Finding my pocket knife, I withdrew the blade from its ivory hull and dovetailed into the long rows, hands feeling stalks until I found one that suited. On my knees, I'd cut a reed close to the base and let it fall to the ground. Then I would chop away forearm lengths of stalk, preserving the joints where pockets of delicious sweet juice gathered, to take home and drink later. Sometimes I'd linger on the old road with time to kill, eating roasted cashews from my pockets. Maria long gone, arms and legs darkening in the sun and covered in bruises, every now and again I'd whisper my three birth names to myself just to make sure my father's daughter was still there.

5. Bhutto's Muse

Sugary green juice running down my chin, I chewed at the cane. A bundle of reeds tucked like a batch of kindling under one arm, I stepped into the coolness of our clay-floored house, such a contrast to the heat outside that my head throbbed. In the cold darkness, I heard my sister's voice traveling through the depths of the quiet rooms, and I followed it out into the backyard.

Clad in a soft draping of white cloth, Ayesha stood as sure and ramrod-straight as a queen on the pitted cement patio. She spoke in a loud, clear voice, enunciating with a clarity and purpose that belied her nine years, delivering a speech about women's rights that she'd been practicing for days. Somehow, my sister already knew that she was destined for a life in politics. By the age of seven, my father had taken her to debating and speech competitions all over the country. At the Government Degree College for Boys in Miranshah, she took first prize, though she was the only girl there as well as the youngest by almost a decade. While the other girls played with dolls and I ran amok, Ayesha honed her oratory skills. Her great ambition, she always told us, was to become secretary-general of the United Nations and work to bring peace to the world. As in all of our aspirations, our father encouraged Ayesha with unwavering enthusiasm. He helped her fine-tune her delivery, and shuttled her whenever he could to debating tournaments all over Pakistan. And when Ayesha had a chance to compete, she always came home with a trophy.

Scabs covering my battered knees, field dust coating my short hair, I could not move as I watched her—white *hijab*, ironed just that morning, so bright I had to squint, Ayesha held her arms at her sides. Before her, in many ranks, stood an army of upended red bricks, placed in perfect rows like checkers on a board. As Ayesha spoke, she addressed the bricks, staring down and taking carefully measured breaths, motioning with her hands, which fluttered in the air. Every now and then, she stopped as though meeting actual sets of eyes, reaching real human ears. I wanted to laugh but knew I should not, catching sight of my father watching from a folding metal chair off to one side, hands on his knees and eyes proud. The air was so still, the sun seemed to shine only for Ayesha. And so I listened.

"Today in this world, in the fight for the liberation of women, there can be no neutrality. And let me tell you this: the best *hijab* is in the eyes of the beholder."

My father had hauled all the bricks from a nearby street in a rusted wheelbarrow, bought in exchange for two sacks of rice from a man who wanted to build an outdoor oven, but changed his mind at the last minute. I remember wondering what my father was going to do with all of those big crimson blocks piled like a second wall along the side of our house. I had no idea he was turning our backyard into a makeshift assembly of UN delegates. He was always making plans; sometimes he concocted wild notions, like letting one of his daughters live out in the open, wandering Taliban country as a boy, or having a wife who wore a jean jacket, read books, and held ambitions for a master's degree. He still hadn't shaved his sideburns.

From his flimsy chair, my father scrambled up, clapping. Making a quick study of the scene, he adjusted a brick or two like a stagehand. Then he turned to me.

"I see you there, eating the grass that makes honey without bees."

And he slid a long stalk of sugarcane out from under my arm, bit a piece off the end, and held the reed out, pointing to the rows of bricks.

"Now, Genghis, listen to your sister as she addresses all the buffoons in the United Nations. They start wars with loaded guns and try to end them with empty words."

"Those are just hard bricks Ayesha is talking to, Baba. Not people."

"Yes, Genghis, you have it exactly. Now, bring out the big laundry basin, and I'll take you on a trip around the world."

In the kitchen, my mother sat at the table, scribbling over sheets and murmuring in a language I didn't understand, a dictionary open, its corners frayed from frenzied thumbing, a half glass of mango juice next to her. As I passed the threshold, she silently held out an open palm, never once lifting her eyes from the white page, her other hand still scrawling with abandon. I placed a sweet reed in her hand and watched her slender, hennaed fingers curl around it, nails lacquered pink. She took my sugarcane and nodded as she bit down, a coy smile and the syrup coating her lips. She turned the pages fast and searched the printed columns. I knew she was writing Ayesha's speeches; it was how they both learned English so well. And I learned it by osmosis, my ears alive on the periphery. Just by listening to my mother and sister speak it, I started to learn the language myself, one word at a time. My father always said that our family was like a factory, working to make intelligent human beings.

Without a word, I hurried to the corner and pulled the big metal basin down from a hook; it clanged like a steel drum beating against the floor. My mother turned, looked at me, eyed the basin that was nearly my height, and grinned.

"I see Phileas Fogg is about to take you around the world. Let us hope it doesn't take him eighty days."

Up and down the lawn, searching the flower beds, my father gathered rocks, and I filled the basin, upending buckets of water until the line reached two inches deep, no more. Beyond our walls, I heard the *clack-clack* of a man cleaning his rifle in a neighboring yard; the slow hum of another decorating his *dhol* drums. My father assembled his rocks around the basin, giving each a careful study, then placing them one by one in the water, each surface like an island projecting above the waterline.

"Now, Ayesha, the biggest rock is which continent—do you see it?"

"Asia. Africa over there is perfect, Baba. Even the horn. You should keep that one."

"And Genghis, the smallest rock. What is it?"

"Antarctica, right there. Let's not go there today. Too cold."

"Yes, you both know your bearings—let me get my boat."

The pitted, cleaned-out hull of an avocado served this purpose, and my father moved our great merchant ship by fingertip from one end of the world to the next. Storms over the Bering Strait rocked us back and forth. Sailors drowned. We were Vikings in Greenland, Marco Polo's companions trading for spices in China, jade from Japan. Ayesha stood over the basin, which reflected bits of her *hijab* across the rippling water like the white chevrons of waves, reciting the names of leaders from the present down into the past, in and out through time, as we traveled from rocky shore to rocky shore in the basin.

"Margaret Thatcher, John Major, George Bush, Bill Clinton, Mao Tse-tung, Fidel Castro, Mikhail Gorbachev, Abraham Lincoln, Mahatma Gandhi"—she turned to me and grinned—"Genghis Khan."

Our hull full of exotic treasures, from pearls to peppercorns, we docked our avocado at the port of Gwadar in the western Pakistani province of Baluchistan along the shores of the Arabian Sea.

Later, my father would go out onto the grass and spread a sheet over the wide base of a twenty-foot *jamun* tree, whose oblong-shaped and purple berries grew in abundance. Hoisting us up with interlaced hands, he sent us climbing high into the full branches, and we felt like explorers in some prehistoric Himalayan world. Fruits so rich and purple and hanging like dark juicy gems.

"Now, my children—jump!"

And we did, Ayesha and I both giggling like birds up there and the branches shaking, ripened fruit coming down like purple hailstones over the clean white sheet.

"Why are leaves green, Ayesha?"

"Chlorophyll."

"How do leaves make food, Genghis?"

"There is a kitchen in the trunk."

"Answer now, my boy, or I will make you memorize ten *suras* instead of five."

"I already know ten today, so it's no matter. But I will tell you, Baba. The answer is photosynthesis, from Allah's great big sun."

And my father let out a roaring laugh. And as he laughed hard, he waved his arms wildly like a conductor, and we jumped high up and down on our branches, arms holding on tight, the fruit raining down all over him, pounding against his head, shoulders, and back, and he caught one in his hand, bit into it, his lips instantly going purple, his tongue dark, as though he'd just dipped it into a pot of ink.

"Ayesha, tell your warrior brother up there on his *jamun* throne the three best words said together in any language."

I could see Ayesha above me, sitting among the leaves and branches. When she grinned at our father's command, I glimpsed the pearls of her teeth. Even now I can still hear that elegant, booming voice. And the thuds of three *jamun* fruit hitting the ground at my father's feet, one for every word.

"We the People . . ."

*

Later, on a television screen—a black-and-white Zenith whose speakers crackled in rhythm to the whirring tape rotors of a VCR borrowed for the weekend from a teacher at the college—stood a woman with big eyes and high cheeks, all in white, speaking. Long arms spread like wings, gaze unflinching. Once, we counted to ninety-nine before we saw her blink. Scouring university libraries, my father brought home tapes of all her famous speeches. I knew her face well, the sound of her voice a torrent of strength as familiar as my mother's; she was the daughter of our once-great leader Zulfikar, and the first female ever elected to lead a Muslim state. Benazir Bhutto—the only hero Ayesha and I had ever had.

As the ninth prime minister of Pakistan, her father had opened over six thousand schools across the country, and Benazir had raised the bar of that legacy to inspire all girls, from one end of the tribal lands to the other, to seek an education. Benazir Bhutto made us believe that we too could aspire to and achieve greatness. Ayesha stood tall in her own veil, facing the grainy screen, speaking. In perfect pitch, she synchronized their voices and mirrored every gesture even adjusting her white *hijab* to punctuate a particular point, stopping to tilt her head and then speak again. Her voice, humming with a power so beyond her years and stature, took all the air out of the room. Suddenly our house was transformed into an auditorium, where I sat with the rest of my family on folding chairs my father had brought back from the college. Then my sister turned to us, Benazir behind her addressing the US House of Representatives back in 1989, both their faces slightly turned, held high; and they said together, as though meeting within a fold of time:

"We gather here to celebrate freedom, to celebrate democracy, to celebrate the three most beautiful words in the English language . . . We the People."

Within a month, Ayesha was sitting next to my father in the pick up, singing out *suras*, hurtling along the Suleiman Mountains and down into the quiet valley of our native village. Benazir Bhutto had accepted an invitation to speak at an assembly of Pashtun leaders deep inside FATA (the Federally Administered Tribal Areas). My father's extended family, who were influential and politically engaged in the region, were key organizers of the event. My father had heard about the meeting and made up his mind to attend it with Ayesha. It might be the only chance she would ever have to actually meet her hero. My sister was determined that she would do more than attend; she told us all that she was going to deliver her best speech to Benazir. My mother and Ayesha honed her speech; cleaned and pressed her whitest veil. Then my father gassed up the pickup for the long, winding journey back to our tribal land. Despite appearances, they were not really welcome there—someone had ratted out my mother for abandoning her domestic duties to go to college. I would be next. But Pashtunwali code demanded unreserved hospitality.

Baba knew it would be just enough—they needed less than one day, even one hour.

Armed guards in convoys surrounded the village on all sides. My father needed no papers—you could tell from his eyes and the way he spoke that he belonged. With offhand waves, the guards let them in. My father and sister could see the tent was up, hear drumbeats and a rifle discharge several times. Ayesha unfolded her white *hijab* and draped it over herself, my father making adjustments here and there. He knew his cousins and uncle would be mortified to see them.

By the time my father and nine-year-old Ayesha, in her clean clothes, entered the tent, it was far too late to turn her away. No one wanted to risk a scene at such an important event, and they all knew they could count on my father to make one if anyone crossed him. Heads whipped around, mouths opened, but no one dared do a thing. Who could say a word when the only other female in the room, invited to address the most powerful families of FATA, was an ex–prime minister and the progeny of a great liberator? My father said as much, laughing when he later told us every detail of the story.

Within minutes of their entrance, Benazir Bhutto took to the stage. Her eyes commanded the room. Ayesha started counting in her head, and she told me that she had reached forty-three when those eyes locked on her own. They blinked in tandem, touched their veils. No one made a sound when Benazir spoke; all that could be heard was her voice rising like a great tide washing over the assembly. Cameras flashed. Guards lined the perimeter, on the lookout for gunmen, suicide bombers; there was always a multitude of threats. After a few minutes, one or two older men groaned, but most were still; a few feet shifted on the bright silks of the Afghan rugs laid out over the gravel.

The assembly rose as soon as Benazir Bhutto was done speaking. The boom of a rifle sounded, and the crowd closed in as she descended the dais to greet several people in person. Our Wazir cousins, who should have taken her small hand, pushed against Ayesha, letting her know that her presence was unwelcome. She might have gotten away with sitting in the audience, but they were determined to keep her from getting anywhere near Benazir Bhutto. Somehow, as the gathering surged, she'd lost my father. The men were raucous and shoving one another to get in closer. Female or not, the woman up there was powerful, and just to touch her hand they would have severed another. Twenty-five men in each row, fifteen rows—Ayesha had counted. Seeing my father through the mob of bodies, she held out her hands to slice her way through. She told us later that it felt as though she was squeezing through a narrow tunnel, there were so many people all pressed around her.

My father grabbed Ayesha's hand and pulled her through the heaving throng. Then, a row of figures, Ayesha spied through the flutter of a white robe slip over a red Afghan rug—almost close enough to touch. A second was all it took for the woman to see that small rose blooming in the forest, and Benazir turned.

"There is a child here. Let her speak to me."

"Your Excellency, I have written a speech for you. In English. May I, please?"

"Make her a path up to the dais, and let us all hear her."

When Ayesha spoke, her voice poured in waterfalls of perfect pitch and cadence over the assembly:

"Why should a girl not learn in university, see a doctor, travel the world as Benazir Bhutto has? Why marry a man at all, if a girl chooses not to? Why should a gun decide where the mind should hold dominion? Where did our choices go? Allah didn't take them—men did. Nothing anyone can do will stop me from saying these things. I will speak for women's rights and against injustice everywhere. Try to stop me and I will say it all, even louder."

When Ayesha was finished, Benazir, sitting on a silk-draped seat, beckoned, her gold bangles singing.

"I have ten thousand rupees in my purse. I give them to you, as I believe that must be your price."

Ayesha, with a soft smile, said:

"Excellency, as you are no longer our prime minister, I cannot accept such a gift. You must need every rupee in your purse."

Benazir Bhutto turned her head to one side, considered a moment, and stared a long time at my sister, who stared back straight-faced, unblinking. So many minutes passed, the crowd held in a hush, my father thought they might be speaking in a way no one else could hear. Then Benazir laughed. Those intelligent eyes, those perfect teeth and *jamun* lips; with her Harvard and Oxford degrees and bulletproof mind, she was the embodiment of every dream Ayesha had for herself.

"Child, do not call me Excellency. From this day, call me Mother."

One encounter with her hero heightened Ayesha's resolve to fulfill her political aspirations, and she never once wavered from that path. By the time she was in her early teens, she had a job working as a current affairs host on a national television show filmed in Islamabad. Sitting before the camera all grace and poise, no one would have guessed that she was still a child. When my sister had a dream, she reached for it with both arms. And she never gave up on the dream of meeting Benazir Bhutto in person again. As soon as she was of age, Ayesha joined the Pakistan People's Party (PPP) and stepped onto the political stage as though she owned it. Over the years, there had been letters back and forth, the gift of an Oxford dictionary as big as a cinder block, two lavish dresses.

Nine years after that first encounter, Ayesha's dream would be realized in Islamabad. Then, at just eighteen and once again draped in her pristine whites, but with ministers and members of the national and provincial assemblies surrounding her instead of tribal elders, Ayesha was in another crowded room waiting for Benazir to address the crowd. If my sister was nervous, she never showed it. Someone once said that when crossed in a debate, Ayesha could bring about an ice age with a look from her eyes— though she melted more hearts than my father could count. When she was barely ten, a rich Pashtun who wanted her as a bride for his reckless son offered her full weight in gold to my father to make the promise.

That day, Benazir Bhutto was sitting in a chair when Ayesha

came forward, sun streaming behind her through a wall of tall windows; her figure glowing white, that crown of black hair just visible against the edge of her veil. Bhutto later told her secretary she thought in that moment she'd glimpsed an angelic vision of herself, years before, when she'd come back to Pakistan from Massachusetts and Oxford to cash in her lofty dreams.

"I have seen you before, but you are not me."

"No, we've met before, half my lifetime ago. I'm from South Waziristan and I won't call you Excellency."

Bhutto brought her hands to her face, the polished gold bands and bangles shackling her fingers and wrists flashing. Later, they said, she left the room to weep, as that small child coming back to her as an educated woman was a manifestation of all the work she had done to liberate young girls in Pakistan. After that meeting, people began to say that Ayesha was Bhutto's muse. The minute my sister had uttered the first word, Benazir Bhutto knew exactly who she was.

"What will you call me then?"

"You remember—I will not call you Excellency, I will call you Mother."

*

Muslims believe in predestination, or *qadar*—that everything that has transpired or will come to pass was written out in a divine decree at the inception of all life. Our births were written before we were born. The very hour and manner of our deaths were foretold millennia before we take our last breath. And my father always taught us that great leaders are granted only a flash of life to set the world on fire, such was their written destiny—Mahatma Gandhi, John F. Kennedy, Martin Luther King, Nawabzada Liaquat Ali Khan, a founding father of modern Pakistan—Zulfikar Ali Bhutto. We never wanted to consider that his daughter might one day join that list, though we feared it—courage in Pakistan is often a fatal virtue. In our hearts and minds, Benazir Bhutto was smarter than the others, special, and her work to emancipate the women of Pakistan and to rid the tribal region of extremists was not nearly done. When her political rivals drummed up corruption charges against her in the late 1990s, she left the country for eight years of self-imposed exile in Dubai and London to assure her own safety.

When she returned triumphant, with an amnesty from President Musharraf, my father said it was a mistake. "Go back, go back," he said, as he watched news footage of her plane landing in Karachi. We all knew her life was at risk—two suicide bombers tried and failed to kill her shortly after she left the airport, massacring 136 people. Even now, I can hear my father pleading with her exquisite image, as she waved to the masses, to leave our country. She did not, and all we had for solace was our faith in *qadar*—Benazir Bhutto's time, as it was written long before time itself, had come. We saw it happen in our living room. It was 2007. We sat on a semicircle of rugs, and when the screen showed blood, we saw it for what it was.

Thousands of people were gathered in the garrison town of Rawalpindi, the elections just two weeks away. Everyone there believed our new leader had come home for good. There she was, standing alone on the lectern among a sea of chanting men. Big smile. Unafraid. White veil—translucent this time; the glasses she wore more often than not; royal-blue dress, satin sheen. She glanced at her watch before leaving, as though time didn't matter anymore. Or perhaps it did, each squandered second a lost linchpin to survival, though she didn't know it. She tripped on the hem of a long scarf, a drab thing that might have been dipped in mud, going down the steps, flanked by people singing her name again and again all the way to her car. I remember thinking that had she not slipped on that fringe, she could have gained the seconds needed to cheat the echo of her father's destiny. Not checked her watch. Not waved to the crowd that one time. Not been there at all. Never come back to us from her exile. A man stepped forward and helped her with a flourish, and she stopped to thank him. Another four seconds—far too late.

She took a white armored Toyota Land Cruiser. But she stood up through the open roof hatch, head and shoulders exposed to greet the wild, jubilant throng. Hundreds deep, arms raised, bodies swarmed the car. Voices called her name, chanting out into a great roar of adulation. The video, grainy and crude, showed her white veil, her face turned away when it happened. Amid the chanting, the chaos of the crowd—three quick shots. One pistol, one clean-shaven man. And Benazir Bhutto, our high hope, her smiling picture adorning the walls of our rooms all our lives, wherever we lived, however we suffered, went straight back down into the hatch. My father played the video back again several times to listen to those shots. Closed his eyes, held up his fingers. One, two, three. He pointed out the way her head moved and her *hijab* shifted just as the gunman fired. Immediately following the bullets, a bomb blast detonated and the screen went white, then black. We knew already from her sudden lifeless fall that the wound was fatal. The news stations reported that Benazir died in the hospital some time later.

There was carnage in the aftermath. Cries of pain through smoke. The exuberant scene one moment before suddenly transformed into an abandoned battlefield. Everywhere, parts of people, parts of cars, parts of buildings, all scattered in bits like garbage strewn over the rally square. The black, blood-spattered floor of an abattoir in hell. The living walked like zombies among the dead and half dead, the whites of their eyes bulging, stains on their clothes. Some of them were soaked red from limb to limb. Pant legs shredded, one man sat in a daze against another, missing his feet. He was pointing to another man, still able-bodied, walking past, and somehow I knew he was sending him out to find his shoes, his incinerated feet. When I asked my father, he said the man was in shock and wouldn't die. The heat from the blast had cauterized his wounds.

Later in the week, we saw footage of the interior of Bhutto's car. Blooms of blood stained the seat where she had fallen back like an angel, unconscious. A gush soaked into the cushion. Her black leather shoes, the insides pink, lay on their sides. Two shots hit her, my father said, one in the neck; he called it a mortal wound. At the time, I thought a fatal injury should be called immortal, because we all know our bodies die but we do not. There were two men—the gunman and a sidekick bomber. Plan A and Plan B. The first got Bhutto point-blank; then the second man got himself and twenty others, just one second later. Dozens were maimed. All those half-ruined limbs lying in puddles of blood belonged to people now dead or only partly alive. The meticulous bomber must have packed all of his clothes with lethal shrapnel—mostly nails, packets of razor blades, metal pellets designed for BB guns. Just one through an eye could kill.

The government tried to control the information about the method of death, and their narrative changed by the week. They said Benazir hit her head, cracked her skull open on a window lever. They showed X-rays on TV. It did not matter one way or the other, not to us. Not to my sister, who had pinned her very soul to Benazir. We saw the end of the thing we cherished most, our high hope—vanquished.

"Why do they care how, Baba? She is gone."

"Maria, everything is in the how. A gunshot makes a martyr. An accident makes a fool."

Then we turned to see Ayesha sitting against the wall, gold dress, adjusting her veil, busying her hands to quiet her breaking heart. I knew she was counting up the seconds before she blinked.

"Bhutto's Muse, tell me one thing as you sit alone over there like a child I knew years ago who made the fruit tremble on a *jamun* tree. Tell me before we all start to cry, though we know things are just as they were written. It is all Allah's will."

"I'll tell you whatever will help you, Baba."

My father moved away from the screen, stepped up to his daughter, pulled back her veil, and took her pale hands.

"What are the three most beautiful words ever spoken in any language?"

Ayesha looked up, black eyes shining.

"Call me Mother."

6. The Wall

Not long after my father's and Ayesha's fight with the elders at Benazir Bhutto's speech, we were forced out of our own tribe and told that we could never go back to our native valley, not even for a day. Whatever transpired at the *jirga*, the elders' decision was final—transgression would be fatal. My family's acts of heresy and dishonor were far too many now to count, or ever forgive. Over the course of many years, my father had persistently and publicly raised his voice for women's rights. I was seven years old and living out in the open dressed as a boy; my mother was still attending college; and all the members of our family lived as equals—male or female. My father often did household chores with my older brother, Taimur. The elders gave him many warnings, but my father refused to submit to their conservative patriarchal code. As the eldest son of an eldest son, Shams held a position of influence in the clan that his renegade views began to steadily undermine. Soon a proud and power-seeking uncle saw a chance for his own son to take my father's place in the hierarchy and plotted Shams' demise.

In the middle of the night, a group of cousins went to shoot my father, but a firefight ensued that lasted until daybreak. In the end, my father survived, but two cousins were dead. To this day my father believes that Allah had protected him against those who conspired against him, so that he could carry on his work to achieve justice for his daughters, and all the daughters who had no father to speak out for them. He could not bring himself to see any of us subjugated any more than we already had been—it simply wasn't in his heart.

"Look at the bird tending its nest. Does it feed the male birds first, or tend to their needs before the females? No. They see and know no difference between their offspring. I am the same. I love and treat my sons and daughters equally. I believe this is what Allah truly wishes for our race, and I will not yield out of fear."

I know my father said as much to the elders at the *jirga* and in that moment relinquished his privileged family ties and all the trappings that came with them. The only thing that saved him from a swift death sentence at the last tribal meeting he would ever attend was his noble lineage. Despite the consequences, he was willing to surrender blue-blooded wealth and power to emancipate his wife and daughters. I remember well how my father explained his predicament when we learned that we were truly outcasts and would never see our many cousins and other relatives again. He read out loud a quote from Friedrich Nietzsche, holding a beat-up hardcover book of philosophy in his hands as though it were a holy tome, and each word went straight into me like a courage-tipped arrow.

"The individual has always had to struggle to keep from being overwhelmed by the tribe. If you try it, you will be lonely often, and sometimes frightened. But no price is too high to pay for the privilege of owning yourself."

*

Our pick-up truck was piled higher this time, with every possession we could fit. My mother had been offered a position running a local school, and my proud father moved us all so that she could accept it. Within months, she was promoted and sent to administer girls' schools as well as teach all over the region. I sat in the back, muscled legs tanned to a molasses shade, big arms hard as granite. I had one of my father's tattered old T-shirts on—Led Zeppelin. Signposts flew past us like giant playing cards: TOCHI MATCHSTICK COMPANY, KHYBER-MATCH. From the open back of the truck we could smell the fragrant air—

cardamom and sulfur. Shams turned to us, smiling through the back window from the driver's seat; he had to shout over the racing wind: "It smells like the fireworks on Independence Day!" It was not quite dusk, and flocks of cranes flew across the sky like living boomerangs. Beyond us in the valley, jet planes sat parked along the army airfield like giant resting birds themselves. Several times, we had to pull over and stop at military checkpoints, my father always affable with the questioning Frontier Corps officers, showing off his Soviet-era Makarov pistol and multilingual books. They were on the lookout for smugglers, extremists, opium dealers, addicts—anyone with trouble on their minds or blood on their hands.

Soon we approached Fort Miranshah, whose high stone walls rose from a rocky ledge along amber-colored ground like a vision out of the colonial past with ramparts and lookout towers. The massive edifice stood as so many others the British built across the frontier lands to concentrate their legions and subdue the wild Pashtun—yet there we were, a whole family of Wazir exiles, tearing toward the city perimeter in our rusted truck.

As pious as ever, five times each day on the journey, we got out of the truck, washed our hands in streams or with wet cloths, and knelt over our mats to pray, remembering each time who we were and what we believed, as those two things were one and the same. At the entrance of the main boulevard we stopped for the muezzin's melodic calls, recited our supplications, and then made our way into Miranshah, which spread out in a mass of low buildings, shadowed alleys, and packed streets.

The Government Degree College, where my father had found a job as a professor of auto engineering, skirted the eastern rim of town. Teaching positions at universities were scarce and often only temporary, lasting a few semesters or a few years. When my father's application was accepted, he was jubilant. We had a good home to go to, my parents both had stable jobs, and my siblings would continue to go to school while I took care of the twins—though we could never go back into the fold of our tribe.

Every campus building in Miranshah looked new, and to me

the patches of lawn between them seemed so green, I thought they might have been painted. We were close to the air base, and I felt the booming engines of a landing jet thunder in my chest. My father laughed over the deafening roar and said the runway was seven thousand feet long. Our truck bumped along streets lined with posts and wires. My father had a city map unfolded across his lap, but he didn't look down once.

His position came with a house in what was referred to as the "college colony," homes usually reserved for professors and their families. It had views, he said, of open land on one side, the dense and sprawling cityscape on the other. When we pulled into the neighborhood, I knew right away we'd lucked out. Government posts in Pakistan had their perks. The compound had tall iron gates and long stone walls that surrounded a garden full of trees—mulberry, bottle brush, apples, apricots, purple plum-like *jamuns*, and a half-dead pomegranate off to one side. Our bunga-low was made of cool cement and had running water, which was clean, and we could use as much as we pleased. There was a room for each of us, and others to spare. The size of the house made up for the fact that we had so little to put inside it. Right away, my mother sent us out into the plain with sacks to gather dead leaves and make our mattresses. We had electricity, but nothing to plug in except a fan.

My mother's job teaching girls and overseeing their schools often took her all over the region. For a short time Ayesha and I attended one of her schools in Miranshah-Bazar, which was a half-hour journey on foot through mountain passes where we would often stop to collect fossils. Several times each week, after our morning *fajr* prayers, we would set off next to Aami out into the quiet dawn, barely a whisper of light to guide us. When we reached the main road, the local horse carts that served as public transportation would take us the rest of the way. Once my mother received a new post as the principal of a school in Darra Adam Khel, our routine suddenly changed. The journey between her new school and our home was nine hours by bus; she also took master's classes when she could—English, literature, history, and politics. We saw her on weekends, while during the week she slept on cots in back rooms at the schools she administered. She wore her jean jacket inside, her face as enchanting and unashamed as ever, but outside she went everywhere in a *burqa* and was wary. In her absence, I often ran the house like her understudy. Ayesha continued to excel academically, but helped with the chores when she came home from school. My family always worked as a team, each one doing what they could to help the others. Thankfully, I took easily to learning at home and looking after the twins. Playing mother, washing clothes, killing quail with a slingshot. I de-feathered and gutted fowl in the yard, then I'd roast the delicate birds on spits over red coals for supper. We ate chutneys made from mint and guava. I served scrambled eggs, fried-up tomatoes and onions in spice, and fruit from the plentiful trees— whatever I could reach that was ripe.

As night fell, the house cooled, and wind rushed through; sometimes we could hear storms pounding mountains miles beyond the Tochi Valley like the restless ghosts of the Hindu Kush. My sister, who feared no man, was terrified of thunder; flashes of lightning would make her cry out. All through her childhood, she believed that the world would come to an end through a massive bombing, and each new storm stirred that terror. Often between thunderclaps, and in a breathless voice, she would teach me to recite *ayahs*, calming herself in the faith that Allah would protect us. Five mornings each week I was up before dawn, and if there had been an overnight storm, I often found Ayesha all tangled up in her nightdress and lying fast asleep next to me.

Every morning, I made the rounds of the house—the corridors and the many shadowed rooms where my family slept on their makeshift beds. I checked every one. I could hear them, father and siblings, breathing like pumps in tandem, so that it seemed that the house itself was a single living thing or an engine moving us all together. I felt my mother's absence then, as I took on the sacred tasks of her morning rituals.

I would venture to the courtyard to pray out in the open, as was my way, and then to the kitchen. Fanning the smoke from the cooking fire, I could hear my mother call to me by my rarely used middle name: *Gulgatai, Gulgatai*—rosebud, and I never understood why she sometimes called me that, her hotheaded seven-year-old girl masquerading as a boy and hardened from head to toe. She said she was only giving the name to what she knew of my soul.

My father's classroom at the college was a vast warehouse full of machinery, whole vehicles, trucks and tractors, engines on blocks, dismembered cars spread out in greasy bits and oily chunks over long work tables. I'd often visit him at school, where I would find him wandering his domain, ferreting around with tools, untangling clumps of wires, crouching under engines, always talking—if not to himself, then to a cluster of captivated students.

"Henry Ford said that failure is a chance to begin again, but the next time more intelligently. So fail here all you must, but always start again. That's how he built the V-8 engine on a single block when all of his engineers said it couldn't be done."

Often I brought my toddler brothers with me to the warehouse, and we'd spend hours playing in the gutted cars and trucks, dusty rays streaming in from the high open doors, while my father taught classes or dismantled engines. Roaming the periphery, sucking on sugar cubes I would keep in my pockets, I picked up bits of knowledge here and there like dropped coins. Before long, I could name the basic parts of an automotive engine: cylinders, pistons, spark plugs, valves all working together for a singular purpose—motion. And that's all my family ever seemed to do—move.

Mesmerized, I watched my father perform miracles at the helm of his classroom. Igniting drops of gasoline in a small tube, he directed the massive eruption of energy to catapult a single mango several hundred feet and straight over the heads of his spellbound students. Hitting the door of a white Datsun, the fruit instantly pulverized. "Behold, combustion! Do this one hundred times in a minute and you have a car engine. Do this with your mind and you'll change the world." At that moment, I knew that my father was a marvel. He made me feel rich when I was with him, poor while he was away. He taught me every single thing I knew. Fearless and genuine, he was honest to the core, with his mass of dark hair, unruly sideburns, and infinite grin. It never occurred to me for a moment how little my professor father was paid, how hungry he might have been, skipping lunches so we could have shoes.

Hands coated in grime, my father often came home in the evening with treasure: a single square of Turkish delight dusted in sugar and carefully cut into small pieces and shared; ballpoint pens from the college; a sack of scuffed-up marbles; postcards of the Egyptian pyramids, the Eiffel tower, Big Ben; an old Rubik's Cube with some of the stickers missing. My father had a way of finding and bartering for dilapidated curiosities that were like tiny windows out into the big world. He got the run-down Rubik's Cube at a roadside stall for a bag of fruit from our trees. Sometimes he came back with people instead of things, inviting them in with a flourish and telling me to put on a pot of black tea.

"Meet my new friend. He's an oncologist from Lahore and he's going to explain how our body can rebel against us if we rebel against it. Five minutes with him and you'll never touch a cigarette."

Sitting on the cold clay floor of our living room, we were introduced to film actors from Iran who told us wild Shakespearean tales; a dentist showed us models of rotten teeth; we listened rapt as poets read out couplets, painters explained the variances of light. Once, he brought home a pair of American backpackers, two men from New York City: "Take note, you won't see this kind of human again for many years, if at all. I discovered them both eating figs under a poplar tree, and couldn't believe my luck."

The young men sat on mats in our living room, showing their perfect teeth within easy smiles, and jabbering beautifully on and off for three days, drinking tea and eating naan with dal with us.

Every now and then, from the deep recesses of their big packs, they handed out sour candies and lollipops that changed my tongue from red to green. They slept on mats inside long cloth bags, like butterflies in chrysalises. The Americans' stories were wild and impossible to fathom: strip malls, escalators, elevators, dishwashers, vacuum cleaners, jury duty, the Peace Corps, Yankee Stadium, making choices like traveling the world, getting tattoos, marrying for love alone.

It was the first time I'd seen hair the color of maize, skin so white you could pour it into a glass. Freckles. When I cut my knee, they gave me a sticky strip of fake skin called a Band-Aid. I taught them to recite my favorite *suras*; they sang me "The Star-Spangled Banner." I remember thinking that being star-spangled meant smiling like an American. It meant having everything. Being American, they said, meant being free—my father had already taught us the word "democracy."

Late one afternoon, my father brought home a derelict he had picked up on one of his rounds of Miranshah, running errands, people-watching—always on the lookout for teachers. We were never sure how he got the frail young man across town, and conjectured about it for a whole hour—splayed across his shoulders, stuffed in a borrowed wheelbarrow? It turned out they'd just walked slowly side by side—my father was a patient man. Without a word, he led his guest in by the arm, gently, as though unaware of his putrid clothes. We all stepped back as they moved past us. The foulness that came off his skin like a living death made us touch our own faces. I held my breath—hard to believe that a human being could reek from the inside out of garbage.

In the kitchen, my father fed him first—a plate of steamed white rice, roasted goat meat, and a ripe pomegranate. Then he filled a big bowl with warm water and carefully washed the man's feet with sandalwood soap, talking softly all the while; he touched his trembling hands, cleaned off the grit, and gave him a fresh shirt and let him take his time. He was clean but still dazed and disheveled. We all congregated in the living room and waited for him to speak.

"Please tell my children how you came to be all alone in this world, living on the streets as a beggar. May Allah make an angel of you for letting your sorrows nourish their minds."

That was the day I learned about heroin—how to get it and why not to try it. The man my father led by the arm through our front doorway to the only cushioned seat we owned, a fake-leather desk chair borrowed from the college, was an Afghan and addict from the Khyber tribal region. He hadn't started using until his mother did, after a neighbor gave her a small hit for her sore throat. Instantly, her pain was gone, vanishing in an unexpected rush of wild euphoria. Soon she started to smoke the drug for every ailment and twinge: headaches, insomnia, fevers, and the shakes; to drown out her crying babies, color in her boredom, or dull the depths of her loneliness—she'd been married off to an uncle twice her age.

My father's guest became an addict by proxy while sitting next to his mother as she lit up globs of black tar in her long glass pipe. The curling smoke infiltrated his system like silken tendrils, seducing every ounce of him. First opium, then heroin. He tried a full hit when he couldn't sleep, melting the opiate down to gold liquid and injecting himself with a needle borrowed from the woman next door. She showed him how to do it, tying his bicep and tapping veins. They all believed heroin was just medicine, like aspirin or a cup of Virgin's Mantle tea. It was everywhere, sold by the spoonful in every village, so much of it and so cheap. Miles of poppy fields barely a hike away. Before the plunger hit the bottom of his syringe, the serpent had called him by name. Instantly, his skin flushed with an embrace of warmth he told us was so much better than love. Better than the finest meal, money, a whole future. Before long, he slept every afternoon with heroin; she was his lover, his best friend, his new mother—the other one had descended so far into her own living trance that she hardly spoke to any of them anymore. Their combined stupor carried on until one baby was dead.

At fourteen, with nowhere to go and little to eat, the man told us he'd taken a job as a poppy picker in the crimson fields of

Kunar, and was soon promoted for his nimble feet and innocent face to cross-border smuggler. They nicknamed him "Marathon" for his speed, and for a while he was a star—until he grew useless from "the curse" of addiction. Then they beat him senseless in the back of a jeep and dumped his used-up body on the barren route to Miranshah. Mother dead from an overdose, father long gone, his siblings who knows where—there wasn't a living soul alive who gave a damn about him. By the time Marathon sat in our living room, he'd been to jail twice; a deflated creature, not really a man at all, open sores oozing along his arms, hands like claws, face pummeled from poison, we could not guess his age.

"Seventeen."

My father held the boy up to us like a huge red flag—*you live in the most heroin-addicted country in the entire world*. We started to see versions of him all over town: shadows huddled around fires in the Tochi Valley, lying on benches by the playing fields, wandering alleys behind the mosque. Those were the future recruits of extremists, willing suicide bombers culled by the thousands from the streets, all of them only half alive and plied into complacency with dope.

Not long after that visit, my father walked through the front gates with a red flower and held it out to us like a teacup sitting in his palm. Dark center, I could smell its ruby sweetness—the Red Sea, I thought, must be filled with poppies. My father pulled out a seed head, slit it open with his jackknife, and told us about the poison inside that had lured poor Marathon and his mother.

"The worst suffering is born of the greatest beauty. Kiss this red bloom just once and she'll suck out your soul."

All of us wondered if my father was able to do what he'd promised and deliver that drug-eaten man to a treatment center in one of the big cities, where they made such people whole again. But Marathon could not outrun what chased him. My father said he knew already from washing his infected limbs that the boy had AIDS.

*

The world beyond us had always seemed immaterial, until my father started to invite it in, bit by bit, person by person, story by story. There was evil out there, I already knew that much. In defiance, I made my body stronger, like reinforcing a building against an impending hurricane. Fifty chin-ups in the courtyard became two hundred. One hundred sit-ups, three. My father bought an old red Sohrab bike with a deep basket for me and Taimur to use to run errands. I cycled the streets sometimes for hours at a time. I lifted buckets filled with stones. Mostly, I ran, hard and fast, mile after mile.

Then I discovered that from our flat rooftop, I could jump to the one next door, and the one after that, and soon I was hurdling from roof to roof for hours; there were so many houses in the colony. I grew so muscular and fast that it felt as though I'd grown another body altogether. At barely eight years old I looked well over ten. When my mother was home, I thought nothing of running the roofs all afternoon, even when I heard her call me back. My time was all mine, and I took it with me.

My rooftop vantage gave a beautiful panorama: boys dancing over the gulley playing soccer, running with wild abandon, flying kites. One September day, I watched several figures in the distance hold a big yellow diamond of taut silk between them, silky tail dancing over the ground. The kite's shining skin trembled in the wind, ready to go. One boy positioned himself as anchor while another continued in a wild sprint over the ground, holding the kite straight up over his head. I thought the running boy might take off, so powerful was the wind. Then, as though signaled by some instinctive cue, the child let go. The kite took off, taking my breath with it. The silk ship climbed high toward a sliver of pale day-moon. Then the boy with the spool ran with the kite, pulling down hard to maneuver it. The wind blew harder, and riding those gusts, the kite swirled. I left the rooftop and ran too, legs pounding cement, and I saw that he saw me. Soon we were running in unison, he across the Tochi Valley, me along the roofs, and all the boys behind us shouting.

I was the only boy without a kite of my own. Somehow I knew

better than to ask my father to pay for such an extravagance—though I hated the feeling of wanting what I could not have. It never occurred to me that my father was an engineer and knew everything about the physics of flight. A man who could build a car engine from bits of metal, or make a cannonball out of a mango, would have no difficulty fashioning a kite from scraps of silk and bamboo.

The yellow kite continued to climb until it ran out of line. Then the boy stopped and began to reel it in as though he'd caught something from the sea of sky. I stood there panting, and watched all the other boys cluster around their pilot. I could hear their excited banter. For the first time, I thought I was poor.

The boy brought in his precious plane, and I watched the lazy descent. I could see the yellow shape coming down toward me, growing steadily bigger, shedding altitude in increments. Again I ran after it, the boy still anchored to the ground. The kite came down lower and lower, and the boy looked over and watched me running. He pulled down on his spool, every movement strong and deliberate. Then he shouted and let his kite swoop in like a seagull over me. On raw impulse alone, I jumped high, hands practically reaching the thin scythe moon. A satiny tail caressed my open palms, and I grabbed at it, pulling down the beautiful thing that I suddenly hated. The boys called out, shrieking. I snapped the thin bamboo scaffolding and threw it to the ground, stomping at it as though it were a living thing. I ripped the yellow silk to shreds. All motion in the field ceased; for a moment, there was only the gusting wind and my fury. Then the boys looked to one another and began to run. I watched their approach and counted fast—thirteen of them, racing toward me in a collective rage. Panicked, I took off. And never looked back. Not once.

I ran for more than an hour—up and down drainpipes, across town, I just kept going. Fight or flight—if they caught me, I was finished. Out of breath and panting, I knew I'd finally lost them. No one was faster than I was. Palms pressed against my knees, the sweat dripping off my forehead and spattering the concrete, I stood up on a high roof in another unfamiliar neighborhood; parched beyond pain, my brain crackling from heat.

A line of unmistakable blue caught my eye. I knew it was still too far to reach before the sun receded, but the next morning I packed a small sack with fruit and headed out. I didn't even think about the kite—I thought I would touch the Arabian Sea by high noon. Mountains were my markers on the long hike, and sometimes I ran. Dusty gusts blew into me with the sound of crashing waves. I made myself believe the air was salty, and imagined how the water would foam over my toes.

But it wasn't to be so—I could see a hard line cutting along the landscape before I ever reached the place where my shoreline should have been. Sprinting, I ran straight into a wall rising from the ground, more than twice my height. I could not see past it. Plumes of black smoke from the other side billowed over the top of the barrier. There was the smell of scorched meat and an ominous perfume of filth and squalor. A voice inside my brain shrieked out a warning, but the blue vision from the day before haunted me.

I walked the base of the long wall, listening to the low human din that came from the other side. There were people over there, lots of them, maybe a whole town I'd never heard of. Maybe someone in there would know how to find the ocean. I'd seen maps of the valley, checked one just the night before, and there was no town, no village—and no ocean, though I still wanted to believe in it.

Along one section of the barricade I found a breach. The wall was made from old cinder block, and someone had pushed out several bricks to form a small way in. Or out—I could not tell. Examining the opening awhile, I made grim calculations. Strange how the body foretells danger. Against every instinct, I knelt down in the dirt.

Snippets of Dari and Pashto, wails of babies, and a strange human clamor grew in intensity. Smoke filled the air and my eyes stung. I held my breath and pushed all the way through the wall, tearing a small hole in my *shalwar kameez*. I'd worn that white shirt reserved for feast days especially to greet the ocean, as though it wasn't an elemental body at all, but a king. Standing up as I stepped out, I gazed a long time at the scene—and knew I'd made a mistake.

The blue I dreamed of was not the ocean, wasn't water at all, wasn't even real. What I found was a series of man-made tarps, patched together one after the other for at least a half mile, blue and billowing, like sails filling with wind hanging above make-shift sets of scaffolding. The tents ran a hundred feet from the wall and parallel to it in a long row that seemed to have no end. The camp was huge, and housed hundreds, if not thousands.

Children sat bone thin and listless in the dirt, or wandered like half-dead creatures. By appearance, the women were all one and the same, caged in the fabric of their *burqas,* every face obscured behind a patch of mesh. The few men walked the lines of dilapidated tents in small groups, some with sticks in their hands like police batons. Aimless. Every now and then, one would reach out and hit a woman. No reason.

Then, as though someone had flicked a switch, all at once I heard every sound, smelled the overpowering foulness, and felt it hit me hard like a punch to the gut. A filthy needle was at my foot; I'd nearly stepped on it. Standing there, immobilized, a wave of nausea went through me. That was when I heard the boys calling out, and at first I wondered how they'd found me—one day later and miles away. By the time I turned around, I was sur-rounded. But these weren't the colony boys I knew, looking for an explanation and a replacement kite. They weren't like any boys I'd ever seen.

For the first time ever in a gang of males, I felt physically weak. Not because my strength was less, but because my horror reduced me to a coward. Somehow, I knew just by looking at them that I would never defeat their hatred. I simply stood there in my clean shirt, that small tear suddenly a mockery.

It didn't last long. Maybe two blows straight into my abdo-men. Maybe three. Then I was on the ground, on all fours and vomiting. One kicked me in the ribs and I went all the way down, flat on my stomach. Then they tore at my clothes in a frenzy. I thought they might be so hungry they were going to peel away my skin, eat me alive. One small boy already had my satchel and was digging in. His mouth tore away chunks of my half-eaten apple. I watched him rip into the fruit before anyone could take it from him. Wounds like bite marks covered his forearms. The others were still on me. I wished they'd just slit my throat and get it over with. I could feel their sour breath on my face, which was now wet with blood and spit that mixed with the dirt from the ground until I was coated in a thick, ugly paste.

My clean shirt was the crime. The breakfast of naan and dried apricot I'd had before leaving. My satchel full of food, however meager. The house I lived in. Clean water—so much of it. My third-hand sandals, which they snatched from my feet. My squeaky-clean Pashtun blood. Those boys were united in rage, dragging themselves down the food chain straight to the bottom. I made up my mind not to move as they kicked and slapped— not so much as a muscle in response. I made no sound. Eyes closed, I just lay there taking it until they were done. *None of this would have happened*, I thought over and over again, *if I hadn't snapped the yellow kite*.

When at last they tired, which didn't take long, they simply slowed their pummeling to a few pathetic pushes, a final kick, and they wandered off. Not a word was spoken; no one so much as glanced back. I never saw a single face that I would remember. And I lay there in the dirt a long time, until I thought it was safe to crawl back out through the hole in the wall.

Later, my father taught me the word "refugee" the way he taught me everything else, but without bringing treasure home. I had walked right into it myself.

"They lost their humanity when they lost their homes. The Russians chased the Afghans out, then the Americans promised them a way back with free weapons. They used to give them food and clothes. So did the Saudis. But once the mujahideen got rid of the Russians, everyone stopped sending anything. Just abandoned them to those camps for Pakistan to feed."

For years afterward, those faceless boys chased me across the plains in nightmares like a pack of coyotes. I would wake up panting and terrified. Just once, I stopped to face my predators. Standing in the ocean of sand, I turned in my dream and beheld not that gang of wild things but just one boy, who stood behind me in the dirt. He looked right into me with sallow eyes and was so vivid in his filthy clothes that I thought he was real. I bolted straight up, straight out of sleep, practically out of my own skin, his name passing over my lips from illusion into the waking world in a breathless cry: *Marathon.* I stared into the night, my heart pounding, and saw no one. At that moment, I somehow knew my father hadn't saved him.

7. The City of Guns

By the time I was barely ten years old, we must have relocated all around FATA four or five times. This time, it was a long ride north, 150 miles on the curving Indus Highway, which ran parallel to the great river like an asphalt twin, to Darra Adam Khel, where every man walked with a weapon and a swagger, and where my family moved after living in the relative tranquility of Miranshah. Just as Miranshah is known for matchsticks, Darra is famous for guns—one thousand a day, made in the bazaar running right through the center of town. I saw the perimeter first as though from an airplane way up along the teetering pass, the city scattered over a ledge of flat terrain at the base of sandstone hills. My first thought: *Switzerland, but more beautiful.* (Not long before, my father had brought home postcards of Europe from the market.) The truck descended fast, so that I had to hold on tight to the rails, and for a while I lost that view to looming cliffs and shadow. As we drew closer, dust clogged the air. There was a steady tick in my throat, and I reached again and again for the silver canteen of water wedged at my feet.

I remember the air vibrated—I actually heard the town through the dirty haze. We rounded a turn, and a great uproar descended upon us from all sides. Hundreds of guns discharging one after the other: *Boom! Boom! Boom! Boom!* The shots combined into one massive cannonade, like a storm charging forward, set upon destroying everything in sight. Shocks threw me to one side of the open flatbed, tossed us against one another, and we laughed together, not hearing our own laughter. My father had given us fair warning that we were moving to a rowdy munitions town. For a while we could not hear anything at all, though my whole family was talking a mile a minute.

Soon the hellfire stopped, giving way to staccato bursts detonating in short, controlled patterns. The floor of the truck no longer shook, and we each took a breath. We only had about a minute of peace, then a massive roar cut open the heavens, so loud it might have been tearing apart the sky and splitting mountainsides. Then I saw it—a small white missile flew straight out over the plain. Faintly, we heard men shouting in its wake. After it was gone, I could still feel it rippling in my chest. My father slid open the back window, his hair wild in the wind.

"Welcome to the Wild West of Waziristan! Don't be afraid. No one is shooting at us. They are just testing the new weapons— that was a small rocket. Business must be good!"

As we approached the limits, our truck slowed to join a creeping line of filthy vehicles—open jeeps, hatchbacks, vans and trucks, horse-drawn carts, boys riding donkeys, tribesmen on motorbikes, and a wandering white lamb. My father let his big hairy arm, the sleeves of his *shalwar kameez* rolled up, rest along the open window frame. His long fingers drummed to the distant crackle and beat of a car radio playing.

At the sound of distant muezzin calls echoing from the town minarets, every human being within earshot stopped whatever they were doing and quietly found their mats; we knelt together in the dry dirt to pray, all of us facing Mecca. For those sacred minutes there was no uproar of weaponry; not even an engine idled . . . just the low chants of holy murmurs. The air was so dry it seemed to be raining dust over every bowed head. I felt it on my lips as I kissed my mat. Everything and everyone seemed to be coated in it.

I don't remember feeling anxious; I liked the idea of new adventure, and all through my childhood our family had been on the move. We'd moved to the gun town where my mother ran her school for girls so that we could all finally live under one roof. At the time, I didn't know what an act of bravery that was in a place like Darra, but I believe Aami chose that particular town for that very reason: if she could forge a girls' school in a munitions hub in FATA, there was hope for the entire region. Without hesitation, my father supported the idea. From the beginning, he'd raised us with the understanding that we were from a noble Pashtun family—to him, being a blue-blooded Wazir didn't mean living better; it meant making the world a better place. If I asked one thing of Allah that first day in Darra Adam Khel, it was that we would be safe.

Dressed in dark gray uniforms members of the Frontier Constabulary (a paramilitary force deployed on the borders of Pakistan's tribal regions and settlements) patrolled the road, big semi-automatic guns in slings strapped to their shoulders. They wore red berets, sunglasses, and black boots, scuffed from kicking around day after day in the dirt. They walked around half-grinning, a few smoking cigarettes, eyes roving the traffic as though they owned the road. Back in our pick up, we moved at a snail's pace, having to stop again and again at paramilitary checkpoints, jump out of the flatbed, wait around, open our sacks, explain ourselves.

There were many more guard posts stationed along the road going in the other direction. Tanks sat parked in the dirt off to the side, soldiers standing in the open hatches, holding up binoculars. The paramilitary was on the lookout for munitions smugglers, gun bandits, narcotics dealers, members of kidnapping gangs, all of whom my father told us slipped right through the lines daily by the dozens. I saw groups of men lumber out of big covered trucks, slap shoulders, and slip big wads of rupees like decks of cards into the sweaty hands of smiling soldiers. They were waved right on through. Before we moved, Shams explained that Darra Adam Khel was the biggest illegal weapons market in the world, and in the age of the burgeoning Taliban they were making a brisk business. Still, nothing he said could have prepared me: entering Darra was like driving straight into a movie—but it was all real. Everyone I saw on their way in and out wore a big smile. *They smile here like Americans*, I thought.

Our small adobe house was tucked between others running for a full block, side by side, along a pockmarked road. My mother had secured our accommodation through a stipend from the government of Pakistan, which encouraged open education in the tribal areas as part of a long-term strategy designed to stifle extremism. All of the dwellings were brown and nestled low to the ground, the foothills so close that at each turn you could see their shadowed faces rising in a forbidding wall beyond the flat rooftops. When my mother released the long bolt and pushed our front door open, I stood quietly in the threshold awhile and took in the sweet smell of tamped mud that for a moment took me back to the fragrant floors of our first home. The air was so cool, though space was limited; I remember thinking that it was like standing inside a rain cloud. All that cacophony outside didn't bother me much; my father had settled my mind before we'd even pulled into our street—we were simply going from a matchstick town to a gun town. I knew already that my father would be at home most of the day to care for my siblings, and my mother would be home each morning and night. Baba had been transferred to a college for boys in the city of Kohat, which was not far from Darra. Meanwhile, based on a series of competitive examinations, the government education board offered Aami the post of principal of the only high school for girls in the area. I couldn't have cared less about gunfire and the dust—in Darra Adam Khel I was free of my childcare duties. More importantly, our family was together at last. Back in Miranshah, my mother had grown weary of her nine-hour stop-and-start bus commute just to join us on weekends. Back then, I had no idea how much traveling she undertook for her work across FATA: writing exams in Peshawar, submitting papers in Kohat, recruiting students village by village, and then taking a break to see us for a day or two in Miranshah. Once my mother received financial backing from the government, my father handed in his resignation to the college and we packed up the truck.

My first full day in town, I was dressed as I always was—shorts and a T-shirt. My family accepted my boyish ways with open arms. To them, I was just Genghis—a tomboy—and out in the streets I was just a regular boy. I lived quite easily under the cloak of that public assumption, never having to outright lie about my gender.

Wearing Taimur's old clothes, I took the dilapidated bicycle out into our dirt-covered street. I never referred to that fast two-wheeled contraption with its rusting handlebars and flimsy tires simply as a bike. It was my freedom and my friend and I always called it by name—Sohrab. Pumping fast on the bicycle, I rode down a long alleyway. The roads were narrow and short, and huts and adobe homes flanked each one like a perimeter fence against which I reflected my shadow and the moving wheels of the bicycle. I skirted the edge of town along the looming foothills, ridges, and land folds, the fossils of a million rainfalls that had cut veins deep into the mountainsides. Positioned on a low rise overlooking town, I stopped pedaling and peered into the alleys, listening. Gunfire shook the ground beneath my feet. A sheen of sand vibrated over the pavement like a shifting curtain. I knew we were in a formidable region of the world, among outcasts and hooligans, and yet I felt that because I was free, I was safe—my father had given me that assurance—and all I had to do was keep quiet and away from trouble. No one would bother a kid on a bicycle—they were all too busy with the business of arms dealing and jihad. I pumped hard, shifted gears, and rode straight toward the heart of town.

The busy gun bazaar teemed with characters: men on horse carts riding at a lazy clobber, others drifting on soft-buzzing motorbikes, some just moseying the route on foot, window-shopping for weapons. Customers tested merchandise from rooftops adjacent to the hillsides. You could see them chatter-ing, making considerations, studying pieces of the firearms and passing them around. They test-fired every variety of gun—automatic, semi-automatic, pump-action, even old-fashioned gunslinger pistols. Standing on makeshift rooftop ranges, men shot blindly into the surrounding hills, or they drove in large caravans out into the plains to try out heavier munitions.

Slipping into a side alley with dozens of small workshops, I swung my leg off the bicycle and walked. In the first arcade I passed, the size of a closet, a man sat cross-legged in the sand. He was chattering to himself and stopped when he saw me there. He gave me a once-over and then a toothless grin. He had a carved wooden rifle stock in his lap and was sanding it down. The next moment, he got up and put the smooth piece on a table. He motioned with his hands for me to touch it, and I propped my bike against the wall. The mud-and-timber hut smelled of freshly cut wood, and I saw against the wall behind the old man a dozen shaped and sanded stocks.

He took a metal rod from a crate and sat down again to rifle a barrel with the long cutting tool. He tapped the length over and over again, in and out, twisting and turning his wrists in deliberate movements, employing some physical equation obviously perfected over years. Once finished, he placed the piece in a pile with all the others. Most workshops had walled-in brick spaces at the back that looked like doghouses, where they fired off ammunition to test each newly made weapon before it was put out into the open market. Hundreds of rounds were shot daily inside those huts. My father explained that at the end of the day, someone raked up the spent metal casings to be used again. The hellfire of Darra was as incessant as a holy war. The walls all over town were covered in bullet holes.

Over weeks, stopping on the way to the dairy farm to buy milk or just wandering the town, I learned all the parts of guns the way I'd learned about cars and combustion engines in Shams' college workshop in Miranshah. Any man-made thing could be broken down into components, and the very idea of that fascinated me—outside in, from big to small: truck engines, gear-shift bicycles, television sets, a VCR, an original Khyber Pass rifle, Smith & Wesson Magnums, a yellow kite . . .

In the forging shops, I watched blocks of steel—called blanks—being heated and then pressed into the shapes of handguns. Several thousand pounds of pressure dropped down over them one by one with the pull of a lever—as simple as cutting out cookies. The manufacturing methods appeared crude, but the sum process was highly sophisticated—a Darra gun counterfeiter could outwit any MIT engineer. They were master forgers, replicating—with nothing more than simple lathes, presses, drills, hammers, and fire—even the most complicated weapon, from James Bond's PPK pistol to a Soviet RPG, assembled piece by piece, working barefoot in the dirt in cramped, sweltering conditions. The older men were often deaf. Many were missing parts of themselves—fingers, toes, a slice of cheekbone, a whole foot, an eye. Still, they sat or squatted in that squalor and worked, tools in their laps, fashioning guns by the thousands. Maimed or not, there was something indomitable about those men. The Afridi clan who populated Darra Adam Khel were famous among the tribes for their prowess; they'd crushed whole contingents of the Mughal dynasty, torn the British to pieces in the Anglo-Afghan Wars, and they ran FATA. If the Wazir were warriors, then the Afridi were the kings of warfare. Nevertheless, throughout history, from the time before Jesus Christ, invaders thought they could send armies through the Khyber Pass and subdue those hard-to-the-bone inhabitants of the Valley of Humans. As my father said: "What were they thinking?" The Afridi were invincible—then as now.

*

Somehow, in those echoes of gunfire, in addition to her position as a high school principal, my mother had founded a small school for girls. Five days a week, she taught classes inside a ramshackle building on the periphery of town to two dozen wide-eyed girls. She transformed the dingy hut into a vibrant classroom—big maps and flags from around the world adorning the mildewed walls in a colorful patchwork quilt; she had notebooks and paper, a blackboard, dictionaries, and colored pencils. The Pakistani government sent money for supplies, which my mother had to supplement regularly from our own meager family income. She was an expert at pestering government officials—if she could fill enough desks, she'd been promised scholarship money to help attract more students. She was just one woman, but there were thousands of illiterate girls out there.

Darra Adam Khel was a labyrinth of hazards, and not just because of its deadly trade. My mother was running a school for young girls in the dark heart of terrorist country, where they made deals and collected their arsenal. At that time the Taliban ruled Afghanistan and had strong links to every corner of FATA. By anyone's estimation, she was out of her mind. But she knew how to make herself fit into places and with people. She could be funny or dead serious, quiet or gregarious—whatever made headway. And what made headway in Darra Adam Khel was wearing a pristine veil and staying under the radar. Dressed conservatively, a satchel full of religious books tucked under one arm, she kept her head down. She simply allowed people to make convenient assumptions, as I did walking around in my brother's clothes. She never mentioned the history, geography, literature, and language lessons she taught. Meanwhile, people imagined hours of sewing and cooking classes. If questioned, she simply explained that she was keeping young, impressionable girls busy until they could be married off—pious and conscientious, which only increased their value. Within months, even the warlords referred to their local principal as "Madam." Monday to Friday, brothers and fathers accompanied daughters and sisters to her school—on foot, in horse carts, and occasionally in hired pick-up vans or old cars. She stood waiting at the door, greeting each student with a smile as they filed in. Inside, the girls washed their hands and faces in large clay bowls and assembled to pray together. Then they got to work. Aami did her best to create an engaging and peaceful environment for her students—even starting a drama club and athletic teams. Pupils took active roles in student government, debating tournaments and in celebrating holidays. At the end of each day, the girls all made their way out with smiles hidden like secrets underneath their *burqas*.

Traveling the Indus Highway by bus, I sometimes accompanied my mother on her weekend recruiting missions in the villages clustered all around town. Often we would travel in the local pick-up vans that took passengers from village to village for a small fee. Even when we had enough money for a tank of gas, she didn't dare take the pick up. Many tribesmen saw the benefit of keeping little girls occupied in classrooms until they could be put to work at home or were married. A woman commanding the wheel of a vehicle, however, was a gross offense. Sometimes, marauding male gangs of hooligans on missions to defend their "ancestral Pashtun culture" hauled a female kicking and screaming by the hair through the driver's side window and beat her courage right out of her for all to see. Other times, they pulled the woman out and didn't bother with the beating. During that time and in the ensuing years, many teachers who ignored warnings about returning to a life of dutiful confinement in their homes were routinely kidnapped and shot. Fearless as ever, Aami got up every morning, washed and prayed and went straight to work.

On the first recruiting trip I took with her, wet spells in Darra had transformed its landscape; giant white clouds descended in big masses right over us, settling all along the ridgeline, briefly dampening all the browns to pale greens. Rain didn't just fall there, it hung in the air, turning the dry dirt to a thick layer of mud. If you had good shoes, you put them away for a while.

After over an hour, we got off the hired van somewhere on the winding southern road to Kohat, nearly fifteen miles away. Up and down hills, we walked for a long time and were soaked right through to the bone. I didn't say much as I kept pace with my determined mother. She'd find houses with young girls in them by some instinct I never could explain. She had a similar instinct with people, and that was my only way of explaining how she accomplished the impossible—talking conservative fathers into agreeing to the absurd and sending their girls in dilapidated vehicles to a school in plain sight of those violent gangs. The government's promise of three thousand rupees per child was also very good bait, and Aami always saved it for last.

The first girl I remember wasn't much different from all the others. Six years old, tall for her age and ancestry. Her grand-mother was a hunchback, grandfather a coal miner, mother not much of anything—as was the custom—father who knows where. My mother delivered her short, impassioned oratory at their doorstep. The startled occupants had no choice but to listen as there wasn't a door, just an opening cut through mud bricks. Within a moment or two, their faces softened from blank stares to awe. I was behind, peering around my mother. They looked at her the way I must have looked at the maimed men making guns in town—they could not believe their eyes.

Soon we were sitting on straw mats inside, drinking yogurt from earthenware cups, and my mother was pulling storybooks from her satchel. She read *Little Red Riding Hood* to the child—I remember how the little girl sat before my mother, her first teacher, still and rapt, hands folded like a bird's wings in her lap, never having seen a book at all, or heard a nursery rhyme read aloud. Then my mother pulled a sack of chalk from her bag and showed the girl how to print her name on a slate board. At the very notion of forming letters into words and words into things—into the meaning of her very self—a whole world took beautiful form in that child's eyes. The little girl stared in wonder-ment at the letters scrawled over the slate held between my mother's hands.

"What is that, Madam?"

"A-T-I-Y-A, Atiya. It means gift—that is you."

Again and again my mother performed the same miracle—she went into mud-and-stone huts tucked along the rocky passes and gave blind girls their sight.

*

I don't remember which student started the backlash, or if she was even one of my mother's, though I heard the story many times. The girl was one of the older ones—fifteen—and pretty, they said: green eyes; raven tresses like an oil slick running down her long back. Too smart for her own good. She fell in love with the school bus driver, a wiry boy from Kohat. Apparently they discovered each other without a single word—just a warm smile to greet her as she climbed onto the bus. He shouldn't have looked at her so long in the first place.

Lovers on the run often tried to hide themselves in cosmopolitan Peshawar, but they never got very far—including that couple. The highway that ran the passes in long curving roads carved into mountain bedrock, skirting deadly cliffs along the switchbacks, was the only sure way to get there alive. The posse from Darra that went after them were expert trackers and had plenty of guns.

When they found the couple riding together on horseback in a rutted-out path off to the side of the highway, the girl slipped down from their saddle, losing her shoes. Then she ran out, barefoot, along a field of sunflowers. Hopeless, she dropped to her knees in the black dirt. She dug her hands into the earth and put her head down and shouted for them to get it over with. The men all stood there, stupefied to hear her beg for her own execution—most begged for their fathers first, and then for forgiveness. They didn't shoot her, though she'd already been sentenced. Tribal laws could be finicky. In that moment of stunned silence, the girl's cousin, who'd been part of the armed contingent, stepped forward and unslung his rifle. He put it down in the dirt. The shamed bus driver sat paralyzed in his saddle, gawking, as the cousin held out his hand to the girl. Without hesitation, he turned and made an abrupt offer of marriage to her father, who was standing off to one side. The girl's father accepted the cousin's bold proposal wordlessly, and the girl took the proffered hand and stood up with her betrothed. Everyone could hear her quick, shallow breaths. For a long time, she could not look up, just stared at her soiled bare feet sinking into the earth. Then she turned to her cousin and whispered, though they all heard her.

"*Maherbani, Maherbani*—thank you."

It didn't matter that the story had a happy ending—from that day on, educated tribal girls were marked, and their principal was the primary target. My mother had often invited students to our home to study books or watch videos. My father taught a few of them grammar and literature in the living room, or brought in a parade of motley characters—Frontier Corps officers, coal miners, philosophers, and down-on-their-luck Pashtuns—to teach them as he had taught us all our lives. When they shuttered the school, my mother went underground and kept out of view. It made no difference—everyone knew where *Madam* lived. Over a period of several days our home was routinely stoned, and in the night passing gangs of "Holy Warriors" shot up our walls using pistols and AK-47s. I remember my sister telling me how those men referred to themselves as devout Muslims, but seemed to ignore the tenets of the Holy Quran, which demand that every man and woman should seek out an education. Considering the very real threat to my mother's life, for a time the government sent an armed guard to watch our house. Apart from the evil few, most of the locals still held a great respect for my mother. Even today, with her school long turned to rubble, the villagers in that region invite her to return to their homes to celebrate special events, such as the wedding ceremonies of their children, at which she is always given a place of honor.

After the uproar finally died down, my mother started looking for another building far away from the perimeter of town.

*

The man who somehow broke through the bolted front door and into our house had an American 1911 .45-caliber pistol and a clear agenda. I knew the gun instantly when I saw it, the way I knew Datsuns or Nissans or 9mm Berettas. I also knew he was after us because of my mother's school—we'd received warnings in the form of letters tacked to our door. To teach Muslim girls anything but domestic duties and lessons from the Quran was heresy and would not go unpunished. None of us were sure what that meant—until we saw the man's gun.

The intruder stood before me, handgun poised; he thumbed the safety. I heard it click. The only way to evade a bullet at point-blank range is to run—fast. I was at home with my siblings, and we all did just that—scattering through the house, our lungs exploding into screams. We raced out back and into the pounding spring rain. I had one boy in my arms, Ayesha had the other one. Taimur made sure we were all out and then chased after us. Somehow we scaled the back wall and hurtled along the slippery road, not stopping for careening cars or trucks or the Frontier Corps soldier who shouted out at us but never asked if we needed help. Not for anything. When my father found his children at last in an alley behind the gun shops, we were wide-eyed with terror and huddled into a single trembling form behind a dumpster—all of us encased in a thick sheen of mud.

The next day, my father handed me a replica Makarov pistol bought at the market, perfect right down to the Soviet-era star stamped on the grip. Simple. Easy to shoot. Accurate. Then he taught me how to strip it piece by piece and clean the components. Cradling the weapon in my eight-and-a-half-year-old palms, I felt its primitive power as though it were a wild thing, barely tamed. Seeing my awe when I first held it, my father placed his hands over mine, which were wrapped around the pistol. When I looked at him, he closed his eyes a long time. I knew he'd given me a thing he hated—not the gun itself but the capacity that came with it: life or death in the matter of a nanosecond.

When I had learned how, I removed the magazine, checked the breech for a glint of brass, and deftly withdrew the single round my father had left chambered as an initial test. He nodded, expelled a breath. Together we cleaned out the barrel with a long brush, alternating between a scrub patch and cloth, and then coating the inside with oil. He showed me how to wipe the action and lubricated its assembly. As I polished the full gun with the cloth, I let my fingers slide along the grip, felt the filed grooves, understanding with each touch every deadly mechanism. We filled the magazine to capacity. Nine bullets—eight in the magazine, one in the chamber.

I became a good shot, practicing with empty Fanta cans on the rooftops in the public firing area. I adopted a bit of a swagger; when you had a pistol tucked at your side, you walked the streets like a god with a chip on his shoulder. Of course, every man I passed had a packed holster and years of practice. Instinctively, most of the kids in town knew not to mess with Genghis Khan; some of them called me "Levanai," the Pashto word for insane, because of my temper. But there was one Afghan boy who just started following me. I'd heard rumors that his uncle was a big shot in the Taliban and assumed he'd been sent to spy on my family.

Every day from the first day, it was always the same thing—me walking, the boy tailing a few paces behind, sometimes hurling insults that I never bothered to listen to. I was sure he was a peon of an extremist group that was trying to intimidate my family, and I made up my mind I would not let him get to me. One day, I saw him coming down the road and I could feel the blood in my veins go hot. I ran a hand through my damp hair, shorn to spikes just that morning when the traveling barber made his rounds.

I slipped over a low railing into another alley and took off in a wild sprint. I tried to disappear into the labyrinth of the town and the mantle of dust blowing in from the dried-up flood plains. Usually I could outrun that boy, the way I could outrun anyone. Still, I wished I'd taken the bike.

On foot and going at a good clip, I skirted along the arcades, past the mosque, street after street. Glancing back again, I could still see him not far behind me. Sweat soaked his red shirt right down the middle. I heard him call out "Little Madam's boy." Up and down the alleys, where toothless men were sawing off bits for rifle stocks, small boys fashioning pistol hammers and squatting in the dirt; past a smiling mullah, behind him a herd of goats on their way to the slaughterhouse; past the poor begging by the fruit seller's stall; past the rich bandits with their gold teeth and expensive sunglasses. The deaf. The blind. I kept going until I was too out of breath to go on—the kid was relentless in his pursuit. I figured that this time he'd been sent to do more than intimidate me. Usually, he'd give up after such a long, pointless trek in the heat. My mind swam and I stopped in my tracks, turned, and waited. I'd had enough of him—no matter who he worked for.

In a moment he was right there, and we stood before each other, panting, tongues loose and hanging in our mouths. I said nothing for a while, just stared him down. He was a head taller than I was, but thin—practically skin and bones. The minute you have a gun, you start planning how to use it. I didn't have a desire to kill; I just knew that I could if it came to that—if that was what he was sent to do to me, I'd made up my mind already that I'd shoot first.

Gently, I pulled up the sweat-drenched hem of my shirt and fingered the polished black grip poking out of my tight waistband. Firing just an hour before, I'd hit the Fanta can right through the first letter A, and I could smell the fresh oil coating the barrel. My lungs wheezed from the exertions of our run. The boy was staring back at me hard, like he didn't care one bit what I had by my side. So I let my full hand take the grip and bit my lip, never blinking. The boy's eyes shifted gears as he took in my small movements, and he stopped panting. He stood stock-still, holding his breath, and watched me slowly move the safety. Then I saw that one of his hands was out of sight behind him, but my gun was already out. He didn't move.

For a moment, I was back home at the kitchen table, and I felt my father cover my hands with his own. In the slow suffocation of those seconds, the hot air buzzed and I was propelled to a place I never thought I would be. The tip of my extended muzzle was barely two feet from him. I had the boy's fast-beating heart in my sights. Ever since my father gave me the Makarov, I'd had fantasies about using it. I thought about what I could have done with it when those men had taunted me—the ones by the willow tree during the volleyball game; the man on horseback who slapped me with his whip. I turned to the boy and looked him in the eyes. Whatever happened, I had a gun now. Whatever they'd sent the boy to do to me, I was ready.

"What do you want?"

"What are you doing that for—haven't you been listening?" He blinked twice, swallowed hard.

"What do you want?" I said it louder, index finger hovering at the trigger.

The boy swallowed again. "The bicycle, the ten-speed."

"What?"

"I just want a ride—that's all."

"You keep following me. Who sent you?"

My open hand was so wet that I could feel the grip slipping. Remembering the slug nestled in the chamber, I moved my finger away from the trigger. I could feel the muscles all along my forearms twitching.

"No one sent me. I just want a ride on the Sohrab. That's what I kept telling you. I want to ride your bike."

It was so absurd that I didn't quite believe him.

"What do you have there in your back pocket—a gun? Show it to me. Do anything stupid and I'll shoot this thing."

He was shaking his head fast. *No—no way. It's nothing.*

Then, from his back pocket, he carefully pulled out a pack of chewing gum. It looked to me like he'd had it for a while—the packaging was worn and bent out of shape. Who knows how he'd gotten it. He offered the pack to me from his flat, open palm and nodded, all his fingers trembling. Then he turned all the way around, showing me that he had nothing else on him.

Slowly, I lowered my arm and pushed the safety back into position. I shook my head and he carefully put the pack of gum away. Then I loosened my palm from the slick grip, tossing it like a dead thing to the ground at my feet, my eyes never leaving the boy. We were lucky the gun didn't go off.

He watched me do those things, his chest rising and falling fast. When my Makarov hit the ground, he let out a long breath, and his eyes flickered. Then he shook his head, held out his arms, and shrugged.

"So?" Sweat poured down his face.

"So what?"

"So, can I have a ride? I won't steal it—if that's what you were thinking."

For a moment it seemed that I'd stepped out of my own skin. I fell to my knees. I looked up at the boy again, his face staring back—I'd actually been a hair away from pulling the trigger. It was just a rusted ten-speed. I had a bicycle, he didn't—just like the yellow kite in Miranshah. Simple as that. The voice I heard then, as I knelt in the dirt, was not my own. It was the voice of someone who'd been to the very edge of hell and back again.

"Okay, follow me home. I'll have to ask my father—he bought the bike."

8. Deities, Temples, and Angels

While we were living in Darra Adam Khel, my five-year-old brother Sangeen often asked me to tell him stories about all the places we had lived. Those simple memories kept me calm amid the perpetual violence. After a day of kicking around the streets and foothills, I'd walk through the front door to find my brother sitting cross-legged on the floor, waiting. If it was late afternoon, Ayesha—who had entered her teens—would be somewhere in the house, studying and looking after him and Babrak.

"Explain to me again how I got my big Pashtun lips, Genghis."

"You know that already. You got them from the Afridi woman who was visiting the house near Baba's college in Dera Ismail Khan."

"No, no, no—tell a story—the way you do."

"All right, sit down with me right here, and I'll start from the beginning."

The last time I had sat with Sangeen and repeated the tale was just before I ran into trouble at the mosque. I would need that story for my heart, far more than he did for his ears. I would need it to remind me that the world is full of people, not religions. Deities and temples don't make us good—our actions do.

At barely a year old, Sangeen had a cry that could stop God in his tracks—full-mouthed and earsplitting. On an afternoon when it rained so heavily the stream broke its banks, turning the roads to rushing brown rivers, he woke in tandem with a thunderclap. I held my brother by an open window, watching the deluge, and he shrieked as though he'd made a pact with the tempest. Whenever anything went wrong, I prayed to Allah—we all did. My family were devout but open-minded Muslims. Until then, I only knew of one God—my own. I believed that when I called him, he listened, and as I stood rocking my fitful brother, I called out desperate *ayahs*. One hour, then two, then three passed that way: "Peace be upon Him, peace be upon Him, peace be upon Him," as Sangeen screamed along with the raging sky. When the weather cleared, I hoped his heavy heart would too.

But no matter how I tried, I could not calm him. I had little money that week, and I'd used the last of the milk at breakfast. There were no more rupees left in the jar. So into Sangeen's mouth I poured spoonfuls of water and dropped soggy bits of stale naan. But this only seemed to fuel his ire, until his body grew so rigid with rage that I could barely hold him, his face turned beet red, and his quavering lips squeezed so tight they went bloodless and white. Again and again and in a panic, I gave him water, and he guzzled and belched only to explode anew. It amazed me then as now how a tiny living thing could emit such power.

The Saraiki woman across the way caught his bloodcurdling cries and came in from the street. I heard her clamoring down in the front hall, yelling my name and my brother's. Then she tore into our kitchen, where I stood exhausted and pale and half out of my mind with fear. Inconsolable Sangeen paused and stared at her, mouth hanging open, his voice eclipsed but for a moment as our neighbor unleashed a barrage of incomprehensible Urdu. Then he started up again, and the woman grabbed him from me by the armpits and hoisted his flailing body to her chest. Together we ran out into the waterlogged street.

She bolted toward a neighboring house and darted through the open door. From the first step inside I felt the pungent warmth of Masala chai tea envelop me, and heard the delicate clanking of cups. I followed her into the strange front room, where a Pashtun woman of the Afridi tribe sat on a raft of cushions. I knew her clan from her colorful headscarf, her robust body, and the bright paleness of her smooth face. Right next to her on a long silk mat lounged the woman whom I had seen before in the streets and knew lived in the house. She was another Saraiki lady with high Tibetan-like cheeks and dressed in reams of robes—all pinks and burnt yellows—both women looked up startled in the dim, shuttered light. The visiting Afridi sat back and quickly adjusted her heavy shawl, rings on her fingers flashing. Her eyes darted from the sight of the two figures standing in the threshold, panting, to the sleeping Pashtun infant cocooned in the makeshift cot next to her. I don't remember what was said, if much of anything. My neighbor simply walked up to the Afridi and handed over a whimpering Sangeen.

His eyes widened as he went from one woman to another, and I waited for him to wail in protest and wake the sleeping newborn swaddled barely a foot away. Then he groaned and let out one last feeble bawl, no doubt at the sight of the suddenly proffered milk-laden breast. He opened his mouth wide and latched on, eyes rolling back in his head and his chest fluttering as he breathed. He guzzled so violently that his cheeks filled and overflowed with milk, and the woman nursing him, whose name I would never learn, chuckled. As they settled into her island of soft cushions and robes as one together, she leaned way back and let out a contented sigh. A moment later, the woman of the house closed her eyes and started chanting—half song, half whisper—a mantra filled with a lulling translucent poetry. Somehow I felt her meaning, though I couldn't decipher a word. Every now and again she opened her lids and looked over with a smile at her Afridi visitor and the suckling child, as though at a work of art gracing her home. Sangeen kneaded his fingers into the doughy skin, humming out gulps as he drank, and she repeated her steady refrain from her corner of the room. The Afridi smiled down at my brother, whispered a prayer and rocked him to the chanting rhythm. They all made a soft, sacred music together until he fell asleep, still drinking.

Relieved, I took a seat on a thick mat with my neighbor, who poured me a cup of the heavily spiced tea from a small red pot with a bamboo handle. She crossed her legs, took a sip from her porcelain cup, and smiled broadly through a cloud of perfumed steam. I languished there a long time in the sweet air, watching smoke spiral up from a flickering candle positioned on a corner table. The flame danced before the smiling brass figure of Buddha, big belly polished to a gold sheen from the touches of so many fingertips. Off to the side, a white lotus flower hovered in a bowl of clear water, delicate petals like the pale upturned palm of a goddess. I examined all of the beautiful things surrounding me, each placed there with some mysterious intent. The entire room felt like a shrine to spiritual worlds, some of which I knew nothing of: gods and goddesses in framed paintings and figurines, pictures of holy men and prophets, a hanging brass bell in the shape of a coin, a cross fixed to the wall, and well-thumbed books lined up on shelves. Deities seemed to whisper through the house. An aura of strength also hovered over the woman who fed my brother from her generous breasts. The Afridi were as formidable as the Spin Ghar mountain range from which their tribe originated. She'd taken Sangeen and nourished him from her body without a word, simply because he was hungry and she had in plentiful supply the very thing he needed. We were all Pashtun, but to her, I believe, it was simpler than that—he was a baby and she was a mother. I still remember the steady melody of the woman chanting by her, caressing my ears in that Masala perfumed temple of stillness: *"Namo Gurubhya, Namo Buddhaya, Namo Dharmaya, Namo Sanghaya . . ."* She said it several times, at first in a halting voice as though practicing a line in a play, looking down and reading from the leather-bound book sitting in her lap like a second infant in the room, drawing her finger over the line of text and nodding. And in between, my brother's hummingbird breaths and sighs.

By the time we meandered back home through the damp streets, Sangeen's head, dizzy with so much milk, lolled about in his blanket. I watched my Saraiki neighbor slip into her house across the way, vanishing through the door as though into another world. After that day, Sangeen grew stronger and his mouth swelled, as though he had developed the Afridi woman's full, beautiful lips, like a memento of her generous heart.

While I was still telling the tale that day, my father appeared. Smiling, he stepped through our front door with an overstuffed satchel at his side. The sounds of gunshots echoed behind him. He stood listening as my brother sat transfixed in my lap. My father liked to hear me tell my brother stories, perhaps because I spoke to my younger siblings just the way that he did. When I was done, we were all quiet for a long time. After I recounted the strange events of that rain-soaked afternoon, I ended up with a head full of questions. My mind drifted to the vision of the lotus floating in the bowl, dainty and beautiful, and the glinting of the smiling Buddha's round belly, the cross, and paintings of holy men and all those books. Above all, I heard the incantations of the woman sitting in bright robes beating in my head.

As Sangeen slid from my lap, I turned to my father. Then I stood up and asked him right there and then if Allah was the only true God as we professed on our knees five times a day—the Buddha, after all, was not Allah. And what about the Christian God and his son, Jesus, who was also one of our prophets. I had vague notions of other religions and knew there were many ways to reach God, but I'd made an assumption about the Almighty: there could be only one—mine. Otherwise, what were we doing going to the mosque, kneeling on our mats, and memorizing *ayahs* and *suras*. My father took me by the shoulders and smiled a long while, as though he saw a sun shining deep within me. He asked me to meet him in the kitchen, which is where we always discussed big matters.

In minutes, he joined me, and with a ringmaster's flourish rolled out a giant map of the world, unraveling its four corners over the ground and weighting them down with earthenware cups. Then he turned on a bright overhead light.

"Our planet—full of countries, full of people. Allah has a plan and a place for them all."

And he put a pin into Pakistan.

We studied the many borders surrounding our landmass,

crooked ink lines veining out—the printed names of places I might never see. Afghanistan to the west. India to the east. Iran next to Iraq. China eating up terrain all the way to a coastline that ran to a trio of overlapping seas; beyond those, the Pacific, spanning the globe past island chains to the wild continents of the Americas. Billions of human beings living and dying.

"I am a devout Muslim, but I am an academic, and academics like to ask questions. Where did we come from, Genghis Khan—where will we go? Why are we here at all? I don't actually care, because I have my own faith. The pure wonder is the thing I love best about being alive in the first place."

Side by side, we stood together over the map, peering down at our pinprick. Then he chanted the words that had only just danced through my memory: *"Namo Gurubhya, Namo Buddhaya, Namo Dharmaya, Namo Sanghaya . . ."*

"Yes, Baba, that's it. She said it again and again like a *sura* while the Afridi woman fed Sangeen. But she is Saraiki, not Buddhist, and follows Islam as we do. It was a strange house, full of books and pictures. The whole room was like a holy place, but it was just a room. If it wasn't holy, then why would I remember it so well?"

"Ah, you were in the home of a religious scholar, an academic like me who has as many questions as she has books in her house. The Saraiki follow many religions, mostly Islam. No matter. She was reciting a Tibetan chant—'I take refuge in the Spiritual Masters, my Gurus; I take refuge in the Awakened One, the Buddha; I take refuge in the Truth, the Dharma; I take refuge in the Spiritual Beings, Sangha'—it is like a thread that leads a Buddhist to their truth, what we would call the Straight Path. Our truth as Muslims is in the single phrase: it is written."

"But in truth I don't know anything."

"Yes, you know much. Maybe what you're reaching for is still too high, like fruit way up in a tree. You can't get to it unless you climb or it falls and hits you on the head—that's how Newton discovered gravity."

"Now you've only given me more questions, Baba, instead of answers."

"Yes—almost there, keep going. You're about to reach the highest form of all human knowledge."

"What is that?"

Just then, Ayesha's thin shadow spread over the map. She had a leather-bound Quran tucked under one arm; I could see the green ribbon from her page marker poking out from the gold-leafed pages. She spent hours each week at the mosque studying, while I roamed outside. Ayesha looked down at the pin, and I wondered if she felt our place in the world reduced to the infinitesimal, as I did. She laughed.

"Uncertainty—am I right, Baba? The thing that binds us all together."

"Yes. Uncertainty—it's a wonder. It lets you live and love with abandon. It doesn't mean that I don't believe in our one god, Allah—my Muslim faith is how I reach beyond myself. I also know that many people have many ways to reach one God. Just like the Saraiki woman, I like to know what they are. Every person must find the way for themselves or they will be lost. Now, Ayesha, tell your brave-heart brother here how many religions there are scattered like seeds all over our oblivious planet."

"Well, according to the Encyclopaedia Britannica, more than twenty—including ours. It's almost as though there are more than twenty gods, but that can't be true."

My father chuckled. "Why not one god given many names by many people?"

My father reached over and took Ayesha's copy of the Quran. He held it, flipping back and forth, a fan of soft paper opening and closing between his big palms. I knew he had nearly every line within it memorized, 114 chapters, the *suras*, told in poetic verses and written in order of decreasing size. As the eldest son of a blue-blooded Pashtun family, my father had spent his youth studying the Quran in order to make himself worthy of his full inheritance of landholdings, wealth, and esteem. On his father's death he would have become the representative of one of the most powerful families in FATA, but he gave up a life of prestige so that our entire family could live as equals and experience the world for what it is—a wonder.

He often told us that taking up his position as a tribal elder would have given him far less influence than the honor of sending open-minded children out into the world. To the Pashtun, honor is the greatest wealth; unlike his forebears, who found it in war, he found it in fatherhood. In that sacrifice alone, he lived closer to the Muslim faith than most any man. Every day, he made us recite a new *sura*—by the Day of Judgment, we'd have each one committed to our hearts—and yet he could see sacred truths in the beliefs of others. Tolerance was the greatest gift he would ever give me. There were millions of people the world over who knew nothing of our book, and I might know nothing of theirs, if they had one. It didn't matter; we were all going to the same place on different paths. Maybe all a Buddhist had was the Lotus Sutra. Maybe others had nothing more than life itself. Shams closed the covers, whispered a prayer, and handed the book back to Ayesha. That afternoon, I understood for the first time what it meant to have faith in my god: Allah anchored me to my own soul—and to everyone else.

I went to a fruit bowl that sat on the table and took three *jamuns* for us all to eat, leaving the pomegranate for my brothers. I missed the days when we had a proper garden and grew peppers and beans and every month my father would come home with meat to cook over the bricks in the fire pit. In Darra we had to buy everything at the market and cook all of our meals indoors. When I gave my father the piece of fruit, he kissed my hands.

"God never speaks directly to people. He sends angels, both good and bad, to teach us. The woman who fed Sangeen all that time ago was your divine messenger, and you are mine. *Inshallah*, may you never run into the other kind."

I went to sleep that night with my father's words and the day's events playing out in my mind, lulling me into a deep ocean of vivid dreams—Sangeen and Babrak running through a strange land of shooting stars. Trying to keep up, I chased after them stumbling over stones as the earth began to quake. My dream turned quickly to a nightmare as the ground before me tore open, cracking apart like a great dropped tile. We all fell into a cold abyss in which I could see and hear nothing. As I tumbled down through the blackness, the air thinned until I was struggling for every breath. Then in the midst of that terror, I felt the heat from a beam of light swell behind me. Somehow, I turned to see a tall man sitting on a stone with his hands held out to me. Through that dim hollowed out world, I found my way to him. Then I placed my head on his knees and wept for my lost brothers. I still remember the man's voice, which was as sure as a thunderclap. Again and again he said to me—"do not be afraid." With a strange certainty that can only come in dreams, I knew he was Jesus Christ. Then behind him I saw that there was a long line of other prophets waiting. When I woke I could still feel warm hands on my head, and hear the sound of his voice that I held onto like a life ring in the cold sea of night.

Not long after, God sent me two angels, one that belonged in heaven—and one who would have been cast out of it. Ayesha was carrying the same leather-bound Quran under her arm that my father had leafed through in the kitchen. As Genghis Khan, I could take my sister anywhere she pleased, but the only places she asked to go were to school or to the mosque. Ayesha studied in a prayer room several times each week with a group of girls, all of them draped in veils. I was not sure what she learned there that she could not ask of our father. My job was to wait around until the lesson was finished and come back with my sister and a pail full of fresh water. We had no plumbing in Darra, but the mosques required water so that every Muslim man, woman, and child could complete their ablutions and enter the immaculate state of *wudu* before kneeling down in the segregated halls. In hot weather, I went back and forth to our mosque and waited in long lines for water several times each day.

Galvanized bucket at my side, Quran by my sister's, we walked together. I could see the dome of our prayer hall from a distance: a giant pearl rising from a brown sea of flat rooftops, towering minaret, from which the muezzin made his beautiful calls. The sight of the mosque in the dingy midst of Darra always gave me hope—hope for what exactly, I don't know. All around us, men fired their killing machines for sport and with thoughts of jihad—or with no thought at all. The only thing that stopped the bullets was the *azan* call to prayer.

Inside the mosque, the cool air thinned and no sound entered from the exterior. Marble tiles lined the walls and floor. Our footfalls were amplified as we walked the long main hallway, and even our breaths echoed. A whisper uttered in a mosque would soar from one end to the other—no one could keep a secret from Allah in there.

I left my bucket on the bench leading to the ablution rooms and headed back out. First I stopped a moment and watched my sister cross the corridor to her study hall, resplendent in the brilliance of her white *chador*, which never once showed any blemish, even after we'd just walked block after block through a haze of Darra dust. Then I made my way back out into the welter of town; the noise of the streets slapping my ears after the stillness of the mosque. I held a hand flat over my eyes and scanned the crowd, looking for my gang. Wherever we moved, I made friends easily. I was strong and brazen and always attracted a wily group of colorful characters. Sometimes we fought in the dirt, but most of the time we just ran amok looking for things to do—tossing a ball, chasing each other, shooting things with slingshots, sometimes smacking each other around; more than once, a firm friendship had started with a punch. To them I was all boy—no one would have guessed otherwise—and not just because of my cropped hair and masculine clothes. It was a way I had about me. At home every member of my family called me Genghis—we all accepted one another as we were. Just as there was more than one way to reach God, I decided that there was more than one way to be a girl. Luckily, I never had to explain myself to anyone—I'm not sure that I could have.

In Darra Adam Khel, my friends were all boys people referred to as street urchins and rats—they went everywhere together in a pack. If they had homes, I didn't know it and didn't care. Sling-shot in my pocket instead of the Makarov, I'd find them lurking in the backstreets behind the mosque or roving the hillsides. They'd call out from behind a car, a dumpster, or down a dark laneway. I always heard them before they came into sight. One after the other, a parade of boys with loose grins and cheap pistols would emerge from a side alley and wave to me.

We'd slap shoulders and then make our way on foot out of town. Usually I led my ramshackle gang up craggy foothills, the boys swarming around, kicking up dust until we were all coated, issuing insults, exchanging banter. No one ever came close to touching me—they'd heard about the Makarov and they'd seen the muscles in my arms. I could lift two of them at once if I wanted to. The occasional scuffle broke out—bloody noses, a broken finger, lost teeth—nothing serious. It wasn't about friend-ship; we were killing time, killing life, letting our childhoods go. There wasn't much of anything to do, but I was in love with my freedom too much to care. I don't remember the substance of what we talked about, though we spent hours in close company; no one had a television or VCR, there were no books, no maga-zines—unlike me, none of them had ever seen a video or a movie. Not one had learned to read a map, seen a globe, seen their names spelled out—whatever they were—learned the alphabet. The very fact that we all found one another with any regularity in the absence of phones or addresses, even a clock or any kind of plan, was a strange miracle—and yet we did, all over Darra.

One of the boys I knew didn't seem to have a name at all; after I heard the story of how he got to Darra, I called him "Batoor"—the Pashto word for brave. He'd come alone all the way from the city of Peshawar, traveling the Indus Highway on foot—more than twenty-five treacherous miles through barren valleys and along the high passes. It took him weeks—he had no idea how many—to get to where he was sure to find steady work. It was strange to hear of someone running away from the big city, since people trying to get away from anything usually went straight for it.

Batoor had no money, but he had wits and kept them about him; he drank water from streams, talked farmers out of ears of corn, talked women out of naan, talked Allah into keeping him going. He found wild fruit, he nibbled on bugs. Watching the boy sit back on his elbows in the dirt, I thought he must be part animal. A quiet savagery lurked beneath his skin, in the eyes, and in his slinking gait. You could tell just by looking that the boy had seen things—and I wanted to know what. Lounging on rocks, doling out roasted almonds he'd lifted from one of the half-blind merchants who pushed their carts up the market street, Batoor regaled us with stories about the labyrinthine city from which he'd come: so many people you could lose yourself there, and that's what he'd done—for longer than he cared to talk about, it seemed. Batoor left Peshawar to get away from something—I guessed that much.

Batoor came with me when I went to pick up Ayesha at the mosque. He stood while I filled my bucket, his eyes darting around. Then he moved to the long row of sinks, washed himself; methodically he rinsed off his grime, as though he'd been to that place to bathe a thousand times already. Occasionally all of the street boys I knew seemed impossibly clean, though they slept on the floors of gun shops and ran helter-skelter through the dirt. They lived in a world of filth, and yet often their skin was so pristine that it shone. Watching Batoor at the sink, I realized that they all must have gone to the mosque regularly to make use of the plentiful soap and clean water, but in all my trips to fill the family bucket, I'd never seen a single one of them—not once.

It wasn't just their bodies that were immaculate, which I put down to simple piety. From time to time, one or two would disappear for days on end, no word from the others as to why. When I made casual inquiries about the whereabouts of this boy or that one, I'd get a bitter laugh or a long stare, maybe they thought I should know better than to ask—which I did only once or twice. Eventually, the missing would come back again like newer versions of themselves—haircuts, nail beds white as crescent moons, clean clothes, full bellies. When they'd eaten well, they talked about the food for hours, as if they'd been on a journey halfway around the world—though they couldn't have gone far. An invisible line existed between us: there were things about my friends—not just their real names—that I didn't know. Maybe it was because he was so clean that day that I invited Batoor home to meet my father, who I was sure would coax the boy's mysteries out of him. The faucet at the mosque ran for uninterrupted minutes, the soap foamed, but Batoor couldn't quite wash off that sheen of savagery—there wasn't enough free water in the Indus for that. Ayesha didn't so much as blink when she saw him standing in the polished marble hall like a dark prophet. She nodded her head underneath her *chador* and held the Quran tight.

We entered the front door and in five steps or less were right in the kitchen, where my father sat, head cupped in his hand, fingers drumming. Music crackled from an old radio he'd put together piece by piece after scavenging for parts. I looked at my friend, who just gawked at the machine, eyes twitching. For a moment, I thought he might cry. My father said nothing, didn't even glance at us, didn't even know we were there. He took a long breath and sighed—there was opera in Darra Adam Khel. Then, as though sensing a shadow in the room, my father took one look at Batoor and switched off the radio.

"Who have we here, Genghis Khan?"

"This is Batoor."

"Yes, yes, I can see that he is."

My father gave Batoor our best, and he never tried to coax a thing out of him—not the name of a father or a mother, not a home, not his age or real name. Asked him nothing in fact, though that was what I had been waiting for. He simply nodded and looked from the boy to me again and again. They talked a little about Peshawar, about Batoor's long journey up the highway—how cold the streams were at night, though warm as a bath during the day. Batoor had had to veer many times from the main roadway to keep well away from the police checkpoints. Boys caught on the road were sometimes put into prison, simply because there was nowhere else.

When we'd all talked awhile in the kitchen, my father let Batoor mess about with the radio. He removed the back panel and showed him the guts. It amazed us both how nimble the boy was with his cut-up fingers. Working in different gun shops, he'd had to learn fast to use his hands—you could see it. Shams took apart the pieces and lined them up in a row. Batoor reassembled the radio in two minutes flat. Then we flipped around stations, adjusted the antenna, and lost ourselves in music again for a time. While Batoor was in our kitchen, I felt rich; we gave him cashews and pistachios and kebabs of roasted meat. My father told him that there were schools just for making things like radios and that Batoor could make a start before he even learned to spell his name—though he took a moment to teach him that too. Batoor listened between stations, his hands deep inside the workings of another machine my father had scrambled together, fiddling. Silently, he nodded and looked around at our small, two-room house as though it were a palace. His gaze softened in the lamplight, and I thought he'd caught sight of a dream he'd long let go and was just then reeling back in.

My father offered to ask a mullah at the mosque for help in finding the boy a school to start in. Then Batoor pulled his hands quickly from the machine. He got up from his chair and said it was time for him to leave—the way a boy who was late getting home might. He never responded to my father's offer—it was as though he hadn't heard it at all. And he never gave my father the chance to make it again—just opened the front door, both of us trailing him, and ran out into the purple veil of night.

My father watched Batoor long after he'd vanished up the street into shadow, hand on my shoulder, squeezing. Both of us stood in our open threshold, home warm and quiet behind us as those soft piano sounds swelled from the radio, the pitted road one step away. My father made me promise things in whispers out there that I didn't understand—about roaming around with Batoor and the other boys, never being alone in the alleyways; about not trusting or going anywhere with any man. If I needed rupees, my father told me, all I had to do was ask. He was looking into the dark as though he could still see my friend wandering barefoot up the road. Somehow I knew I wouldn't see my friend from Peshawar for several days, and that he'd reappear with his hair cut and his nails filed down to perfect crescents. Maybe a new pair of shoes if he was lucky. So lucky he would barely say a word. My father looked down at me. We were both silhouettes in the dark. I wanted to know why he never asked the boy his story, as he did every other visitor. After all, it was the first time I'd brought home human treasure.

"Batoor has already lived a thousand years too many. To ask him to tell his tale would be asking him to live a thousand more."

Within a day, I was back at the mosque with my sister and an empty bucket. She went down the hall in her pristine *chador* to find her group, and I went to wash and then to pray. Every now and again, I liked to linger in the prayer hall, as though my soul had emptied and needed filling. I stood under the huge center dome. Above me, the white vault seemed to push straight through the sky, a circumference of half-moon windows surrounding it like a dozen suns. We were meant to see heaven up there, and I always believed that I did. Then, before kneeling, I faced the indentation of black marble within the mihrab wall, which showed the congregation the *Qibla*—the direction in which they should all pray.

If you could walk through that indentation like a secret door and kept going, you'd get all the way to the Kaaba in Mecca. I'd forgotten to leave my bucket in the ablution rooms and thought at once that I should go back and put it on the bench for later. It was then that I heard a cough behind me and turned to see the smiling face of a mullah in a long robe and white turban—a man I didn't recognize, though I'd been to our mosque almost daily. I could smell fresh soap on him as I smelled it on Batoor and the other boys. He was wiping his hands with a cloth. Wordlessly, he nodded to my bucket and motioned for me to follow him.

And I did. We slipped down an empty corridor, and I remember thinking that he seemed to glide across it, as a holy man of his stature should, while I lumbered in shoes that were too large for my feet. For some reason, I felt filth in my hair, on my hands; my skin crawled, though I'd scrubbed hard in the sinks. We weren't going to the ablution rooms; we weren't going anywhere I'd ever been before. The mullah led me to an adjacent building and had me put my bucket down outside a door. He had to use a heavy brass key to open it, and when the locks shifted in their casing I could feel the heavy sounds in my heart. Inside, all the curtains on the four tall windows were shut tight but one, which let in a sword of light. An imposing desk, a silk rug woven to a deep ruby sheen, and at the far end, a long ottoman covered in cushions. It was hard to see, though I noticed a small pair of boys' shoes left behind and lying on their sides like dead things.

Then I saw a tendril of steam spiraling up from a red tea pot positioned in a corner. The Masala chai whisper wandered the room as though it had traveled time, all the way from my old life back in the college town, just to reach me right there and then. No Buddha this time, no floating lotus or cross tacked to the wall, no pictures of prophets or shelves of sacred books—no woman to offer herself up to save me if I cried. No brother sitting in my lap listening to a story—whatever was happening, it was all real. How I wished to be standing in the tranquility of that Saraiki woman's living room again, sipping tea and watching the Afridi nourish my whimpering brother—confident in the kindness of strangers. I could hear the woman chanting in my ear and then my father explaining that scene to me later. My mind was grabbing on to memories as though to flimsy rafts. Standing in the mullah's office as he tried to lure me into his shadow was like stepping into the foreboding threshold of a nightmare. Then in the cold darkness of sheer terror, I felt warm hands on my head and heard a deep voice come back to me like sureness itself—"do not be afraid". Later, I'd realize how peculiar it was that in my moment of confused terror, inside my own mosque, I hadn't reached for *ayahs*. Instead I had conjured a tableau of peaceful women sitting in a living room, and then the prophet from my dream. Just for that, the mullah might have whipped me.

The mullah went to his desk and I hovered under the threshold, feeling the coolness of the mosque behind me spread out like an ocean, the darkness of the office so hot you could barely think in it. The mullah was rummaging in his desk and licking his lips as though he were thirsty. He had a pile of rupees in his open palm—I could see their burnished gold glinting. I looked at the money, more than I'd ever seen in one place, right there for the taking. The mullah chuckled and talked to me about the boys I played with. He'd seen us many times and knew them all—all but me, he said, and he'd like to take some time to get to know me better. He was moving to the ottoman and motioned with his hand for me join him on the deep crimson cushions. Through the dimness, he gazed at me—not at my face but along the whole length of my body—and right then I knew full well what he wanted.

As though a hand were pushing me—the hand of God, the hand of my father, the hand of Jesus Christ whose sacred voice I still heard—I started to back away. The mullah frowned and continued talking, jangling his shiny pile of change and touching the red cushions. He beckoned me in again and told me to shut the door. Then he reached down into the darkness and pulled a ripe pomegranate out for me to see. In the soft air of the open corridor, I leaned down for my bucket, swinging it so hard by the handle that the metal hit the wall. Clangs reverberated through the mosque like a broken bell. I stopped then, stood my ground for a moment, and said what I had to say before running.

"When I need rupees I ask my father, and when I'm hungry for fruit he gives me that too. Bother me again, and I swear he will kill you."

Moving fast up the corridor in the clean light and high polish, I went all the way past the prayer hall, running under its heavenly dome and around the pillars. I raced out the main doors, dropping my bucket but not hearing it. I just kept going, not stopping—not once.

The instant I stepped outside, the filth and clatter descended upon me. I stood in the street and gulped the air as though it was clean water and I hadn't had a drop in days. I thought my lungs had forgotten how to breathe; I could not catch my breath. Across the road, I saw a few of the boys I knew lurking around. One of them had on an ironed shirt, new shoes. They hadn't noticed me yet. I scanned their faces for Batoor, but he wasn't among them. Not two minutes before, I'd been one step over a threshold away from that boy's dark world, and I knew it. I didn't wait long enough for them to catch sight of me. Running, I felt my father's hand pressing down on my shoulder and heard his voice in my ear. Every word pierced me.

"Batoor has lived a thousand years too many already."

9. Out of the Tribal Lands

Everyday life simply became too dangerous in Darra Adam Khel, so we loaded up the pick up once again, this time in search of peace. From the flatbed, I gazed down from the Indus Highway into a circular valley the size of a sea. And when I saw it—a metropolis spread out in a great hive of tall, clustered buildings—I thought Peshawar was a city to be reckoned with. I was right. Straightaway, I would struggle to find my place among the masses there, where I had nowhere to run free and didn't know a soul. It was 2001, I was barely ten years old, and it felt as though that final move of my childhood, out of the bad and beautiful tribal lands behind us, signaled its end.

Before our departure, my father had described the capital of the Khyber Pakhtunkhwa province, which would be the first real city I'd ever laid eyes on. The ancient texts of the Parsi described the region as the sixth most beautiful place on earth, and it must have been true at one time, when it was still the jewel described in my father's history books, nestled along the eastern end of the Khyber Pass. Now it was a sprawl of soulless buildings, as though the bygone valley had sprouted a boundless forest of huge, colorless trees, all rising half dead to a pale yellow haze. My father told us about the colleges, modern hospitals, markets, and parks. We were moving there for opportunities that we couldn't find in the tribal belt: good schools, medical care, stable work, and no more guns—a better life. It sounded too good to be true. Maybe it was. All I saw slipping past the truck rails as we veered off the highway and onto Kohat Road was an imposing urban jungle. When we finally reached the heart of the city, the streets of Peshawar hummed with the angry clamor of jammed traffic; its cliff walls of buildings loomed for miles. The city seemed to have no end—*if I let it*, I thought, *it could swallow me whole*.

Our new home was a stucco building, a washed-out mustard color that rose up several stories. I remember staring along its face, my neck craned, mesmerized by its height and the many windows that punctuated the facade. It would be like living inside a giant honeycomb. Our apartment block ran right alongside a sidewalk full of hustling pedestrians and fruit stalls selling lemons, oranges, limes, mangoes, all arranged in pyramids. Every time someone bought a piece of fruit, vendors swiftly rearranged the pattern. A parade of motorized rickshaws rushed past the curb. So many cars clogged the street that there was barely space between bumpers. The city buzzed like a hive.

A wiry teenager stood by the gutter, watching us unload our bags and crates. He jumped forward and held out a calloused palm, and I saw right away that his wrist had a stippling of raw sores across it—another heroin addict. It seemed that in Peshawar addicts and vagrant children were everywhere. My father nodded and handed the boy a small coin, promising one more after he'd finished helping us carry our possessions into the building—the few things that signaled home. With no room for chickens in this new apartment, all we brought with us were clothes and books, my mother's box of mementos, two fans this time instead of one, and the Sohrab.

During the first few weeks in Peshawar, I had difficulty finding my bearings. We'd come from a landscape of wide-open flood plains where all the landmarks were purely of the earth—mountain peaks, a bend in the river, an acacia tree, boulders, sunflower fields, an abandoned eagle's nest. One glance at the position of the sun and I could guess the time of day. Now I was lost in a chaotic grid of roads and buildings all jumbled together. My father gave us each a street map and a watch. But I didn't want either—I wanted to go back to the valleys. I longed to see the

Indus again, to breathe unspoiled air and to run barefoot across the rooftops and plains.

The apartment was clean and sufficient. We had a proper bathroom, a nice kitchen with cabinets, two bedrooms, and a living space with a pullout couch where my parents would sleep. Taimur and the twins shared one bedroom, while Ayesha and I occupied the other. My siblings took to city life immediately, slipping right into the routines that school provided. At first, I was still taught at home, but between their jobs teaching, my parents had little time to devote to my lessons. Most days, I stayed inside, staring out the window, waiting for someone to come back. When you opened a window, the city spilled in, all noise and heat. It was a strange sensation living closed-in, so many feet above the ground, and sandwiched between floors. Outside, all I could see were other buildings—no sun to offer my face to. I felt as though I was suffocating. Sometimes I wept myself quietly to sleep. Often, I thought I should just leave and walk the highway passes all the way back to Darra Adam Khel, where I could roam the mountains with my slingshot again. My family could see that from the first day in Peshawar I had grown sullen; my temper thrashed at the slightest provocation. I lurked about our rooms like a creature caught in a net. Moving to the city was a clipping of my wings.

The government education board, whose headquarters were in the city, sent my mother for training courses and on teaching assignments all over the area. My father commuted most days into the tribal regions to lecture at various colleges. For the first few weeks, my mother took Ayesha and me with her in the jingle bus, a colorfully decorated truck with benches inside, to the school for girls where she had taken a temporary post. The journey on the lumbering school bus was happy and loud, full of girls chattering on benches while I sat silent, pressed between my mother and sister. Every now and again a few girls would turn to look at me and stare.

In Peshawar, at my parents' behest, I tried out Maria again, wearing the school uniform of dark, itchy dress and a veil draped over my head and shoulders. The only way I could go to a school for girls was to dress like one, and now the only way I could get a regular education was to go to school. Taimur had started at a fine high school at the other end of the city, and Ayesha was just two years away from going to high school herself. The twins attended kindergarten a short walk up the road from home.

Every morning, slipping on the wool tunic was like putting on someone else's ill-fitting skin. My hair was still razor short, and I was a tall plank of hard muscle inside that ironed dress. The uniform made my skin erupt in painful rashes. My big square hands showed their history of slinging rocks and shooting arrows. It didn't take long for the other girls to size me up as I squirmed at my desk chair trying to concentrate on the lessons. There were rumors that I was actually a boy. But no one said a word against me, as I was a Madam's child; they simply acted as though I wasn't there. And in essence, I wasn't. Throughout those long, torturous school days, I retreated to a dream world, walking the deep, fertile gullies between mountains, taking long drinks from streams. I had no interest whatsoever in reading textbooks or learning things from words scrawled on a board. Up until that point, I'd loved learning at home and couldn't imagine acquiring knowledge any other way. My mother had taught me in the warm kitchen, my father in the soft shade of fruit trees, sitting on the cool clay floor of our living room, or taking walks through the rocky plains. Every day, Ayesha would come to check on me in my classroom, always shaking her head. She said, "I feel so sorry for you, Maria. You don't belong in here." She was right. I was completely out of place and wasn't learning a thing. And so my father set me free from the prison of that suffocating uniform, gave me lessons when he could, and found me something else to do.

My new job was to run errands for the family—purchase groceries, school supplies, medicine, toiletries, newspapers, books. Whatever we needed. I had to get to know that map of the city like the back of my hand, and over the course of several months, I did. When I had my bearings set, my father let me take Sohrab out in the city, and we attached saddlebags to the sides and a bell to the handlebars. I loved to race along the paved streets—zig-zagging through traffic; taunting drivers; ringing the bell; ignoring traffic signals, road signs; never stopping for anyone or anything. I dressed in shorts and T-shirts, pumping hard and bumping over potholes. The city streamed alongside me in a blur of white buildings as I rode past the ancient town gateways, playing fields, and stadiums, along the Kabul River Canal. But every single time I climbed onto the bike, I still thought of cutting right across Peshawar and dovetailing onto the long road all the way back to the wild tribal lands.

On any given day, my father might send me out for any number of things—toothpaste, razor blades, or a bunch of bananas. On one particular afternoon, he asked me to buy a bag of flour. Most of the time, I knew he was sending me out just to get me outside. If he couldn't think of a thing for me to find, he simply directed me to a place—the beautiful gardens of Ali Mardan Khan, the narrow pitted alleyways of Old Peshawar, which were so fragrant with spice that I came back giving off heady wafts of saffron and clove. Once, my father directed me with a sketchpad and pencil to take a tour of the old monuments—Bara Bridge, built by the Mughals; Cunningham Clock Tower, built by the English. But eventually he ran out of ideas, and that's about when I started to run amok.

It started at the site of Kabuli Gate, the most prominent of the sixteen that once led into the old city. My tire punctured on a piece of broken pipe and I had to stop at the curb, sweating and breathless, to patch it. After I fixed the tear, I couldn't quite get my breath to steady. My mouth was parched and rough, and my heart hammered. I rubbed my temples against the din of cars, mopeds, and lumbering trucks. I hated the city more than ever that day. Thirsty, I had no water left in my canteen and no money to buy anything but the sack of flour my father had sent me for. In the city, if you didn't have rupees, you had nothing. It wasn't like living out in the fields where water ran free for the taking in brooks, and trees dropped ripe fruit right into your open hands.

I was in the heart of Old Peshawar. Stone walls divided the area into three neighborhoods—Sard Chah, Gunj, and Dhaki Nalbandi. Who knows which one I was in when the boys began following me that day. When the first one called out to me, I looked back and got on my bike. Many of them got onto their own bikes; they must have been standing around waiting for someone to prey on. Some of them started out on foot, running, and then somehow their small cluster multiplied to a swarm. When I felt the wind from their movement, I pumped harder, legs moving like pistons. I could hear them jeering. They thought I had something they wanted—my watch, the shoes on my feet, the old Sohrab. Their sport was in the taking, I knew that much. They had no idea how strong I was as I rode just ahead of them. It occurred to me that they were soft-muscled city boys who spent their days loitering in the streets. I knew just by looking over my shoulders in angry glances that I could take them all, one at a time. And I wanted to. Turning into a side alley, I stopped pedaling, and I stepped off the bike.

The stench of the city sewers hung in the air. The boys all pulled up alongside me in the alleyway. Wordlessly, one or two of the half dozen who were still following me got off their bikes. One of them called out something in a language I didn't recognize. I said nothing back. I assumed the strongest among them would step forward. He wasn't hard to spot—there was always an alpha dog in a group of males. In Darra Adam Khel, the alpha had been me.

The boy who walked up to face me was a head shorter than I was but he was stocky, like a bag of cement. Big hands, wide shoulders, he would put up a good fight. Still, I figured it would be fast. We'd hit each other a few times. He'd try to take something from me. Probably my watch. I wouldn't let him. Instead, I would get him in a choke hold, scare him a little—simple as that. The others would watch, shouting, placing bets. I'd seen that show of male dominance play out many times in Darra.

For a few seconds, everything was quiet in that narrow, dark laneway. I could hear water dripping from a pipe behind me and felt my thirst again. I was calm and swallowed hard. My heartbeat was steady. Standing there, surrounded by nameless boys holding up bicycles, their leader drawing in closer, I curled my fingers into a loose ball. The boy came up to me, and we stared each other down a moment or two, both of us lit for a fight. Then he nodded, eyes never leaving mine, and spat at my feet. That was just the way he wanted to start things between us.

I didn't think hard about what I did next. The outcome was already clear in my mind—no one could beat me, not there, not ever. I pulled back my arm jackhammer-style and shot my fist straight out and into his jaw. He stammered out a cry, his head going back, but he squared himself fast, stood his ground, and shot me right back dead center in the mouth. I felt a tooth loosen and a spurt of warm blood, used my tongue to jam the tooth back into the gum line. Soon the boy and I were tangled up, wrestling arm to arm, forehead to forehead, breathing in grunts against each other like sparring bulls. Before long, his endurance waned—all it took was a slight weakening of his grip and I had him down in the choke hold, one knee on the ground boring into the paving, the other bent to prop up the boy I had subdued. He was wheezing from the squeeze of my arm muscles wrapped around his neck. The unsteady staccato of his heartbeat pulsed against my flexed forearm. His sour sweat stank.

One by one, the boys in the alley quieted down, got on their bikes, and slowly pulled out into the road. The show was over; I watched them go. Still, I held the boy tight and waited for the last one to move out of the alley shadow, round the corner, and disappear. Finally alone, I let the boy go, and he fell away, off my knee to the ground at my feet. Gulping the air for breath and clutching at his bruised neck, he never looked at me once. A water bottle sat in a holder on his bike, and I walked over and grabbed it, taking a long drink. Then I went up to the boy and upended the bottle over his filthy sweat-soaked face. I felt good standing over him, seeing his weakness. In my mind, that kid panting for breath on the ground wasn't a person at all: I'd just beat up Peshawar in the first round—but I had a feeling there would be others.

*

I walked through the door to our apartment with blood trickling down one side of my mouth—pretending nothing had happened —slowly took off my sandals, put them side by side in the closet. My father took one look at my swollen lip as I handed over the sack of flour he'd sent me to the market for, and nodded. I think he believed that in my first big-city street fight, I was getting something out of my system—but whatever that something was, it had already infiltrated my veins. The fact was, I'd enjoyed the raw excitement of the fight. I'd also loved the feeling of winning.

"What were you doing out there today, Genghis Khan? Fighting back a horde of invading Mongols?"

"Something like that, Baba."

"Well, then my timing is both unfortunate and perfect."

I trailed my father into the living room, trying hard not to touch the bruises blooming over my face. I saw the television set and VCR sitting on a stand in the corner. My father always found a way to hustle vendors and rent equipment and movie cassettes; sometimes he came home with as many as seven movies in a big paper bag. Over his weekends off, my family would sit sprawled in a mess of blankets and cushions all over the living room floor of our small apartment and watch together. Sometimes we screened television shows from the United States. I was never sure where he found such rarities. My favorite of them all was *CHiPs*, a series about two highway patrol officers with impossibly white teeth, who rode around California on motorcycles, fighting crime. The dry sierras framing the Los Angeles basin looked just like the beautiful rolling brown foothills of Darra. When my father slipped *Rocky* into the VCR and pressed the PLAY button, he turned to me and grinned. I don't know if he intended Rocky Balboa to become my new hero, but from the moment an underdog Rocky agreed to fight the invincible Apollo Creed, it was too late. I was riveted. Right away, I identified with the strong and aimless hero battling his demons for recognition in a callous city. What he was doing in the ring, I had just done in the streets. My father was right; the timing was perfect.

Rocky Balboa's Philadelphia slum-world wasn't all that different from mine. I was miserable living in Peshawar and saw only its blemishes: pitted roads, neglected gateways, dilapidated curbs, the overfilled dumpsters, the overcrowded buses—the utter absence of anything green. You could walk a mile and never once see a tree. Nothing could subdue my rage against that city for caging me. Peshawar was the Apollo Creed I had to vanquish but already feared I could not—the city was simply too massive. And when Rocky Balboa spoke onscreen, I thought he was speaking right to me. His words, which I had to read in subtitles, made my heart beat stronger.

Let me tell you something you already know. The world ain't all sunshine and rainbows. It's a very mean and nasty place and I don't care how tough you are it will beat you to your knees and keep you there permanently if you let it. You, me, or nobody is gonna hit as hard as life. But it ain't about how hard you hit; it's about how hard you can get hit and keep moving forward.

And I was always moving forward, from town to town, valley to valley, neighborhood to neighborhood, past mosques and shrines, hospitals, schools, the ghettos, the Afghan refugee camps on the outskirts, the alley slums in the old city. The next time I went out on the Sohrab, I went out as Rocky Balboa looking for a fight. And it didn't take long for me to find one.

I had no gang of my own—and still no invitations to join one. I raced my bike up the main arteries of Peshawar all the way to the outskirts, where the traffic and roads thinned. In my mind I was in Philadelphia, running the streets. I shuttled through scenes in the movie, which I had watched several times already—Rocky Balboa pounding meat carcasses instead of punching bags, the way he took eye-splitting hits to his face and kept coming back for more.

Along the rim of the city, I passed crowds of young men

loitering. Some were Afghans, whiling away the months until their official repatriation back to their homeland. The United Nations had just granted those displaced by the Soviet war official refugee status, although that's exactly what many had been for well over ten years. Others had only just gotten to Peshawar, on the run from the Taliban who were in power on the other side of the Durand Line. My father had shown us pictures of the sprawling Jalozai encampment, an ocean of huts and makeshift tents planted in a wasted dust bowl twenty miles outside of Peshawar. The new UN-designated camp Shamshatoo was fifteen miles away off an unpaved road into the wilderness, and officials were in the midst of moving people from one camp to the other. I'd seen the long, beaten-up dirt road leading all the way to the camp, and the water trucks lumbering up it carrying rations and stirring up yellow clouds of dust, and then the people coming down into the city looking for work or more food. You didn't have to be dead, I thought, looking into the voids of their faces, to no longer be living. Baba said, *Bureaucracy kills more people than bullets*. And he was right.

I turned down a small residential street where laundry hung from lines above. Children wailed through open windows; a lamb bayed. I didn't know I was being followed—and could have been for hours and miles. Ever since I took that boy down in a choke hold, a bull's-eye was on my back. All those boys knew where I lived and had been waiting for me. Inside Peshawar's urban labyrinth there was a whole network of wily street gangs, I would learn. And once they targeted a kid for a fight, you didn't have a choice. Unwittingly, in beating one of their own, I'd started a war.

Some of the streets in the old part of the city were a narrow no-man's-land. Many of the buildings—shabby bungalows and corner shops—were shuttered. Garbage littered the curbs. As though they knew something I didn't, several old men who had been sitting outside under awnings went quietly indoors when they saw me. I put my foot down on the pavement and looked up to the strip of blue sky in time to see a bird beat past.

I felt someone coming up from behind me like a low electrical current, and the air suddenly changed. Turning, my hands slipped against the handlebars. A checkered scarf covered half his face. The look in his eyes told me everything I needed to know and what he was after: nothing I had, no material thing he could take—just me. Other boys came sauntering into the roadway with their bicycles or on foot. A few came out of houses just to watch. They had the cool look that came from knowing that you own the ground and the moment itself. I counted them up fast—got to ten and stopped. The boy facing me was so close I could smell his caraway-seed breath. Casually, I walked over to a pock-marked brick wall, propped up my bike, and then went back. I was poised: they didn't know I was channeling Rocky—it was the main reason I was still there.

The first boy started jabbering at me about the mess I'd made of his brother. There was no explanation I could give. His brother had come after me first, not the other way around. I shrugged my shoulders, saying nothing. Two boys slid to either side of me, and I figured they were all just going to take me down in a riot of kicks and punches. Then, my opponent held up a hand, shaking his head, and they backed off quietly. That was the moment I felt as though I really was Rocky—in the ring, ready to go the distance. I had nothing to lose but my pride, and that was all I had worth keeping—it was the thing that had kept me at the top of the food chain with the boys back in Darra, and I had no reason to believe the pecking order would be any different here. People were watching like shadows from behind their shutters. I could hear their voices and the shifting of latches. The desire to win spiked my nerves. My mind grabbed a line from the movie; I may have said it in my head or uttered it aloud, I can't remember now. "You're gonna eat lightning!"

Then he shoved me hard—with one hand—testing me out. His breath escaped in a quick *huff*. I shoved him back with both palms hitting flat against his torso, and he fell back—and we were in the thick of round one. I thwacked him in the face again and again, and he did the same to me. I feigned weakness for a while, seeing what he had in mind, and we toyed with each other, dancing around, hitting and jabbing this way and that in the alley. I knew he was trying to imitate my choke hold; the other boys and his defeated brother must have described it to him. He kept coming at me with a bent arm, trying to loop my neck. I knew that would be his undoing—fixating on a single endgame maneuver while I calculated against it. Every adversary hid a fatal weakness; you had to find it and dig your way in—this was what my father had taught me long before I learned about the proverbial Achilles' heel. All I had to do was grab that bent arm fast, pull it straight, and jam it back with two hands, popping out his elbow—just like breaking a hinge.

His joint made a hollow sound when I cranked it. I held his limb firm, considering my next move. Then we looked at each other as though seeing one another for the first time. I noted the pain cutting through his black eyes, and we exchanged a sure knowledge that if I wanted, I could snap his arm in two. I was one pulse away, and he knew it—another half inch and he'd need a cast. Those wide wet eyes begged me to stop—and that was enough. I let go, tossing him down like a sack of flour. We were done.

Music from a radio floated in the air. Drumbeats, an electric guitar. I thought of my father and what he would say when he saw my knuckles pummeled and wet with blood, the gash on my top lip. All the air was gone from the long, filthy street, as though we'd sucked it away, using up every ounce of oxygen in our brawling. We'd been at it for a long time, maybe a half hour. It was suddenly hot. Already, the other boys were slowly leaving on their bikes, like an audience exiting the auditorium, all of them mute in their beat-up shoes just as before, and abandoning their comrade to the ground where he cradled his elbow. This time, instead of simply vanishing, one or two of them looked back and nodded at me. Silent approval, respect—it was all I needed. I turned, held out my bleeding hand to help my Apollo Creed up, and then went for my bike. I walked it up the street.

When the brick hit my head, it split the skin straight down

the back of my skull. Blood gushed, I could feel it and smell it. I stood there teetering, let go of my bike. It fell in a clatter to the ground, one wheel spinning. Then I was on my knees. The back of my T-shirt was suddenly sticky and warm, and I thought one thing—*honey*. All of the adrenaline from the fight was gone from my body. The Hollywood spell was broken. For a moment, I thought the boy might have hit me hard enough to kill, but I could feel my heart stampeding. At first, pain didn't come from the wound but erupted from my gut and spread right up my throat. I lurched forward and vomited. Glancing up the dizzy street, I focused just enough to see a pair of ripped-up running shoes stop before me a moment. Then everything simply went white, just like an old tube television does when you turn it off. My head fell to the ground with the rest of me, and I closed my eyes.

Sometime later, I somehow got up and wobbled home. I remember seeing my building rising from the roadway, setting sun shooting off the honeycomb of glass windows, and not knowing how I'd even gotten there. By some miracle, I still had the bike and was pushing it along. A grime of blood, sweat, and filth coated the handlebars. I don't want to know how I looked when I stumbled through the door to our apartment and called out for a glass of water.

It didn't matter how it happened or where. I don't think he even asked me. All my father saw was my blood. Our arms intertwined, he took me to the couch and checked me over, limb by limb. Asked me questions: my name, our address, to count backward from ten. No one else was home. Often, my parents traded off days taking care of the household between their teaching shifts. The living room filled with our murmurs and nothing else. I kept my eyes closed as my father talked to me softly, using a cloth to tamp down my wound and stop it from gushing. I've never forgotten the way he sounded, like a much younger version of himself, like a man tending to his infant.

At the hospital in Peshawar, the doctors gave me stitches and administered pain medications. They ran tests and let me go.

Before we left, my father came into the examination room and stood before me; drops of my blood spattered his white *shalwar kameez*. I was pulling dried clumps of blood from my hair and tried not to look at him. I felt ashamed. He talked to me about anger, how I needed to grab it by the reins and pull it in. He was back to himself, a solid baritone of strength now that his daughter had been put back together again. After he was done, he took my shoulders and held me close to his chest, so that I could hear his breathing and the sureness of his heartbeats. Just then, I wanted to fold myself up and into him. Peshawar wasn't home: home was my father—I didn't need anywhere else.

"Maria, don't you remember what Rocky Balboa said about what you're doing?"

"He said a lot of things, Baba. A lot of things about trying to win."

He stepped back and looked at me half-smiling. Then he touched my beat-up face.

"You gotta be a moron . . . you gotta be a moron to want to be a fighter."

10. The Capital of Empires

Fourteen stitches didn't deter me, nor did my father's sentiments in the hospital, though at first I did try to clean up my act. The story of the brick splitting open my scalp took on legendary proportions among the street kids, and soon I couldn't walk the pavement without a new contender following me. It seemed like everyone wanted to fight the new Pashtun. I didn't feel as though I had a choice. One after the other, I subdued boys quickly and with as little blood as possible.

Fist fighting became a sport to me—and, strangely, it was a sure way of making friends, which I desperately craved. Brawling was how poor boys in the streets both socialized and protected themselves. I'd figured out from watching that once you'd proven yourself, you would be invited into a gang. That was how the system worked, and I waited for my turn. At the same time, those sweaty brawls cured an insatiable drive to exercise my physical strength. I became a master of the slick one-two punch, always landing it right between the eyes. The first hit stunned, the second sent them to the ground—ten seconds flat, maybe less, and it was all over. I split lips, smashed teeth, broke noses, and I never turned my back on any of my opponents again. I pinned them down but never pulverized—that was a deal I made with myself. Sometimes I fought for rupees or food; most of the time I just wanted to win. Not just the fight, but a position of respect among the gangs. Those gangs weren't unlike tribes, and I knew I needed one in order to survive living day-to-day with nowhere to go and little to do in the city. When I was done, I'd hold out a battered hand and help my adversary to his feet, pat his back, offer pleasantries, and we'd make our way onto the market street, where I'd buy him a conciliatory mango if I had enough rupees— no hard feelings.

Soon, I roved the neighborhoods with a gang of ten boys, all of whom I'd beaten. After that, it was accepted that I was one of them. We all had nicknames and talked in our own slang. They took me from one end of the city to the other. People called us bandits, though we didn't break any laws—never so much as stole a piece of naan. None of us ever asked each other personal questions, and I liked it that way.

Then, in July, on the cusp of a summer storm, along the street of storytellers, Qissa Khawani, I fought my last fight. I should have known that my father would pass through, walking the bustling market roadway where he often bought books. A black sky and gathering winds warned of the coming ten-day deluge. People crowded the bazaar, stocking up on last-minute supplies: batteries, kerosene, flour, and basmati rice. Or in my father's case: paperbacks, magazines, and American movies.

I was standing in a side street between apartment blocks. It was so damp outside that it felt as though we were living inside a heavy cloud. Flocks of black crows congregated, perched on rails and on rooftops, lining the criss-cross of electrical wires by the dozen. They were cawing about something in an eerie chorus. Their relentless racket was enough to drive a person to madness, and some of the boys took to shouting back at the birds, called them loudmouthed infidels, kicked them from their perches, picked a few off with slingshots. Right then, I knew something was wrong. My sister would have called that scene an omen; my mother would have said what was to happen was written—maybe they were both right.

My adversary was a thuggish Afghan with arms like hams, sent on a mission, he said, to take me down. I assumed he was a member of a rival gang. He kept telling me about his cold-blooded crew back at the refugee camp. We stood squared and stared into each other. I kept quiet, never blinked—my usual routine. Then, just as the birds started up that melee of squawking again, I pulled back my fist and shot it out into the breach—one-two. Nothing but air. Maybe he flinched; I was too stunned to notice—he just stood there grinning. I pulled my fist back again and stepped right into a harder punch—one-two. Glancing blows, my fists never finding full purchase. One-two, again. This time, I connected solidly, but I felt my knuckle crack like a wishbone. I might as well have slugged a brick wall.

My turn to take a hit came fast—his arm hammered back, and a second later my world blurred. Within minutes, it was like fighting underwater. A single thunderclap and the rain came, falling as though the sky had torn open, releasing a warm sea down over Peshawar. I could barely see a thing. Somehow my opponent was all over me, and I felt the ground hit my back. We were on the pavement, fighting like dogs. Then the Afghan used his weight to keep me down, and no matter how I squirmed he had me cinched. My forearms were up, shielding my face, and I felt the wound along my head scrape against the wet ground, but the scabbed skin held fast. The birds were all lifting away, black forms spreading out into the darkening sky, over which they scattered like flak. For a moment, I registered the sheer beauty of those fleeing birds and the senselessness of what I was doing. One breath later and I was back at it—I had his hair clenched in my fists.

It was then that my father happened to pass, stop, and stare down the road. He might have heard the gathering crowd shouting under awnings and umbrellas along the perimeter. I turned my head to the side, and our eyes locked. He had a set of paperback books cradled under his arm, protecting them from the elements. Momentarily, I thought he was not my father in the flesh but a manifestation of my humiliation—somehow conjured, not because I was fighting so soon after the brick incident, but because I was in danger of losing the fight. Methodically, my father shoved his books into his satchel and then put the sack on the ground. The thug had me straddled and fixed, but as my father cut through the line of bystanders and entered the scene, I found a split-second maneuver and swiftly turned the tables. All it took was one quick jab into his eye socket. Stunned and struck temporarily blind, he reeled. Then I shoved hard, arched my back, and hurled him over. Now I was on top of the Afghan, clawing desperately at his eyes with my hooked thumbs—that's when I felt a pair of big hands on my shoulders heave me straight up and away.

Despite appearances to the contrary—his clean, pressed *shalwar kameez*; the dignified roll of his head scarf; those long, elegant fingers and limbs—my father could be an aggressive man. For the first time in my life, I felt his raw physical power as he hauled me by the scruff, calling back to the bewildered boys that I was late for dinner. Then he dragged me by the collar straight up the street, stopping only to get his bag. I didn't get a chance to look behind us, but part of me was relieved. I knew I'd come out on top. I could still hear the Afghan moaning.

Out of the bazaar, my father released my ruined collar but kept his hand clasped to my shoulder as we dovetailed into the river of pedestrians. If he said anything, I don't remember it, but there wasn't much we could say to each other. I was still catching my breath. All of that interrupted rage suddenly had nowhere to go and it circled my mind like a trapped animal, leaving me out of sorts for a time. A rickshaw pulled over, and I heard my father utter an address that was not our home as we slid into the covered seat, heavy rain slapping our faces. My father sat back and looked at me then, studied my face, which, despite the savagery of the match, barely had a mark on it. He took my beat-up hand and scanned the row of bruises, found a cloth in his pocket, and wiped away smears of blood. Then he reached into the sack burrowed behind his feet. Muttering under his breath, shielding his precious used paperbacks from the storm that spit at us from all sides through the flimsy tarp covering, he pulled out a book—frayed covers, cracked-up spine. A single name stood out—Plato —second only to Socrates as his favorite among the ancient Greek philosophers. My father thumbed through pages until he found what he was looking for and tapped a line with his index finger.

"For a man to conquer himself is the first and noblest of all victories."

Confused, I had to look away from him. In my father's resolute calm, I saw my own shame. "Are you angry, Baba?"

"No, not yet. I'm looking for a solution."

"Where are you taking me?"

"I'm taking you to a place where you'll finally get to fight your own demons instead of all those useless hooligans out there. *Inshallah*, we will make something of you yet, Genghis Khan."

*

Even seen through sheets of pouring rain, the sports complex, which included a stadium and several other large structures, was massive and imposing. Because of the downpour, no one was outside in the wide cement quadrangle or crossing the many walkways, and I feared that my father was taking me to a juvenile prison or to sign me up at a school for delinquents. He still hadn't told me precisely what he had in mind. I'd only ever kicked a soccer ball across open plains years before. At my age, most boys had already chosen and honed a sport. So far, I'd only fallen into street fighting. It was time, my father said, for a change.

Inside the main building, all the fluorescent lights were on, but the huge foyer was empty except for one man sitting back in a chair at the far end, reading a newspaper. Every time a thunderclap hit, the lights flickered. At first, I thought the man was fast asleep, because he didn't so much as twitch, despite the interruptions of the violent weather; but then he looked up and smiled as we approached. The man had a friendly face, big smile, white teeth that made me think of American television shows, and he waved us over. He stood up and had a look at me from head to toe, and then walked over to one side and had a brief conversation with my father. I heard the words "strong," "brave," "boy," "fist fights," and "twelve years old." Then the man approached and studied my bashed-up hands; he motioned to the jagged scab along the back of my skull and looked up at my father.

Rain-soaked and pummeled, I was a sight to behold. They shared a laugh.

"So, you're a pretty strong kid. How would you like to lift weights?"

I thought about the idea for a moment, looked over at my father, who nodded and crossed his arms.

"Okay—why not?"

"What's your name, boy?"

"Genghis Khan."

"Ah, the Great Khan." He laughed out loud, his head going way back. "Perfect."

From the start, I was a natural. It turned out that the man sitting in the chair was the center's weightlifting coach, and he was short a few boys for his provincial team. One look at my muscled arms, strong hands and frame and he knew I'd have the right kind of prowess—the strength to lift loaded barbells and the gift of stubborn tenacity. The next day, my father signed me up with my older brother, Taimur.

Until I took up weightlifting, Taimur and I had spent very little time together—he was four years older and always out studying with his high school friends. But once my father brought me to the sports complex, we trained together almost daily. My father didn't trust all the sweaty men exercising at the gym and worried that I could be caught out as a girl. It was Taimur's job to make sure that didn't happen; it was also a chance for us to cement our relationship. The only reason he was there lifting weights at all was to watch over me. But if he was annoyed at having to join the team, he never once showed it. My quiet, dutiful brother never showed much emotion, but he took his task seriously. Everywhere I went, he was my unfailing shadow.

Taimur and I didn't meet the other boys on the team; all of them trained one at a time with our coach, but my brother and I were given an exception because we were siblings. I often looked over to see my brother standing off to the side, tall, quiet, and sure, his eyes roving the crowded weight room, back and forth. I knew that if anyone bothered me, my nearly six-foot, soft-eyed, sixteen-year-old brother would pound them inside out. I remember thinking that what little Sangeen and Babrak were to me, I was to him—precious things to be protected at any cost. Having him there with me felt good.

In the sport of weightlifting, a competitor has to master two basic lifts with finesse—the snatch and the clean and jerk. It wasn't just about getting the barbell off the ground—that was the last thing I had to contend with. The first was to figure out how to prepare both physically and mentally. In the snatch, the lifter must raise the barbell from the floor to an overhead position in a single explosive motion. It requires a sudden detonation of raw strength, and the move came to me as though by instinct. I had a mercurial temperament already, and I simply forced that reserve of wild emotion into synchronized bolts of power. Somehow, when I centered all of my fury and executed the maneuver in perfect form—stance, breathing, and movement—a weight that should have crushed my bones was briefly under my command.

The clean and jerk required two motions: cleaning the barbell up from the floor to shoulder level, a short pause, and then a powerful thrust to a full overhead position. It was that short pause that made the lift far more physically challenging. At first I struggled to get the bar up past my clavicle. I tried for days, always dropping it to the floor. When at last I stood in the middle of the weight room with the barbell held high, I felt transformed.

From that moment of victory, I discovered the linchpin of athletics—winning or losing starts in the brain and travels by a single command to the rest of the body. When faced with a stacked barbell at my feet, I would tell myself that I could execute a full lift, and my muscles would naturally agree with me. If I allowed even a sliver of doubt to infiltrate my mind, I would grab the bar and fail fast. I told myself that I was invincible, and somehow my body believed it. I got to know every muscle fiber along my limbs and learned to communicate with each one as though by telepathy. And for the first time, I actually understood that I was a material being, a skeletal frame encased in a living armor of taut muscle, and I believed that I was tougher than any other kid my age—girl or boy.

I'd get a chance to prove it at my first tournament, in Lahore, capital of the province of Punjab and one of the most densely packed cities in the world. Our team, representing the Khyber Pakhtunkhwa region, traveled more than three hundred miles along the AH-1 Grand Trunk Road in a blue and white PAF bus. Taimur sat up front with me, staring out of the wide, bug-spattered windshield. The highway was long and smooth, and the sky above it clouded-over and limitless. Being strong finally meant going somewhere—just stepping onto the bus with my gym bag, wearing a new team shirt, I was already a lifetime away from the pitted back alleys of Peshawar. My family of intrepid Wazirs had traveled the treacherous lengths of our wild tribal lands, but we'd never gone so far into the populated depths of Pakistan proper. There were so many towns and cities along the route: Rawalpindi, Talagang, Kallar Kahar, Bhalwal, Pindi Bhattian, Sheikhupura. On that six-hour drive over rolling verdant hills, I fell in love with my country, my Pakistan—so vast and beautiful, only a god could have made it.

Lahore made Peshawar look like a ragtag hamlet with its high-rises and minarets, hundreds of domed temples and churches, museums and mausoleums, colonial forts, university campuses, and hospitals, miles of flowering parkland scattered between. Lahore has a millennium-long history as a basin of power—from the Ghaznavid Empire of the eleventh century, through the Mughals in the sixteenth, who established the city's many fabled gardens, to the Sikh realm of the nineteenth century and finally the British Raj, when Lahore became the capital of Punjab.

But I was in Lahore to compete and win, and I thought of little else. Weightlifting wasn't a big competitive sport in Pakistan like hockey, squash, or cricket, and tournaments were few and far between. It would be another year before I'd get a chance to compete like that again. To me, weightlifting wasn't about beating the other boys; first and foremost it was about finding the full depth of my strength. I wanted to go home and tell my father that I'd done as Plato had advised—fought and conquered myself—and in the capital of empires.

Outwardly, I wasn't concerned about the fact that during the three-day tournament I'd be sleeping among boys in a crammed hostel room. I refused to think about the fact that someone might discover my true gender. It was a fear so great that, like the edge of a cliff, I didn't want to go near it. Taimur made sure I took a cot in the far corner and placed himself in the one right next to mine. Even though he was competing at the tournament in a different division, he saw his primary job there as making sure I didn't get found out. Meanwhile, I got to know my male teammates, who came from all parts of the Khyber Pakhtunkhwa province, in the usual way—we roughhoused, told jokes, and traded good-humored insults. Five times each day, at the melodic call of the muezzin, we became as one in our faith while so far from home, and knelt down together to pray.

The entire time I was there, Taimur lurked on the periphery, my lumbering and steadfast bodyguard. He was polite to the others, exchanged the occasional banter, but most of the time he stood around the room like an imposing pillar. He made sure I changed clothes in the communal bathroom alone and stood sentry outside the door, arms folded. Regardless, I didn't have to worry about a boy coming in while I was using the restroom. Modesty and cleanliness are tenets of our Muslim faith, and none of those boys would have dared to relieve themselves at a urinal or in a stall while another person was anywhere near. I was comfortable in my disguise and told Taimur many times to relax and enjoy our cross-country adventure. At twelve years old, I'd been living as a boy for nearly eight years, and Genghis Khan had become my second skin. I almost knew him better than I knew myself. Even Taimur hadn't called me Maria in years.

The athletics stadium was near the old walled city, and we walked to it from the hostel as a team on registration day, gym bags slung over our broad shoulders, taking long swigs now and again from our water bottles. We'd bonded the night before, roaming around Iqbal Park, eating kebabs from street vendors, and racing one another around the tall pillar of Minar-e-Pakistan, which rose up into the night lit up like a jeweled dagger. Built to commemorate our country's independence of 1947, it was often likened to the Eiffel Tower in Paris. I'd only ever seen it in books, and I remember looking up into its high cascades of electric light, mesmerized, and thinking that for the first time in my life, belonging to a group outside my family didn't mean getting into fights. When we entered the stadium to register, a group of officials led us to a huge gymnasium crowded with boys from all over the country. I joined one of the many lines leading up to a row of long tables, and put my sack at my feet. The mood in the room was electric. I looked around and checked out the competition. Some of the boys were small and wiry, and I paid them no mind, but others were built like oaks. I met a few of their eyes; already we were staring each other down, just like in the streets. All of us were lightheaded and slightly savage from hunger, as we hadn't eaten since the night before in order to keep our registration weight in the lowest category possible. In matches where competitors fell within the same body-mass category, lifting the heaviest weight in combination with using the proper technique determined the winner. After the weigh-in, the official would divide our teams into classes. In matches where competitors successfully lift equal weight, body mass alone determines the winner—the lighter athlete wins. My coach had already set our weight classes back in Peshawar, but I had to have an official measurement taken just before the competition.

I thought nothing of the process and stood nonchalantly with Taimur and other members of our team. We made plans to go out to eat that night and explore the walled city afterward. Then, as I got closer to the front of the line, I noticed that after signing in, each team was sent into another room. I could just see the row of scales through the open door. Then I watched as the boys inside removed their clothing, placing their shorts and T-shirts on a table before stepping onto the scale dressed only in underwear. I took in their exposed bodies and felt something inside me slip. Beads of sweat gathered along my forehead. I turned to Taimur, who must have seen the same thing—we exchanged a panicked glance but remained quiet. Back in Peshawar we'd always weighed in fully clothed. The air in the room was suddenly heavy, and I sucked it down as though I could not get enough oxygen. Our team was already at the front. Taimur touched my shoulder and whispered

"Don't do it."

The man behind the table motioned to our group and we all moved forward to register. I thought I might throw up. I searched desperately for an excuse in the seconds it took for me to print *Genghis Khan, Male, Age 12* across a form, but all I felt was panic as I walked with the others, mind completely blank, into the room with the scales. I watched a boy get down from the platform and put his clothes back on. My brother was next to me saying something about letting him go first. The man in the room was looking me over. My entire body went hot. I'd had a gun pointed at me in Darra Adam Khel, but faced with removing my clothes and revealing my secret in that room sent me into a frenzied state of fear that I had never experienced. Taimur was right, I had no choice—I could not do it. The official standing by the scale with the clipboard took one look at my pallid face and knew that something was wrong. He motioned to the table and instructed me to remove my clothes and step up onto the scale. My teammates were already unbuttoning. I think he must have said it two or three times before I thought of what to say.

"No, sir—I cannot." Taimur's voice was thin but clear. My big brother didn't care about weightlifting and had only agreed to compete so that he could chaperone me to the tournament. Now I'd put him in an impossible position. At the sound of his voice cutting through my fear, I thought of the missed chance to show my strength after two months of backbreaking training. I assumed that it was over for me—not just weightlifting but playing any sport at all. I'd be back on the streets brawling with my boys in less than a week. And I thought of my brave brother who was willing to sacrifice his own pride just for me.

Then I stepped up next to him. "I cannot either."

The man by the scale stared at us. He was clean-shaven and tall and smelled heavily of soap. I noted his copy of the Quran on the table next to the scale, and a thick prayer mat rolled up in the corner. His eyes, long lashed and dark, moved over me intently. Without a shadow of doubt, I thought he could see right through my clothes. I was about to simply cut and run—all the way back across the park to the hostel—when he came in closer, placed a hand on my shoulder, and looked down at me.

"You are both ashamed. I understand."

We nodded. I looked to the floor, my heart sinking into my chest so that I could barely take a full breath, and waited—for what I don't know. A slap to my brother's face and then mine? A tirade? Some final humiliation followed by the end of my world? But he just led me to the scale by the arm, clothed in my T-shirt and shorts, and asked me simply to remove my running shoes. I kept my socks on. When he shifted the sliding weight and read out the number, scribbled it down, I just stood there frozen. One second later, I was done. I moved off the scale and onto the other side of my fear as though I had crossed a treacherous ocean. Bending down to retrieve my shoes, I was breathing heavily and on the verge of passing out. The man patted me on the back and wished me good luck. I did up the laces with trembling hands and looked up just in time to see my brother stepping up fully clothed onto the scale. When I passed by him, we looked at each other, said nothing, yet exchanged a thousand words, and I saw that stoic Taimur had tears in his eyes.

By the grace of God, the locker rooms were empty when I went in to suit up. Taimur quietly took his post guarding the door. My eyes adjusted to the strange artificial light, the absence of a window—I had never been in a room underground before. There was a faint smell of talc and the low hum of fluorescent lighting. Wet towels and papers and candy bar wrappers were strewn about the rows of metal benches. There was a wad of bloody tissues on the ground. Above me, I could hear the muted din of the crowd massed in the stadium, though the subterranean room was completely still. Every now and then a buzzer went off, signaling the end of a match, and applause thundered overhead like a drum line. I had only minutes to get ready before my name was called. It would be the first time I'd ever competed at anything in my life, but I wasn't afraid—I only wanted to win.

I took a breath, chalked up my hands. Then the stadium erupted above me again; the crowd was pounding the floor in unison. I looked at the ceiling, imagining them all up there, faces filling the bowl of the stadium, the high pitch of their cheers, and felt my heart kick-start. I was still keyed up from the close call at weigh-in, but I could not allow doubt to splinter my mind. I thought of the man in the scale room, the sureness of his decision to save me from shame, and of the Quran sitting on the table right by him, within arm's reach. So I got down on my knees to do the only thing I could think of that would dial me down. I slid all the way to the floor, head bowed. Eyes closed, my hands flat on my thighs, I whispered *suras* to Allah, one after the other, until I could feel my pulse slow and the throbbing at my temples die along with the sounds of the crowd three floors above me.

My steadied mind and closed lids steered me into the past, and I saw my father standing next to me by the cooking fire, a heap of dresses burning. I felt his arms surround me then, and heard his voice whisper my new name and the *azan* call to prayer. His work in the tribal regions meant that he couldn't be in Lahore with me, but I'd brought a piece of him. I reached into my gym bag and found the gold coin he'd given me that afternoon so long ago under the ancient blue dome of Waziristan. Still folded in prayer over the floor, I held the coin hard in my palm. The metal heated and bored into my skin. As though he were right there with me, I could hear my father say my name loud and clear—*Genghis Khan*. And I knew I could beat them all.

I got up and made my way to the competition floor. The snatch lift was first. A bar stood before me. I looked along its length, eyed it as though it were a living opponent, and steadied my breath. I went down into position, feet hip-width apart, back straight, and breathing in and out in a strong, quick rhythm. My head filled with fury against nothing and everything, against the fact that I was there as a boy at all—I felt it course down, shooting into my limbs like a filament of lightning. I gripped the bar—hands wide, spine locked—and separated the weight from the floor. A deep gulp of air, and everything in my body and mind went into the one motion, lifting the barbell up and over my head. I stared out, eyes bulging, and the full weight seemed to vanish as I hauled it, drawing all of my strength into it. I held the weight, arms straight over my head, the crowd roaring to life, until I heard the signal buzzer. Then I let out my breath and heaved the bar down. The crowd cheered so loudly that it reverberated in my chest. I felt my body thunder with pride. Over and over, I repeated the maneuver, the plates loaded higher and higher to twenty-five and a half kilograms—until I crushed every opponent in my class.

The clean and jerk was my last event. I was up against a burly Punjabi, several years older, with cinder-block hands and legs like cannons; he was the reigning champion. I'd told him in the corridor that his time had come, and he'd laughed in my face. Before easing into my stance, I noticed him off to the side and winked. Then, exploding with strength, I executed a series of perfect lifts until he and I were matched weight for weight. By that time, it wasn't about beating that boy or anyone else anymore. I was in my element under the blazing lights, the audience wild, witnessing my show of strength. I'd already surpassed the best of them and myself. Then, as I lifted the weight-to-win, seventy-five kilograms, past my deltoids, my knee torqued and I felt something pop. The bar was just over my head and I dropped it, almost in tandem with the buzzer—off by only a millisecond. The crowd deadened and I rammed my eyes shut, biting my lip so hard that it bled.

A quick round of polite applause met the Punjabi when he went up for his gold—he'd done what was expected of him. He was the oldest, the biggest, and he'd been in training for years. Then it was my turn to cross the stage for the silver. I'd resigned myself to the moment of muted glory. All things considered, I shouldn't have been there at all, winning anything. The announcer shouted out my name—*PRESENTING GENGHIS KHAN OF PESHAWAR*—the underdog, the youngest, competing after barely eight weeks in the sport. And it was as though a thunderclap hit the stadium. The audience leapt to their feet, shouting my name again and again in a wild chant. I stood on the platform, smiled, arms held high like a champion, and bowed my head to the cheering crowd. As far as they were concerned, I won that day. I felt like the strongest kid in Pakistan. I started to laugh, tears in my eyes—I'd done as my father had asked, and won the noblest of all victories. Secretly, I relished the fact that I had beaten so many boys without them knowing I was a girl. I had fooled them all, and that was the best part.

On the way home on the bus, my brother kept glancing at me, but he wasn't smiling. He sighed several times, saying nothing. Finally, I looked over and told him that if he had something on his mind, he'd better say it right then and there. During our trip we'd barely exchanged more than a few sentences—that was his way. Taimur took my hand and squeezed it hard, but he wasn't looking at me. He turned his face and stared a long time out at the scenery blurring past the window, rain pouring down the glass. We could hear sirens and see flashing lights along the side of the road. There were several accidents and we would be late getting home. When Taimur spoke to me, it was in a low murmur that I could barely hear, though I knew afterward that it took everything out of him to say it. He told me that he saw himself as my great protector, and I realized that for three days straight, while I lived and breathed the glory of competition, he'd lived in terror of failing me.

"If they ever find out what you did in Lahore, Maria, beating them that way, they'll hunt you down, believe me—they'll hunt you down, and they will kill you."

11. I Am Maria

Somehow, my reign of glory didn't last. The silver medal went up in our living room, and there it dangled from a hook. I'd also come back from the tournament with a large cut-glass trophy, the grooves so sharp they glinted before the dingy window like thousands of tiny knives. The trophy held a place of pride on a table, and the championship certificate rested in a frame next to it, my bogus name—Genghis Khan—written across white paper in swirling calligraphy. Maybe I expected some significant change to take place after that Rocky Balboa triumph in Lahore—but it didn't. Back home again, time spun on a carousel. Weightlifting tournaments were rare: it could be another year before I'd get a chance to compete onstage in another city again. And there wasn't any point in going out into the mess of streets to muscle the boys anymore.

Several times each week, I was back in the weight room at the sports complex, training alongside Taimur. When my father couldn't be there for me in Peshawar—or anywhere—Taimur was. He didn't have to tell me so; every time I turned around he was looking out for me. We also understood each other. I was more like a little brother than a sister to him—we played sports together and I wore his old clothes. We scarcely spoke, just loaded and unloaded the bar. Counted our lifts. Took swigs from our water bottles. Exchanged the occasional high five. Every so often, the coach might show up to check on our form or take us to another room to step on a scale—I was always dressed head to toe.

My first victory had come as easily as tossing a coin in the air and watching it drop, but as far as pure ambition went, I was a featherweight. One part of me wanted to go back to Lahore to compete for a gold and crush the boy who'd bested me by a hair. The other part of me didn't care so much. I already knew that in actual fact I'd beaten him; the roaring crowd told me so, and so did the numbers—another month back in training at home and I had him by increasing kilograms. The trouble was that I'd have to wait a year to prove it. Emotionally, I was sinking. All I seemed to do was go back and forth on a pendulum, crossing Peshawar between home and the sports center. Most of the time I traveled on a packed public jingle bus, sardined against my steadfast brother.

Weightlifting is also a lonesome pursuit. In all those weeks after the tournament, I never ran into my teammates at the complex or anywhere else. Sometimes I believed we'd all simply come together in a vibrant dream of Lahore; that gleaming city diminished by the day to a barely lit illusion, which itself slipped further from memory as I drifted through my dull routines.

When I was very small, my father told us the ancient Greek myth of King Sisyphus, and I found myself thinking of that king, along with dozens of other stories Baba had recounted, to pass the time while I trained. Zeus condemned Sisyphus to roll a boulder up a hill for having the audacity to liken himself to an immortal. Each time the breathless king was about to heave the rock over the lip of the hill, Zeus made it slip and roll all the way back to the bottom. Until the end of time, the weary king would have to start over with each new dawn, consigned to an eternity of massive wasted exertion. As it happened, every other day Taimur and I went through the same lifts, again and again and again, stacking up the plates—as though sentenced to a Sisyphean fate—and I felt condemned.

Just one thing was different and changing all the time: me. The swells of living fiber rippling along my bones tore against the weights and refashioned themselves like the recasting of cannons. At home, or standing at food stalls in the market, I ate with the voraciousness of a caged animal, scooping up rice and tearing off chunks of meat and naan; and I guzzled water from aluminum bottles in loud gulps. Through Taimur's castoff shirts, my biceps bulged, the sweat-soaked fabric plastered to skin, showing every contour. My neck widened to a trunk. Sometimes I'd glimpse my reflection in the full mirrors lining the weight room as I lifted. My breath would catch and I'd almost let go—*who was that huge boy? Not me, that is not me*. Physically, I no longer knew myself from the outside—maybe on the inside too. People stopped as they passed by me in the training room, or even in the streets, to get a good look at my frame. The cords of sinew flexing along my legs as I moved were like slithering ropes.

I must have trained in that dull tank for hundreds of hours. All around me I heard the clanking of metal plates, the strained grunts of men, and the whir of the ventilation system. Fluorescent light flooded the room and there were no windows. Walls of mirrors. The sour stench of male exertion. Men and boys came and went and nothing changed but the ticking hour. The sheer stillness of my sport held a certain beauty—and, for me, a lethal monotony: I'd never been so bored in my life.

I remember looking over at my brother when I dropped the bar hard and its weighted ends bounced as they hit the concrete floor—*boom*. He tilted his head and said nothing; his eyes were on the disks rolling toward his feet.

"What are we doing in here, Taimur?"

"Lifting weights."

"I don't care for it anymore—do you?"

"No—not so much."

On the way home, men crowded our jingle bus, hanging from the rails suspended off the back, as the vehicle—painted gold, yellow, and pink and covered in ornaments—careened around corners, teetering up and down the streets like an overloaded ferry. Bells on the bus clanged, men jabbered, and the engine groaned, tailpipe spewing soot into the air. Jingle buses never quite stopped to pick up passengers, but slowed and then took off again, lurching forward into the gridlock. Poised on the sidewalk, Taimur and I watched the decked-out bus approach through the hot chaos of traffic. Everything depended on one big jump, getting my sandal in and finding anything to grab—a held-out hand, a window lever, a rail—and then hauling my body up just as the vehicle picked up speed, pushing my way deep into the sweaty mass of bodies. Sometimes we would lose each other, call out, always laughing. I'd find a way to look through the forest of limbs and see him still standing in the road, hands out at his sides, hollering. I would have to force my way to the very back of the bus and jump off the rear. Men called for me to stop, but I'd fly out wide-eyed and grinning, right into the traffic and back to my waiting brother. It was all a game to me, and the only time on any given day that I felt alive.

On the day I knew I was done lifting weights, I stared out as we cut across the city from end to end, all those male bodies pressing against mine—each wearing a *shalwar kameez*, hair combed, dark, and oiled to the sheen of mink pelts. I was dressed in sweaty track pants and a T-shirt. Standing among them, I stuck out like a hard pillar, but unmistakably male. I didn't have to fabricate anything—I just was what I was. I liked dressing in athletic clothes: never once did I wish for a dress. Every man on that bus—in Peshawar, in Pakistan proper, in the entire world— would have bet his life on me being one of the boys. My suffocating existence had nothing to do with my gargantuan lie, or even whether I was a girl or not. In the city, I lived half-starved on faded daydreams of mountains and open sky, eyes closed as we trundled over the tight grid of pockmarked roads. Out there in the bare-boned world with my old friends, zigzagging rock-strewn valleys, kicking soccer balls, chasing kites, no single day ever resembled another. In Peshawar, all I had was the bus.

Lately, I also had the sense that a clock was ticking over my head. Within a year or two, I would no longer be able to so easily hide the fact that I was female. Impending puberty stalked me like a death sentence. I lived on a knife blade. When I looked at Ayesha, already blooming into a confident woman, I was both in awe of her and afraid for myself. There was no escaping hormones and cultural expectations. For a long time, I'd been aware of the inevitable changes that my body would soon undergo. Physically transforming into a woman was a reality that I never wanted to face. It meant the end of Genghis and of my freedom. In the quiet of night, or while standing on the bus, I wondered what would happen to me when I began to change and finally lost the gift of androgyny. The future was an opponent I couldn't outrun.

Every now and then I thought about the Americans who stayed with us back in Miranshah for those few days, telling stories and giving glimpses of their glittering side of the world like pieces of candy dropped into my open palms. My father always said those boys were lucky to have survived their journey into the tribal belt, that he hoped they steered clear of Peshawar. At the time, I wasn't sure what he meant. It never occurred to me that we lived in a region that was dangerous to foreigners, because there simply weren't any around. Ever since getting back from Lahore and my victory as Genghis, I wondered if I wasn't just as fortunate as those visitors from New York City. They might not have lasted thirty seconds on that jingle bus without some sort of trouble—and yet there I was, standing in plain sight in my short hair, camouflaged in my brother's old clothes. On that bus, city men surrounding me, I was as foreign as they come.

When I arrived home, I threw down my gym bag and went straight to find my father. In those days, he gave lectures a few times a week and then came home. I knew he missed my mother—we all did—who seemed to be working all the time. My siblings were still in the middle of their school day and would return to a full meal, which my father and I cooked together. Often we made simple meals of potatoes fried in oil with chilies and tomatoes. It was my job to bake the bread. We would set a plate aside for my mother and then do the clean-up together. I found my father alone at the living room window, his tall silhouette gray and slightly hunched as he stared into the pane as though into a giant television screen. He held a pair of binoculars to his eyes, and I thought of men on safari in the depths of Africa; but he was just my father standing several floors up above the teeming streets of Peshawar.

"Where did you get those binoculars, Baba?"

When he turned to me, his big white smile in the dim light almost knocked me over. No matter where he was, my father lived as if he were born for some great purpose. He loved life, and it rushed out from his whole body as though he were made of light—even there.

"I borrowed them from a friend. I wanted to get a closer look at things. Tomorrow, I have to give them back."

"Everything here is all the same, Baba. I bet I could walk every street and see all the same men doing all the same things."

My father put away his smile and looked at me—hard.

"Well, well, well. I was wondering when the weightlifting would let you down."

He roared, laughing at his own joke. He stepped away from the grimy window, wiped off, and handed me the binoculars.

I held the heavy glasses to my eyes and directed the lenses down into the crowded street. It was like scanning the surface of a slow-moving river: vessels sailed along with the current, men walked the wide banks. It was all a blur. I fingered the dial as my father directed and focused the view, zeroing in on the oblivious world below. There was something hysterical about seeing close up the very terrain I'd crossed just minutes before. I stood back and laughed, looking over to my father in astonishment. I'd only once felt such power before—when I'd turned on a television for the first time. I'd pressed the button again and again—turning the world on and off at the whim of my index finger.

My father grinned wide and motioned for me to take another look through the binoculars, and I did. Back and forth, I slowly swept my polished gaze over the paved scene—moving figures, moving things. I felt slightly predatory, tightening the glass on a parade of the absent-minded; people traversed streets as if in a trance, or sat in cars and on rickshaws, bent over motorbikes and hung off buses, expressionless, awake but sleeping—alive but dead.

My father whispered into my ear. He might as well have been reading a page ripped from my mind:

"Zombies."

The horde moved at a snail's pace. A few people stood still on the sidewalk, checking pockets, waiting for buses, or deep in conversation with companions—the drama of lives playing out. I watched two men arguing under an awning across the way, arms gesticulating. Then, as I shifted to farther along the road, a boy reached out and swiftly pilfered a mango off a cart. I watched him do it and giggled. Once the mango was in his hand, he tossed it like a ball several feet into the waiting hands of a wily cohort standing some distance away, who shoved the fruit fast into a tattered satchel. They stole at least six pieces that way, lobbing bright fruit through the air in blink-of-an-eye maneuvers so well practiced that no one but I, watching as though up in a cloud, even noticed their crime.

Then I zoomed in further and scanned up the boulevard. From a fume-choked distance I watched as a group of boys moved down the street, racing toward my building with the current of traffic, shifting this way and that through the breaks between vehicles. I didn't have to look hard to know—they were all members of my old fighting crew. Just watching them, I could hear their sounds: high-pitched shouts, calling back and forth to one another over the din of engines and horns as they veered out like wasps speeding around cars and trucks. They had complete command of the road; and watching them race forward in that scattering swarm without a trace of hesitation, I could see they knew it. It was so strange to observe them that way, while standing in the quiet of my living room. Still, watching as they moved up the asphalt river and into the urban blur, I imagined seeing myself riding among them, always at the front of the pack. We'd all traveled the lengths of the city like warriors, and acted on impulse alone—always on the move. Despite the blood and pain of our brawls, I suddenly missed that gang, though I couldn't remember a single name to go with those beat-up faces racing up the boulevard. I was sure that word had gotten around that I was lifting weights. No boy in Peshawar, no matter how brazen, would ever dare to challenge me again. Those days were over and I knew it. I handed the binoculars back to my father.

"I wonder if this is what Allah feels like, watching us, Baba."

"Allah doesn't watch, so much as know. He has no need for binoculars."

"I would like to know what he wants me to do."

"Whatever it is, Genghis, you're already doing it."

"I'm not doing anything."

My father had the binoculars back up to his eyes, while he glassed the scene below.

"Start tomorrow by looking around. You might notice a fork in the road. I see them all the time myself."

"A fork?"

"Yes. Open your eyes. Sometimes you have to go in the wrong direction to find the right one."

*

Less than a week later, it was angry weather. Sirens and horns blared. People shouted in the streets. Once or twice, I thought I heard a gunshot, or maybe an engine had backfired—hard to tell. I walked the concrete paths outside the sports complex through blinding sunlight. It felt as though the sky was on fire. Clouds were a dream, coolness an impossible wish. I held my gym bag over one shoulder, full canteen swinging into my thigh. I waited in a pool of feeble tree shade for Taimur to meet me after his classes. Sitting on a low cinder-block wall, taking small sips of the lukewarm water in my bottle, I kept wiping drops of sweat from my brow. Boys moved up the walkway and past me, casting glances at my rock-hard limbs—no one ever seemed to look me in the eye anymore.

The hard cement under me chafed against my legs, and I had to shift my weight again and again. I waited for my brother the way a pedestrian waits for a light to change, and for what seemed like hours. I studied the structure at the opposite end of the quad. Tall and painted pale orange, it dwarfed the weight facility. People kept filtering inside in small, exuberant groups. Every time the big front doors flew open, the erratic sound of a game in full swing was unmistakable, but I had to strain to make out the shifting tensions—high cheers, low groans. When the doors shut, the noise ceased, leaving me in the tedium of buzzing heat.

Tired of killing time, I got up from the wall and wandered across the quadrangle—if a game was on, I wanted to see it. I peered through the glass doors, pressing my hands against the cool surface. The glass seemed to vibrate from within, as though whatever game was being played had reached its climax. A tall man came up behind me and pulled open the door. I stepped into the open threshold as he moved past me. He had a racquet bag slung over his shoulder and must have been well over six feet tall. His body was lean, and he moved with a lithe agility I'd not seen before. Perhaps sensing me watching him, he looked back, stopped, and smiled in a way that invited me all the way in. I shadowed him down a long, silent corridor and into the stands. The whole world of heat and monotony outside simply vanished. He went well ahead of me, descending concrete steps two at a time to join his group in the front row. Shuffling along the packed tiered benches, I stared down at a big glass playing box. The air was soft and the light was dim, and I felt that I could breathe again. I waited in my seat for the next match to begin.

It was so unexpected—being there at all. Two men dressed in vibrant athletic gear stood in the lit-up box as though at the center of an ice cube. All around them in the crowded dark void, a silent, expectant energy rippled out. For a while there was no sound. The two players stood and spun a racquet like a top to decide who would make the first serve. It rattled when it hit the ground. A few people called out from the stands. I'd seen squash played once before on the television set with the sound off. Next to cricket, it was the most popular sport in Pakistan, but I didn't know a thing about it except that it was played against four walls.

The first player leveled his serve hard. I'll never forget the hollow sound of him grunting, then the loud thud as the smacked rubber ball ricocheted, propelling the players into a wild rally. The men raced around the box. Jumping. Diving. Running. Shoes squeaked against the polished plank floor. From the initial hit, I was hooked—the ensuing controlled chaos of motion, the ball darting like a bullet. In the thick of that first rally, the players never stopped moving. I didn't care who won. I just watched—stunned—as though my whole world had shifted on its axis in the blink of an eye.

"What are you doing in here?"

Taimur's low, paternal voice startled me, and I looked up slightly dazed. I'd been following the wild trajectory of that rubber ball in a strange frenetic trance. Every time it hit the wall, I felt the beat land in my heart. My tall, broad-shouldered brother had a way of appearing disheveled when he was confused, though his hair was perfectly combed. I smiled—big and wide.

"What do you think of squash, Taimur? It's beautiful."

Taimur squeezed in next to me, put his schoolbag on the floor, his gym bag in his lap, and watched the match. We sat side by side a long time, saying nothing—neither one of us making a move to leave. Several times, I could feel his eyes shift to me and then back to the pounding rhythm of the game. It was hard to tell if he was as riveted as I was. He simply observed his surroundings, the loud, jubilant pack of spectators all around us, their gazes fixed to that bright white box, to the players moving in a blur. When the audience erupted after a particularly long back-and-forth, he showed no reaction. Several times, I shrieked next to him, and I thought I heard him snigger. We should have been lifting weights. I kept waiting for him to tap me on the arm and grab his bags—maybe he knew he'd have to drag me out of my seat. The longer we sat there together, the more confident I became that I wasn't ever going back to the weight room. At last, he breathed out as if he'd made up his mind about something. Taimur sometimes spoke in a definite language of sighs, gestures, and grunts. He took his gym bag from his lap and dumped it on the floor, kicking it back behind his feet. He sat back, folding his arms over his chest, nodding. Then he turned to me and whispered in my ear.

"I like it, Genghis."

"I love it, Taimur."

"We're going to need racquets."

When I found Baba that evening, he was sitting in the dim glow of a reading lamp, sewing up a tear in his *kameez*. A thick cast of duct tape wrapped about the lamp's joint, to keep it together, as if it had a broken appendage. I don't know where he'd found the tape, but lately he'd been using it to fix everything: wobbly table legs, the frayed spines on his books, a fan blade, a toothbrush, and the fractured lamp. My father had large square hands, but his long fingers were nimble with the thread. I watched him with a needle held between his finger and thumb, making stitches, up and down, deftly caressing the air, no doubt to music playing in his head. He was performing a domestic task for which he would have been taunted anywhere outside our home. In a moment, he looked over, eyes landing on me with a half-grin. For several beats, we said nothing to each other. I might as well have been gone on a long trip—in a way, I had.

"Well, here you are, Genghis Khan, back from an adventure at last. Am I right? I can see it in your eyes: you've trapped stars in them."

I hadn't stopped smiling since leaving the sports complex at the end of the match. "I found a fork, Baba. Just as you said to."

"Aha! I knew it. You've always been a very good listener. Let me guess: it wasn't in the weightlifting room."

"No, it was inside a giant glass cube."

When I told my father about discovering the game, describing its fast-paced lure, he listened and watched me intently. After a few minutes, he got up from his chair, and turned off the crippled lamp. My mother had taken a position as the principal of a school near Darra Adam Khel and wasn't home. Five days a week, after we had all kneeled together to recite our morning *fajr* prayers and share a quick morning meal, she would leave for her new job, only returning tired and hungry in the evening. In her absence the rest of the family shared in the household responsibilities, like a cleaning squad with my father acting as the captain. Seeing their Baba participating in menial chores would have been an abhorrent sight to most Pashtun children, but to us it was a gift. I loved coming home and finding him there. Often

My mother and father shortly after their marriage.

My father at twenty-five years old addressing a *jirga*. He spoke out so often for women's rights that he was later jailed.

My father standing on the road to Waziristan in 2012.

My mother sitting in the grass with my brother Sangeen, during a break from teacher training in Islamabad.

Receiving my first squash trophy. I won first place in the under-thirteen category at the 2002 Hashim Khan Junior Squash Championship.

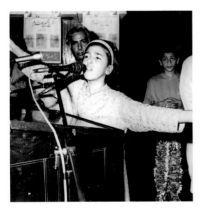

My sister, Ayesha, delivering an impassioned speech in Peshawar to celebrate Labor Day. She was nine years old and the only girl in the room.

At the under-fifteen squash tournament in Quetta. I was the only girl there among over 400 boys.

Above, left. Standing with legendary Pakistani squash player Qamar Zaman at the 2004 Asian Games in Malaysia. It was my team's first big tournament outside the country.

Above, right. Sitting in the dirt in Darra Adam Khel. I am the "boy", Genghis Khan, on the far left.

Visiting one of the many holy shrines outside Tehran. I was in Iran to play at the Women's Islamic Games in 2005.

Jonathon Power coaching me at a tournament in Pakistan, 2013.

I am standing among Pashtun children recently evacuated from their tribal land. Tensions between the army and extremist factions had reached a boiling point causing entire families to flee for safety. Later I organized a special squash event in Islamabad and we brought all the displaced children over in hired buses. Generous sponsors from around Pakistan provided food, clothes, shoes, equipment, and food. It was my way of inspiring those kids to choose a racquet instead of a gun.

When I arrived in Canada my psyche was battered and bruised. On one of my many walks through the city of Toronto, I stopped at an art supply store. I have turned to canvas ever since. I paint to find serenity. One day I hope to use it to promote peace. This painting is titled *Crossing the Cold Valley*.

And this painting is titled *Mosque Morning Mist*.

At the opening ceremony for the 2014 Asian Games in South Korea.

Getting a feel for the court with my coach, Jonathon, at the
2014 Asian Squash Championship in Pakistan.

Here I am with my mother at the players' dinner for the 2014 Asian Squash Championship in Islamabad.

My coach, Jonathon, spending time at my family's home in Peshawar. We were in Pakistan together for the 2014 Asian Squash Championship.

we would sit together sipping tea and wait for my mother and the rest of the children to return.

Wordlessly, we went out the door, moved down the flights of stairs in semi-darkness, and stepped out into the loud city to flag down a rickshaw. My father didn't seem to think much at all about the fact that I wanted to give up weightlifting and take up squash. Resolute as ever, he simply accepted my decision without question, just as more than eight years before he'd accepted the incineration of my dresses in the cooking pit. Later, when my mother balked at the idea of me playing squash instead of going back to school, he talked her out of her trepidation. She had long hoped that, like my sister, I would follow in her footsteps and pursue a degree and an eventual career in education. Having a daughter who played a professional sport had never occurred to her. She had never even come across a female athlete. In our part of the world, they simply didn't exist. More than once, I heard them debating my fate in heated whispers late into the night. Once, I heard my father say: "Maria isn't like other girls. She isn't Ayesha, and she isn't you." In the end, my mother agreed.

Somehow, I knew my father would have been thinking of his sister, as he listened to me rattle on about the exhilarating squash game—he thought of her often when we talked about my plans. Sometimes, when he looked at me, he saw her and said so. Other times, he saw her and said very little, as he had that afternoon. She and I were so alike—in our look, in our aggressive manner, hot-tempered—but we wouldn't share the same tragic fate. When we sat back in the rickshaw, my father took my hand a moment and kissed the top of my head. He whispered something into the wind as the driver steered away from the curb and out into the traffic, but I never heard what it was.

One building over from the weightlifting facility, the door opened to a sea of polished tiles spread over the deserted lobby. I'd been there just hours before, but now the silence that greeted us in the bright artificial light was eerie. I assumed it would be like the last time: we'd find a coach, write down my name, and sign me up. A man sat behind a desk off to one side and we made our way over to him. He was clean-shaven and smelled of orange peel. His hands were wide and rough-looking, and when he looked up, we recognized each other. He was the tall man with the racquet bag whom I'd followed that afternoon.

My father spoke to him in hushed tones for a few minutes while I walked around, already feeling sure of my surroundings. Along the walls, I scanned framed pictures of players holding up trophies. Beaming grins, placards engraved with dates and the names of cities around the world—London, Tokyo, Hong Kong, Philadelphia, New York. I could hear the thudding of people playing in the glass boxes. It sounded as though deep within the guts of the huge building there was a great honeycomb of those playing cubes. An intoxicating energy coursed like a storm brewing, while I stood at its periphery, in the same way I waited poised on the roadway for the jingle bus, ready to jump into the fray. I'd never wanted to do anything the way I wanted to play squash. Just the idea of holding a racquet, hitting the ball against those white walls, made my whole body seem to take flight inside itself.

My father called me back to the desk and the man looked me over, not appraising, just curious. He asked me if I truly had the desire to learn the game and I nodded. He pulled open a drawer and found a form and pen, pushing them over. The man raised a finger as I signed at the bottom. He looked at me. "And now we just need your birth certificate."

At once the blood rushed from my head, and I felt sick to my stomach. I looked at my father and could tell he didn't want to explain a thing—not there, not then. As we stood in utter silence, I felt myself traveling further and further away from the dream I'd only just caught in the palm of my hand. All I had was my identity card, and I heard my father say we would have to go home for the birth record. The man nodded and said it would do for the time being. Still, birth certificate or not, there was no going back. Quickly, with the seconds ticking away like a detonator in my heart, I rummaged through my mind for an excuse, a reason why I could not provide the documentation that would rat me out. Even in profile I could see the strain in my father's face, the veins pulsing in his neck. He never blinked. I knew he was doing the same thing, looking for a way around the red tape—around telling the truth. I was sure that he wanted to leave, right then, without offering a single word as to why.

I don't know what possessed me to take command of that moment, but I did. Gently, I touched my father's arm and nodded. We looked at each other in a profound way, eyes locked—and he knew what I wanted him to do.

"Do you let girls play? My daughter here would like to know."

The man peered across his desk, his eyes twitching, and he touched his face in wonder. You might have thought from the way he looked at me that I'd flown down from the sky and landed there in front of him. When he grinned, it was as though the whole world opened and let me in.

"So, you're a girl." He said it right to me as though my father wasn't there at all. And I felt my father step back, giving me space for my bravery: he knew I was all right—and I was.

"Yes. I am Maria."

The man came around from his desk. In my entire life, I'd never been more grateful for a stranger's smile.

"Welcome."

12. *Playing Like a Girl*

At first, nothing changed. Through a haze of half sleep, I got up and dressed as before—in Taimur's cast-off shorts and an old T-shirt. On the cusp of morning, a cool silence covered everything like mist. I rinsed my face, looked into the cracked mirror over the sink—shorn black hair, sideburns. If I'd wanted to look like a girl, I wouldn't have known where to begin. Gym bag strapped across my back, I rode my Sohrab through the pale dawn rising over Peshawar, feet pumping the pedals in beat-up running shoes. In appearance, I was no less Genghis than I'd been the day before, when I'd said my real name and held my breath. It didn't occur to me to change a single physical thing about myself. The acceptance of my family meant I didn't have to—not for them, and not for anyone else. After so many years living as I had, carefree in my brother's hand-me-downs and comfortable in my tough skin, I existed somewhere between Genghis and Maria— breathing no more as one than the other.

A few people studied me from their cars as I stopped at a light and took a quick drink from my full canteen, one foot on the ground tapping the concrete. I stared back, squeezing the handlebars and showing off the ridges of muscle tightening along my arms. It was so early that most of the shops were closed, and the long roads were wide open. I looked into the dark banks of cloud rising in the distance and imagined the slumbering ranges of my lost Waziristan. It was so still and quiet in the streets that if I closed my eyes, I could be back in the valleys, living under the Abode of God again. Mile after mile, riding between the shuttered facades of buildings, I could see the way ahead for blocks. Along the roadsides, kebab vendors hauled white, headless carcasses from the backs of carts and put them on hooks to hang outside. All through the morning they'd butcher the meat. The gutters in the food streets would run red with fresh blood. The smell of smoke as cooking fires were lit; the scent of rain on the horizon. It was going to be a long, wet day outside—I'd spend it inside, running around between four walls.

I arrived at the sports complex alone, just as the streets began to fill with sound. Taimur was taking exams that month and wouldn't be able to start playing until they were finished. Inside, I could hear only the soft thwack of rubber against a wall. The beat grew louder as I neared the court. The kind man who had signed me up just days before was dressed in perfect whites and hitting the ball against the back wall. There was something ferocious yet beautiful about it—hard and fast like the sharp echoes of a firing range. As before, I felt each slap against the wall reverberate deep inside my chest. Inside the court, his feet covered the expanse of polished floor as he danced across it through the lit-up air. The black rubber ball darted from wall to wall in a dizzying blur, painting hypnotizing angles.

My first squash coach was also a wing commander in the air force and director of the PAF (Pakistan Air Force) Squash Academy Peshawar. He had the split-second reflexes of a man accustomed to commanding things that moved at Mach speeds—he owned that ball. Without a break for breath or a drink, he hit again and again, arm and racquet shearing the air, an electric precision propelling his every move. I could see the tilt of his forearm, the slight twitch of his shoulder blade, the barest movement of the racquet altering angles, changing trajectories. The ball obeyed, punching through the air at whatever speed its commander had in mind. Long and lean, the man's body was capable of a mesmerizing swiftness. He looked like he could catch a bullet in the palm of his hand. Then, as though catching my fleeting thoughts, he stopped in his tracks, raised an arm high, and grabbed the ball out of the very air. He turned around and flashed a grin all the way up to me in that darkness. Then he waved, inviting me in.

"Taimur said you needed a racquet. This one is for you."

He held it out to me.

The handle was warm and damp with his sweat. As the racquet slid into my palm, I felt it connect to the rest of me like a joint fitting into a socket. I look back on that moment now and believe it was like finding a missing limb. My coach stepped back, his face covered in a sheen of perspiration, and looked me over. I knew he was thinking things about me: maybe how boyish I was—hopefully, how brave. I squeezed the grip, moved the racquet, slowly at first, up and down, back and forth. When I held a flat hand to the taut, stringed face, I could feel the tight mesh boring into my skin. I was ready: suddenly, all I could think about was hitting the ball.

"Thank you, Coach. It feels good."

"It's a Jonathon Power signature edition. He's a world champion—*Inshallah*, it brings you good luck."

"I think it already has."

My coach, whom I would often refer to as the Wing Commander, looked at me and nodded, a curious gleam without a trace of malice. I remember thinking that he had eyes like my father's. From the moment we met, I trusted that man with my life. He took my hand and offered me the ball—soft and hot from that unforgiving round of pummeling. I curled my fingers around it, felt the trapped heat—at once every muscle in my body came to life. I thought I had found squash, but I believe now that it found me.

Though I felt the soul of the game, I still knew nothing of the rules. My coach stood me at the back wall and gave me a rundown of the full squash court. In theory, there wasn't much to it; in practice, mastering the game would require a monumental combination of agility and stamina. To chase a bullet, you had to run like one; to control it down to the millisecond required a mastery that can only be described as magic. The Wing Commander positioned me between the lines of the service box. We practiced a few empty swings. I slashed the air with my new racquet, slamming an imaginary ball so hard that I felt like I was splitting atoms. Then he went to the other side and told me to go for it.

"Just see if you can hit it—hit as much as you want, for as long as you can."

From the first shot, I was committed. At the command of my arm, the racquet strings made clean contact. Before I knew it, the hot rubber hurtled through the air, smacked the back wall, and came shooting back. I jumped over to the centerline, tilted my racquet, and sent the ball back to the wall again. It kissed the surface and fell dead to the floor, but I'd made it one full round. The joy of making that first shot erupted all through me, and I let out a laugh that resounded against the four walls of the court— to this day, I can still hear it. Then rain started outside and pounded the roof. Thunder shook us in the tank. We were deep inside a fortress, the world outside at war with itself. Racquet in my hand, feet on the court floor, ball in my sights, for the first time since moving to Peshawar I was in my true element.

When I fell, I went down with my whole body, crashing straight onto the floor like a felled tree. I didn't see it coming; my body simply gave way. I leapt straight up, barely shaken, and went right back into position. My coach stopped me here and there, explained things: the top out line against the far wall, the bottom tin, the center sweet spot I aimed for in my serve. Again, he let me at it—just hitting, sending the ball to the back wall, watching my aim, playing each move as I'd seen my coach do, until my chest heaved. My coach stood far back, calling out to me—

"Watch your feet. Slow down. Get used to the feel. Keep going back to the T."

Over and over, I stumbled as I raced to make a hit, bruising my knees, cracking my sides, but I didn't care: each stroke of pain as I hit the floor and got up again was sweet. The Wing Commander just observed me, arms folded across his chest, nodding with each *thwack, thwack, thwack*. I was playing with an urgency that I'd never experienced, but not well—a big twelve-year-old kid with gargantuan arms and lazy feet. It didn't matter.

When the coach leapt out and grabbed the ball out of the air, he took me out of a trance.

"You're playing against your demons, Maria Toorpakai, and you have many."

"Is that good?" Sweat was pouring down my face.

"Yes. It's the only way to win."

He took up his racquet and we started a game.

I learned the basics, scrambled, tripped over my own feet, shouted out, felt my heart galloping so fast I thought it might just stop. I was like a giant in a shoebox. The ball zigzagged all around me like a hummingbird. Before we knew it, two hours turned to three, and the Wing Commander caught the ball in his hand. Turning his face sideways, he looked over at me—panting. I was already sprawled on the floor, chest pumping hard. The rain overhead was still pounding and the lights flickered over us, on and off. It felt as though there was lightning in the box.

Then I got up and stood tall, spinning the racquet between my beat-up palms. If he thought I was done in, he was wrong. I wasn't any good—I could barely hold a rally for more than ten seconds. In fact, I was a lumbering mess. But I knew one thing— inside that cube, I'd just found my game. I walked over, and my coach gave me a high five. He'd never had a kid take to it like I had, like a warrior, and he said so. That's when I told him that I wasn't just a girl. I was my father's daughter. I was a Wazir—down to my last drop of blood.

*

The boys all crossed the court in new white shoes, more than a dozen of them. No one exchanged names, only shifty glances. I'd only been playing squash for about ten weeks, but over a two-month period of weekly round-robins, I'd encountered a few of them in the courts. The ones I'd defeated readily, I never saw again. The Wing Commander was sorting us out into teams. There were other coaches there, but he was the leader and ran the academy. Taimur was there with me, lurking in the back, doing up his shoes—newer than mine but still as scuffed up as a beggar's.

I stood in front of my brother, stared straight ahead, listening to the echo of all those low male voices against the high white ceiling—so like the inside of a mosque. We were inside one of a long series of courts. A row of benches stood behind the glass back wall, where more kids waited. Our coach walked the length of the courts, assessing his teams. I was the only girl among us yet.

Coach came into our box and checked his clipboard. He lined us up against the back wall and counted heads. When he got to me, he stopped briefly and nodded. I wasn't sure why. Even then, I didn't realize that I was still tiptoeing along a knife-edge —no one could tell by looking at me that I wasn't 100 percent male. I had signed up as a girl, but for all intents and purposes was playing as a boy. The truth was, I was also more comfortable not flat-out disclosing my true gender. I let the others think what they wanted. There wasn't another girl in sight.

Whenever the Wing Commander passed by or entered a court, every voice went silent. In Pakistan, divisions of the military oversee the three main sports: cricket went to the army, field hockey to the navy, and the air force runs squash. The system was set up as a way for the government to channel federal funds directly into their most important teams and affiliated programs. In my country, in terms of national pride and cultural identity, military and athletic prowess go hand in hand. Under the eye of the most powerful organizations of Pakistan, each boy watched himself. Even in such close quarters, with so much time to kill, no names were exchanged, no introductions of any kind took place.

Another coach came in, stood at the center T of the court with a ball held up in his hand, and set us to our first hitting drill. One boy after the other went careening after the ball, then scurried to the back of the line. First we just swatted the ball straight to the back—a standard game maneuver. After a while, we worked on a battery of wild hits, whose technical names it would take me months to remember: rolling nicks, corkscrews, cross courts, and boasts. We all ran around the full court until every kid in the line was panting like a dog. Eventually, the same coach narrowed us down into smaller groups and we were set up for small, one-on-one matches. Taimur was sent off to play with boys in a different division. He glanced back at me, looked over the boys in my group. I nodded and told him to go.

Barely anyone spoke. The silence gave me a chance to keep things straight. I was more serious about playing squash than I'd ever been about anything. My mind was fully engaged on learning the game and figuring out the other boys—who could beat me, who didn't have a chance. I didn't want to bother with the weaker ones—girl or not, I was the biggest kid there. A few of the boys eyed me, and some of the more experienced players—the ones with bright whites and new laces, expensive-looking racquets and their own leather bags—jeered a little in my direction as they stood around the court. It was strange how with one look a boy could make me feel inferior; many had tried in alleys and valleys, but until that morning they'd all failed. During the drills, I'd watch those nimble boys race around the court with a lightness and agility I simply did not possess. They had an aerobic stamina that I lacked, but my arms were like battering rams, and that was the single silver bullet in my holster. I couldn't wait to meet their insolent glowers with one hard hit. Fast or slow, I planned to send them all to the floor.

I got my chance before the hour was up, when I was sent into the tank with another kid, maybe a head or two taller, but far leaner than I was. We didn't so much as shake hands—that just wasn't how things were done. It was better for me that way. What would I have said? I was there as Maria Toorpakai Wazir—but only the Wing Commander and my brother knew it. The wiry boy scrutinized me in my tattered athletic clothes, assessed my racquet. It looked well used, but I knew it stood out; it was a special edition—Taimur had explained the meaning of that to me. In an instant, I could see he thought from my equipment alone that I knew my way around the court, had been playing for years. The spin of a racquet determined that I should make the first serve. When I took a breath and smacked the ball, it punched across the court, pinged against the wall, and shot back like a filament of lightning. The boy next to me lunged, going airborne after it. I could hear the air leave his lungs in a quick, frustrated gasp. He missed, and nodded at me, took a good look at my pulsing arm and the tributary of blue veins that always showed when I'd exerted myself. I went back to the box and served again—same straight dive, same way—killing it. And I did it five times in a row. Every time the ball died before him, the boy exhaled and bit his lip. When I looked back to the glass I saw a row of faces watching. They'd all heard my first serve like a gunshot and dropped their racquets. Then the Wing Commander stepped inside and looked at me.

"Switch." That's all he said.

I tossed the warm ball to my opponent. In his corner, he stood looking directly ahead. I'd set something alight in him—the desire to set me straight, I think. Purposefully, he lobbed the ball, as soft as a baby's breath. I hurled myself forward, crashed to the floor, my racquet outstretched—and missed by a mile. Then he did it again, that same feather touch, and I went for it hard, barely picking the ball up with the frame. When he'd proved his point five times to meet me on level ground, he gave me one nice clean drive. I got to it, hit it back. We needed a no-nonsense rally to get into a genuine game. Right then, I was reminded that this was not a blood-and-sweat fist fight outside in the street; this was squash, and I was a member of a team. Back and forth we volleyed, gently at first. It didn't last long. He had it all: precision and speed. After minutes of criss-crossing the court, I was blinking rivulets of perspiration from my eyes.

In barely a ten-second rally, that kid had uncovered my glaring Achilles heel and exposed it for all to see: I could murder with a hit, but I couldn't chase one to save my life, so he sent me on a futile tear from corner to corner. I made up for setbacks the way I always had—with full-throttled tenacity. The ball came away from the wall and kept dying before me. We were just kids learning the game, but the competition between us had a gripping tribal quality. We shouted out at each other—sometimes laughing, sometimes just letting the other one have it. Taunts meant nothing between boys—I knew that already. Once or twice, I hit back so hard he jumped away from me as though I'd just fired a bullet from a pistol. In between those short-lived rallies, I fell many times, always getting up from my knees with a tortured smile.

The boys assembled behind the glass had never seen anything like me in a squash court. The power in my legs catapulted me far too fast and hard. I couldn't stop in time to grab and command the ball with my racquet, but I ripped into that game tooth and claw. My well-heeled opponent knew how to cherry-pick shots and had all the angles in his mind. All I had was raw power and a cut-throat instinct. Still, I held my own for a long while, even when I was breathing so hard it felt like there was a knife in my chest. The coach stopped us, shaking his head; he looked me up and down, my battered knees and swollen hands. He picked up our match ball, curled his fingers around it, whistling through his teeth, and dropped it to the floor like a burning nugget of coal. I was taking off my shoes and pulling off the bloodstained socks. A few boys pounded the wall. By now they all wanted to play me. The boy next to me was catching his breath, taking a drink, giving me the once-over I recognized from my weight-lifting days. He'd won, but he'd also lost. He handed me a towel. Through the open court door, I could hear the sideliners jabbering away. They were talking about their own matches and they were talking about me. What kind of kid, one of them said, played to the death?

"Look at that big Pashtun—he looks like someone shot him in the kneecaps."

I took it for granted that I was safe in that group. I'd crossed through a rite of passage the way I had from the start of everything, proved my rank among them with a show of force. Regardless of my scuffed-up shoes, I would be a part of the group.

The Wing Commander called my opponent and me to the center T, told us to shake hands. I remember the kid had my brother's name, Sangeen, and I told him so. We smiled at each other as we clasped palms then turned to join our teammates. As

I began to walk off the court, the Wing Commander looked at me and said the thing that changed everything in the space of one breath.

"You'll break that racquet before long, Maria."

He might as well have painted the air red.

Then he slipped through the small white door in the back wall. Before it shut, I could feel the change in the energy inside the tank. My breaths were suddenly shallow and I could hear the blood rushing through me. I waited for one of the boys to say something and strike a match. My head was still pounding from the game. I hadn't crossed so much ground on foot since living out in the open in the valleys. I picked the ball up from the floor where our coach had left it, held it between my hands. No one said a word.

"It's still hot." I spoke without a trace of hesitation. Then I handed it to my opponent.

He took it from me, met my eyes for a second, and then looked away. The other boys were still peering through the glass. One or two had heard my name. I could see it in their deliberate stares through the court window. They were looking right at me like some foreign creature on exhibit. Still, I felt no shame, no fear. If the cat was out of the bag, there was nothing I could do. My days of cutting and running were far behind me. I was there to play squash at the invitation of the Wing Commander, and I'd done that before them all to the very edge of insanity. No boy there could touch me. When I coughed hard into the white towel, my lungs tightened and I thought I was going to spit up blood. If they wanted to confront me—to even ask—they wouldn't dare. Not yet. Not after that game. Blood was running down my knees. They knew from my big square hands and cinder-block arms that what I'd done to that squash ball—whatever I was—I could easily do to them.

My opponent was going to pretend it was a mistake, that he'd simply heard wrong. I could see his confusion in his frenetic blinking as he prepared to leave the court. The others followed suit, just stealing looks over their shoulders as we assembled in the corridor to get our bags from the floor. They peered at my chest, at my careworn shorts, along the length of my stocky legs, looking for clues. I could read the questions in those weighted glimpses. *Let them ask,* I thought—*I don't owe anyone a thing.*

The biggest one among them would step out from the crowd, and I should have anticipated that's how it would go down. Even in the upper echelons of a clean sport like squash, there was an animal code. Someone was always an alpha. He came up next to me as I made my way out, taking confident swigs from my canteen, some of the boys shadowing, quietly listening. I could have picked him out in a second. He was the one with all the perfect whites—the easy life. Even after a morning of hard-core training, he was still pristine. I could smell the sweet sandalwood coming off him in heady wafts like insults to the squalor he assumed I came from. Maybe he thought he could see it all, just from the tears along the seams in my shirt, the old stains on my shorts.

"I should have guessed. You play like a girl. You can't even run."

I thought about stopping and facing him down right there under the bright lights of the lobby. Our coach was at his desk, talking on the telephone. Against the walls hung the framed portraits of champions—five decades—not a single girl among them. Suddenly, I felt some pride in this. I'd joined a nationally revered sport at the invitation of the Air Force; the commander had told me the government was pursuing a mandate to include more girls in athletics. I knew already that I was among the first. The president of Pakistan, for whatever reason, wanted girls in the court.

I turned to the kids, pointed my racquet out straight, and grinned.

"That's right. I'll show you again next week."

*

Nothing I said mattered—after that, the boys were after me. Every time I played, they leered at me through the glass with their tongues wagging. Word had gotten out: there was a Pashtun girl on the courts. Nothing the Wing Commander could say or do could erase that mark from me. Their male pride was too raw. I'd sent more than one of them into a fit of frustration with a single hard kill in the tank. The truth was, they feared me. I could see it. I wasn't like the girls they knew: the veiled diffident sisters, the quiet doting mothers. I was just like them, but stronger. But when the boy in those immaculate whites walked behind me and ran his hands along my backside, laughing as he passed me in the court, something inside me snapped in two. I didn't turn to face him, just went into the corridor with my racquet and beat-up bag and made my way home. The next morning—and every morning after that—I was up before dawn, dressed in an old sweatsuit, pumping across Peshawar to the courts. The only way to beat them was to beat them. That's all I knew.

That's when playing squash went from a game to a full-blown addiction. The janitors always let me in, and sometimes we played together. I'd take up a match with anyone I could find if it meant having a solid back-and-forth game. Taimur was only good for a few matches here and there after school. I played air force pilots, custodial staff looking for a pick-up game after work, teachers, cooks. When there wasn't a willing soul with a racquet around, I just found an empty court and slapped the ball. I knew what I had to master—lithe speed and the precision that came with it. Over the course of frenzied weeks of playing hours each day in the court, sometimes up to eight if I could get away with it, I transformed. It wasn't just a hobby anymore, an occupation that would keep me off the filthy streets and out of trouble, a way to exercise my untamed aggression. Playing squash became the pursuit of my soul. My father didn't question my sudden obsessive drive—gone at first light, back all battered and swollen at night. Better a racquet than a gun or a fist. Better a squash court than a back alley and fourteen stitches to the back of my skull. There is a difference between a winner and a champion. It was an all-or-nothing attitude—and I already had it. Every time I chased that wild ball, I saw those kids in their perfect whites, and I saw myself beating them, one after the other.

*

I was in the stairwell with my racquet the day I heard all the boys coming; some of them were already there, congregating outside the courts, checking the posted game roster. My hands were taped to hide the cracked calluses across my palms, my ruined knees wrapped in gauze. I'd lost two fingernails from falls in the court and shed so many pounds that I had to wear an old pair of track pants, the drawstring pulled tight around my waist. I was still a wall of muscle, but I'd cut enough bulk to give me an edge of added agility. In defiance of every lewd grimace in the glass behind me as I trained, I let my hair grow—let them see me as a girl all they want. I'd gotten an ice cube, held it to my lobe, and pierced my own ears over the bathroom sink with a sewing needle. If those clean private-school boys were trying to get to me, they were going about it the wrong way.

When I walked the corridor along the full benches, heads turned on cue as I passed. I had a bright pink band in my hair. The coach wasn't there at the start of that practice. I put my bag down in the corner and got out my racquet, felt around for a ball. Some of the boys were already starting up—standing behind me, giving looks, daring one another into who knows what. I walked past them toward my designated court, looked around for my partner, and then pointed my racquet to choose one myself. They were all laughing. It was just like in the streets, I thought, even among those elite players in their starched clothes. They all went to school five days a week but were as dumb as they come—that's what I believed, and maybe I said it. I don't remember now.

My first opponent and I stood squared in the court, racquets at the ready. I can't recall who served, only what came after it. From then on, I raised my arm and shot him down again and again. As though it was nothing, I mowed the ball and beat him into a stupor of confusion. That's when I made up my mind: I was going to run down the full rank of them right there and then. Fourteen was the number, I remember it well. Before I got to seven, they were starting to quieten down behind the glass—all of them but the boy in those bleached and ironed whites. He had a mouth on him and pressed his full body right up against the glass. He hollered something about liking my new hairdo and asked if my father knew what his harlot daughter was up to. And that's when I invited him into the cube with me. As he sauntered in, our separate tensions met and electrified the court. He knew if he lost he was done for. I knew if I won they'd all hate me more than ever before. The paradox was a question of survival for me— with that particular hatred would come a distant respect. If I didn't annihilate that kid, they'd never let me play the game in peace.

Deliberately, I took my time with the serve. He was already disgruntled that he'd lost the racquet drop. Almost lazily, I walked to my corner, feeling the ball, squeezing it in my hand and looking him over. The lights kept going on and off, and the boys behind us let out a chorus of moans. I could smell the burn from the electrical system working at full capacity. The air buzzed. Then, without so much as taking a breath, I just took the ball and swatted it, detonating a hit so hard, the ball was in two pieces before it hit the wall. I looked over my shoulder and one of the kids brought out a fresh one. When he did, I noticed that he couldn't meet me in the eyes as I thanked him. It was already starting—the change. I had to follow through putting them down or I was all but finished at the academy.

I'd like to say my opponent put up a good fight, but he didn't do much more than flinch. I'd psyched him out the moment I split the ball on first serve. And I was a girl, right in his face— bright hairband, the small hoop earrings that my sister had found for me. On that day, I looked more feminine than I had in years, and somehow I think that made it harder for him to go toe-to-toe against me. So I did what I was there to do, what I'd been training for daily, hours on end, week after week. I crushed him, one point after another. By the time I was done, I could hear his breath coming out of him in long, angry drafts. Chin buckled, he went to the door, swung it open so that it slammed against the back wall. Then he turned to me—

"I will pray for your father. No man, whatever his sins, should have a slut like you for a daughter."

He crept out. Then, from the other side, he went right up to the glass to face me, all the boys surrounding him. I stood watching as he pressed his pants up to the glass and let his tongue hang out. Some of the boys were snickering; most of them just stared, not sure what to do. The brave among them simply left.

I felt that familiar heat boiling up my neck. I took my racquet, held it high, and shouted at him—at every single boy or man who'd ever tried to torment me. As my fury exploded, I hurled my racquet like a javelin straight into the glass. The boy jumped back when it struck the surface, the frame snapping. Then I invited him in for a different kind of match. He could see that I was dead serious. I stood there waiting, tapping my foot, motioning with my hand. I got right up to the glass wall, our faces eye to eye, and stared him down until I could see the terror creep over him like a sudden illness. I made him know that I wasn't afraid to hurt him—if he'd gotten into the cage with me, I would have torn him to pieces and he knew it. He was already backing away when I screamed at the top of my lungs:

"You want to see how girls play? This is how we play."

13. Smoking Scorpions

Wild dogs used to roam the hills of our tribal lands. After the move to Peshawar, those animals came back to me in restless dreams, sometimes only their eerie sounds and nothing else. I would hear echoes of the high barking calls the dogs made as they hunted along the night-blackened ridgeline. As a small child, I used to lie awake in the airy expanse of our slumbering house, listening to rabid packs chasing whatever creature they were after, round and round the rim of our valley, in and out of gullies and out across the cold plain. I could sense their shifting movements by the rise and fall of their sounds, which increased in intensity as the hounds slowly surrounded their prey. Then came the final series of savage cries when they all closed in and tore whatever they'd caught to pieces. Sometimes the dying animal howled once feebly into the night. The moan of death was unmistakable to me, even then.

When I was younger, my family kept a domesticated female dog in our home. Many families in the village used dogs to guard the house or herds of sheep. Always, in the new warmth of spring, her scent would attract those wild dogs, luring them all the way down into our quiet village. Entering in a long row of ten or more, they moved along the river path like a gang of hooligans— wet tongues hanging, heads low. When they slunk into our courtyard, our dog would cower inside a back room, though the front door was bolted and the windows shuttered. My father told us there was nothing we could do to keep them away, as a hail of vicious snarls fell against our walls. They knew we had a female in there, and they wanted her. Eventually, the hounds worked themselves up into such a frenzy that they attacked the door with a ferocity that terrified me, scratching and growling as though they'd all gone mad. Despite the comfort of my father's arms, I believed those violent animals were after me, after all of us, and wouldn't stop until they found a way in. Once or twice, men from the village came and shot a few of them dead sending the others scattering back into the hills.

Years later, when we moved to Peshawar, I wondered why I dreamed so often of those dogs, always chasing me—and me alone—across a dead sea of night. Between 2001 and 2002 the city of Peshawar, once a vibrant frontier town, seemed to slowly darken. The crowds teeming along the market streets thinned, though the population was steadily rising; passing faces grew gaunt with foreboding, but that meant little to me as a child. I simply noticed that the atmosphere of the city seemed heavier; people lost their tempers more often; refugee children were left hungry at the side of the roads; gangs of addicts multiplied like a virus. At home, my father often fell into long spells of quiet contemplation. I never asked him why. I was too absorbed in hitting that rubber ball as hard and as fast as I could. Already, though I was full of awkward stumbles and missed shots, playing squash was my whole world. I often look back and wonder how my father and mother managed their miracle. They raised our family in a sanctuary of peace on the cusp of a massive war so fanatical that it threatened to destroy everything in its path.

For my entire life and for over twenty years, Afghanistan, with whom we shared a border and ancient bloodlines, had been mired in conflict: the Soviet invasion and occupation (1979–1989), the ensuing civil wars (1989–2001)—the first ousting the communist Najibullah government, and the next ushering in the dark reign of the Taliban. My father had taught me the basics, and I understood that strife was part of the fabric of that country and of ours. But 2001 was a very different year, one that unleashed an unprecedented savagery—and that's saying something for a region with such a blood-soaked history. Across FATA and over the Durand Line, the rising call of war churned our part of the world as though in a huge cauldron. Long-simmering tensions, some of them generations in the making, had reached their apex and, one apocalyptic day, lit a long, never-ending fuse.

I've learned that most Westerners remember precisely where they were when history-making events took place: the first moon landing; the assassination of President John F. Kennedy; the space shuttle *Challenger* disaster; 9/11. On September 11, 2001, when terrorists flew two fuel-packed American jetliners, engines screaming, into the World Trade Center in New York City, then another into the Pentagon in Washington, D.C., and then lost another to the bravery of its innocent passengers over a lonely field in Pennsylvania, I have no idea what I was doing. We were still newcomers to Peshawar, without a television or access to any news whatsoever. It took hours for the story, which at first seemed improbable, to find its way to us. Even when I heard about the attack and saw fleeting pictures at newspaper stands as I rode past on the Sohrab, it didn't register—not the magnitude of the horror or the loss of thousands of civilian lives, which no one told me about, or how you could trace that cataclysmic moment in time back through a series of links, all the way to our pinprick on the map of the world. America was continents and oceans away, and no more real to me than the Hollywood movies my father borrowed from time to time. The home of those fabled backpackers was a dissolving dream of colorful candies and flashy grins.

On 9/11, I was almost eleven years old, spending my days fist fighting for a place on those congested urban streets—angry and oblivious. Looking back, I do remember waking up to find a teenaged Ayesha sitting as though frozen in grief on the floor, her face down, the white *chador* pooled around her, my father leaning down, speaking softly. Taimur was a grim silhouette in the background, staring at his hands. Somewhere, they'd seen footage of the terrorist attacks, gotten hold of the newspapers, sifted through the gruesome accounts, and read the death tolls. My mother found out about it only later, when she came home and my father sat with her sipping tea in a corner of our living room. I heard her sighing over and over again as my father whispered into her ear well into the night. I remember hearing the word's "Al Qaeda"—in a quick murmur, as though it was a forbidden spell—but they meant nothing to me. Later, I heard her offering prayers for all the departed souls and then the sounds of her feet moving over the floor as she wandered from room to room. She didn't sleep that night, none of us did. A few days afterward, my father and Ayesha both went out into the rain, and I watched from the window, their bowed forms dissolving into mist. They were gone for hours, standing in a long line on Hospital Road to sign the book of condolences at the consulate general of the United States. Drenched and sullen, they came home and barely spoke except to ask me for tea; they just sat together in the dim quiet, thinking. They knew what I did not—that we were living in the midst of a powder keg, and it was only a matter of time before it went off.

For Pakistan, as for the rest of the world, 9/11 cut a red line through time. What we lived before would bear little resemblance to what came after. Members of Al Qaeda littered Afghanistan. Their leader, Osama bin Laden, was living there under the protection of the reigning Taliban regime. When the Taliban refused to hand him over to the West, the West mobilized their armies. Just over two weeks after the attacks, Pakistan shifted its long-held support of the Taliban regime to the United States and its allies. It was not a decision without serious ramifications for our country. Since 1947, when the creation of the Durand Line cleaved the tribal region, Afghanistan had refused to accept that border and staked a claim to the Pashtun territory on the Pakistani side. To keep the peace, Pakistan had to make concessions to Afghanistan; they also had to consider their complex and contentious relationship with India on the other side of the country. Political decisions had nothing to do with right and wrong, and everything to do with the survival of the nation. One wrong move and Pakistan could easily have found itself sandwiched between pairs of bared teeth. When the American president,

George W. Bush, declared to the world that *either you're with us or you're with the terrorists*, Pakistan took note—and decided that it would be a bad idea to go up against a superpower.

The US-led coalition's war in Afghanistan was over quickly—in less than three months. After a final bloody stand at a fort near Mazar-e-Sharif in November, the Taliban fell. However people may have rejoiced at the surrender of that barbaric regime, the violence had barely taken its first breaths. My father predicted it, though it would take me years to understand what he meant; pacing our living room, he kept repeating the phrase *Pandora's box* and shaking his head. Militants hell-bent on crushing the Western invaders—Taliban, Al Qaeda, Uzbek, Tajik, Chechen, and Arab, including Osama bin Laden himself, moved stealthily in and out of Afghanistan across the porous Durand Line, as their ancestors had for centuries. They burrowed into the unforgiving terrain under the protection of elders, with whom they shared a history predating Christ, in remote villages all over the tribal belt.

To tribal men, history is far longer than a single conflict. To them, the fall of the Taliban in Afghanistan was a transient set-back. Surrender was just a word—the war was a long way from ending. Pushed back, the militants were simply regrouping and biding their time. This wasn't just a conflict, it was a full-scale jihad—a crusade for God against the invading infidels. There was no ending it with bunker-busters and paper. And it didn't matter that Pakistan was an ally of the invading armies; those militants were free to move about, deep inside the region—a no-man's-land that had never fallen under the dominion of any single power. In the months and years that followed, the militant groups grew stronger and more numerous. Meanwhile, civilian refugees from the war flooded our city. Slowly, over time, dread crept over Peshawar like a fog.

Camouflaged among hordes of displaced Afghans, embittered soldiers of jihad also poured in, gathering a quiet army. They assembled in safe houses or hid within the squalor of the refugee camps on the fringes of the city. Those stealthy fighters hunkered down, built up caches of weapons, expanded their networks, organized contingents of drug dealers and kidnappers, indoctrinated the helpless, the homeless, the hungry, and the addicted—then they hatched their plans and did the one thing they were far better at than their enemies: like those dogs hunting in the hills, they surrounded their prey, closed in, and waited.

*

When we moved to a house in Bara Gate, a quieter neighborhood located southwest of downtown Peshawar, everyday life became easier. The education board provided principals and other employees with housing in pleasant residential colonies when it was available, and my mother had waited months for her name to come up on the waiting list. It was 2002, and I never thought about the war in Afghanistan or the attacks or what was happening in the hills beyond our busy urban valley. It might as well have been a thousand miles away.

Even after 9/11, my father continued teaching at colleges deep inside FATA, which forced him into a tedious cycle of commuting many hours each week in and out of increasingly hostile territory. Though it was far too dangerous for our family to live there, he would not give up his post working and teaching classes in those tiny pockets of peace that still existed. Every morning, he packed a bag, grabbed a piece of fruit, a strand of holy beads, and got on the bus. He crossed the many military checkpoints and changed buses, taking him deep into the tribal belt. No authority questioned his presence there. If you were a full-blooded Pashtun, you were simply allowed in. When he came home to us at night, on the same bus, like any other father coming back from work, you could see in his face, dust-covered and tired, that he'd seen things out there that he wouldn't speak of until years later: bodies full of bullet holes left to rot at the side of the road, whole villages ransacked—not a girl in sight.

Our house in Bara Gate was a modest brick-and-mortar dwelling, but we had windows that let in full beams of light; stairs; a front and back door. You could hear the constant car-

and-motorbike buzz of the city. Just blocks away from the two-lane main street of Bara Road, we finally had the one thing I longed for—our own postage stamp-sized piece of sky. The house nestled within a neighborhood full of local schools, and when I ventured out, children were everywhere—running the lanes, jumping rope in their multicolored clothes. I cycled to the PAF Jansher Khan Squash Complex, and my siblings were close to their schools.

We had little money for anything beyond the basic staples; our clothes were ratty; we took our shoes in satchels to the cobbler until he could do no more. More than once, my small brothers went barefoot for a time. One thing compensated for the poverty, and that was stone's-throw access to a genuine education. Every one of my siblings was going to a good school. My father thought of me as a completely different child from the others, and decided that I needed to be free to learn outside, in the open air as I always had. I simply did not fit with the subdued and studious children around me who could bury themselves in books for hours. Outside, my imagination, which was filled with as much adventure as any Hollywood movie, came to life. My father believed that to keep me alive and happy, I should not be caged. I was smart and one way or the other, he said, I would learn what I needed to learn—and I did. So, I stayed on the sidelines, acquiring an education of a different kind: playing sports; helping out at home; listening to the lessons in math, geometry, and physics as my parents taught my brothers and sisters from textbooks—and roaming the city from gate to gate.

The month of July 2002 was remarkable for its heat and dust. The many Pashtuns who populated our neighborhood had taken to congregating in large groups on the side of the road, in the flimsy shade of awnings and half-dead trees, where they huddled in the dry haze, all dressed in loose white clothes. I watched them through a veil of dust, the hot ground radiating up my bruised legs. When I look back at that time, I always see it the same way, as though filmed through a strange gold filter of dust that still sends a chill up my spine. What those men spoke of—battles and bloodshed—was just background noise. Gliding past them slowly, I heard snippets of stories and words that had yet to find their meaning in my mind—"Taliban" was the most common. I didn't know it at the time, but that summer was a watershed.

For the first time since the partition of 1947, the Pakistani army deployed troops into the autonomous tribal regions. Their presence in a region paranoid about outsiders came after negotiations with the main tribes, but not every clan had agreed to that influx of armed government soldiers. Despite a massive effort by the army, only a handful of terrorists were actually caught or handed over in the villages. Taking advantage of the Pashtunwali code of hospitality, they found safe havens everywhere. Before long, Wazir subtribes saw the Pakistani army's continued presence on their land as a brazen attempt to subjugate their people and take over, and slowly over time, the natural mistrust turned malignant.

My mother returned to her post as principal of the school in Darra Adam Khel. This time, the education board gave her what she asked for: her students had a proper cement schoolhouse, textbooks, blackboards, a badminton set, cricket bats and balls, pencils and paper—just not enough teachers, only my mother and a handful of others were at the helm and taking on as many classes as they could manage. Though the nearby border hills often thundered as tensions grew—bombs, grenades, machine-gun fire—there were still children, families trying to carve out a life in the valleys, to harvest crops, feed and raise herds, run small village shops, and go to school. The future was the only weapon they had. As my mother said as she packed up her satchel each morning and went out to take the bus, which still made the daily journey through checkpoints: *what is written is written*. Our parents were always back home in time to eat with us at dinner.

If I was unhappy about anything at that time, it was about playing squash with boys. I lived just a pleasant cycle up Bara Road from the squash complex, past the booming passenger planes of Bacha Khan Airport and the screaming military jets of the neighboring air force base. The sounds of the planes taking off and landing sucked all the air out of my lungs. Sometimes I had to stop at the side of the road, squinting up as a jet screamed over the city like a blades tearing apart the sky. The main streets were as wide as the Indus and seemed as long. Scooting fast around Peshawar Ring Road, all the cars racing around and around in a huge circle, my feet working against the pedals to keep up and make my exit, the world was just a dizzy blur. When I got to the complex, heart hammering, clothes soaked in sweat, I knew what would happen. The boys would start to come out as soon as I opened the main door, as though predators alert to prey. I kept at it because the sport itself—its swiftness and the feel of my racquet hitting the ball—took me out of whatever torments I suffered. If my brother was around, he'd play a long set. From time to time, the staff at the complex were still good for a game, but I had stopped participating in the painfully awkward group sessions. Still, it didn't matter how I tried to lie low—the pack was after me.

As I passed along the corridor to the courts, the pounding rhythm of games in full swing stopped. Boys turned in their boxes and watched as I went by. I knew they hated me—for my poor clothes, my wild hair that was not quite short and not quite long, for the single earring I wore in my lobe as though to taunt them with uncertainty—for beating them one after the other, and then for throwing my racquet against the glass and breaking it, which I had come to realize had been a colossal mistake. I had let them know that they were getting to me, and I couldn't win once that cat-and-mouse game started. If I kept losing my temper, I could be kicked out of the academy, and all those boys knew it. Unfortunately, their silent harassment was hard for me to explain and prove to the officials.

For months I believed that if I was quiet, they'd grow tired of the routine and just let me play and learn the game. I opened the door into the last court in the long rank, got out my racquet, and hit the ball—just softening up the rubber. In my mind, I was already counting—not the number of hits but the number of seconds it would take for them all to come out like animals lured from their cages. I don't think I ever reached a full minute before I sensed them—three or four regulars usually among them. It always started out the same way: they'd just stand behind the glass looking into my court, running their eyes all over my body as if they were hands. If I turned to look, one might make a lewd gesture with his mouth or his tongue that would set fire to the skin on my face. Playing was impossible with those boys leering at me, and I often fumbled around the court, missing the ball, tripping over my feet. In three months of playing that way, I hadn't made any progress, though I played for hours each day. I could never forget they were there, taking turns, as though in pre-planned shifts, to torment me. Shame kept me from telling the coach . . . from telling a soul. It was part of a campaign to defeat me, and I knew I was losing.

My father was outside when I came home the last day, standing in the open front doorway looking up at the volatile west. A jet boomed past, circled our city, and then screeched off again to the hills. It was almost dusk, and I remember that he had a cup of green tea in his hand and was slowly sipping it. Lately, he was always out there like a sentry, waiting in the soft dusk for me to come home. I set the Sohrab against the house, threw down my racquet bag, tied my shoe, wouldn't meet his gaze. I rubbed my hands together—the rims of my palms were landscapes of cracked calluses. I had cycled home in a frenzy, as I fought my tormentors in my head. I knew that with one blow I could crush them, each and every one, but that that would mean the end of squash for life. The havoc that paradox unleashed in my mind was breaking me. Within seconds, I could feel my father's eyes on me and looked over. I knew a question was on the tip of his tongue—not about my day, which he could read just from the hunch in my shoulders. Sometimes our father would greet us with a quiz.

"Maria, I watched you racing down the street like a Tasmanian tiger and knew I had to ask you one thing."

"Okay, Baba."

"First law of motion—do you know it?"

My answer was instant—I didn't have to think at all. "A body in a state of motion will remain in that state of motion unless an external force is applied to it. Sort of like me riding the bike and then braking to make it stop. Of course, gravity plays a part."

My smiling father nodded and took a long drink. Leaning against the doorframe in his clean *shalwar kameez*, he stood as languid as any man of leisure, though he was anything but—no one could have guessed that he'd been in and out of a simmering war zone that day.

"How is it, Maria, that you know all three of Newton's laws of motion, though you haven't really gone to school? Some kids your age are only just learning to use a ruler."

"You are my school, Baba, and I listen while the others learn. Last night, you studied physics with Taimur and I learned all about velocity."

A small laugh and he put his cup on the ground and came up to me. Saying nothing, he took my hands and held them out flat, running his long fingers across the crusts of hardened skin. Then he looked right through me as though he'd spent the day watching me in the courts, seen the boys assault me with their eyes, and heard for himself the crude words that I could barely hear as I pounded the ball with my racquet while the boys pounded their fists against the back glass.

"When I look at your hands I see a passion for the game. Then I looked at your face when you came back here and I see the opposite—apathy. I've been wondering what to do, and I think I know. You won't like the idea, but it's for the best. It's time for you to try school again."

My father. He taught me everything I knew—and I was weary. I didn't have any fight in me. I could not defy him, not then—not ever. And the truth was, I felt he might be right. When I put my racquet away in a corner, I thought it was for good.

*

The Warsak Model School, where my brother and sister went five days a week, was a short bus ride from our home. It still stands today, the same well-regarded institution, and it was one of the reasons that we moved to Peshawar in the first place. I remember that the first time my mother saw it, she came home, sat down, and wept. A brick building with a clean courtyard and modern facilities: computers, laboratories, and a library. My sister flourished there, fulfilling each dream my parents had for her. Every day, she got off the bus, satchel full of books, mind filled with new knowledge, and she met the expectations that came with her miracle: like my mother, she found herself in the top 1 percent—a tribal girl receiving a fine education. My sister, with her white veil and placid manners, was a model student. And then there was me.

When the school bus picked us up, I was dressed in a scratchy pair of brown pants. Fiddling with the folds in the wide *chador* draped over my shoulders, I couldn't seem to stop the fabric from slipping—I refused to wear it over my head of untamed hair. From the age of four I'd never worn a veil, and I wasn't about to start at twelve. No one made me—it was enough that I was there. Watching the bus pull up, I could hear the cacophony of children's voices singing out of the open windows. Dread sat in my gut like a stone. I looked at my watch: it wasn't yet eight o'clock, and already I was counting down the hours and minutes. Before we stepped aboard, Ayesha explained that the boys and girls were segregated on the bus—the boys at the back, the girls at the front, and the teachers all along the bench in the middle. I heard her, but didn't listen.

As Ayesha nestled into a front row seat, I bent down against the low ceiling, hauling my tattered bag of books and canteen, eyes low over the dirty floorboards. Questioning eyes moved over me like heat lamps. Past the teachers' bench, I walked all the way to the back. Ayesha had told everyone she knew that her sister had just been admitted. One look at me, my big muscled frame, my boyish clothes, and they said nothing—just watched dumbfounded. They must have expected a smaller version of Ayesha and not her hulking opposite in a pair of pants. As I passed each row, the chorus of voices died down. I took an empty seat among all the boys, who simply shifted their weight to give me room. I could smell their male heat rising in the small space as I settled in. Finally, one of the teachers called out to me to move, but I refused—not in words, I just smiled and shrugged. The bus started up and peeled into the traffic. After a moment, the teacher laughed a little, her face reddening as she gave up. I don't know why I sat there—it wasn't a protest. Apart from Ayesha, I'd grown up among boys, a member of their packs, usually the leader. I didn't know a thing about being a girl among girls.

Sitting on the plastic-covered bench as we moved through the main street, I looked up the rows of seats. Every face on that bus was turned to me but Ayesha's. Way up front, I could see the back of her white *chador* as she sat still, looking straight out at the street, her soft hands no doubt folded in her lap. At that moment, I loved her more than at any other time. Somehow, by saying and doing nothing, Ayesha had protected me. They respected her, they respected my parents for teaching the forgotten tribal children, and so they let me be.

*

Monday to Friday at school, I was a failure. My first classrooms had all been rocky valleys, running amok with a slingshot. I'd learned what I needed to know from my father under *jamun* trees, or sitting on clay floors listening to the anecdotes of the motley crew he brought home as gifts for our psyches. The first day of school, I remember sitting at the clean desk, running my fingers over the smooth polished wood. Right away I knew that I was in a different kind of school—a real one. Students weren't all jammed into a dreary room, arguing over pencil stubs and scraps of paper. Electric lights overhead brightened clean white walls. There were long hallways and bathrooms. Bells chimed between lessons. The school had computers, big blackboards, and up-to-date maps. At first, I thought the luster of such prosperity would make a difference. I had my own dictionary, textbooks, and a calculator. My teacher even flat-out ignored the fact that I was sitting in a girls' classroom in pants. The girls surrounding me like exotic creatures giggled, some said hello and talked about my sister, but they never made me feel out of place. People seemed to accept the fact that I had lived most of my life as a boy. The idea was so unfathomable that it was untouchable—permissible. There were far larger problems looming in our world than how I chose to dress. Still, every morning after the first bell, I sat down, notebook open, and within minutes had my head down behind a book—fast asleep.

I had some of the best dreams of my life at that desk: back in Darra fashioning bows and arrows; flying kites; flying planes. The teachers and administration didn't know what to do with the forever slumbering Maria Toorpakai. My ability to sleep through classes with students chattering and bells signaling the hours became legendary. Exasperated teachers rapped me with rulers; fellow students doused my head in water. Nothing worked. Even when I came to school on ten hours' sleep, I still slept through class. I couldn't help it. Even on the school bus I would be fast asleep and drooling in my sister's lap all the way.

Inside my desk a stack of notebooks, one for every subject, gathered dust. After two or three months and a roster of failing grades, my homeroom teacher asked to see those notebooks, stood over me, and thumbed through the blank pages. I remember watching her trembling fingers sifting through each one, almost desperate to see some evidence of attention. She had a look on her face that even now I can't decipher—a kind of horrified disbelief so intense that she said nothing. Over the weeks, that same teacher had tried unsuccessfully to find me a book to read that I might enjoy, an independent project that I might take to—she might as well have tried to catch a minnow in her hand. I had never learned a thing that way, and I told her so.

"I can't learn anything sitting, Madam. I must move around. Sitting here under these lights shuts off my brain."

Not long after that, I was called to the office and expelled. When my father came home, he said nothing, just read the school letter and looked over at me. I knew he was running out of ideas, and so was I. For the first time, when our eyes met, I saw fear. The fact was, my family simply did not know what to do with me.

No longer bound to school, I bicycled all over town. It was during my return to Bara Gate from a long trek across the city that I discovered that the world was off its rocker. A lazy glide; I wasn't in a rush as I moved from the main street into the narrower roads, avoiding a stretch of closed sections. Until riding around and zeroing in on home that day, the war hadn't touched me. Before I got to the end of the lane around the corner from my house, drifting, feet off the pedals, legs stretched way out, I would feel the war in my bones. If for Americans the war began with those horrifying visions on 9/11, for me it started with an interrupted bike ride.

Just ahead, leaning against the sidewall, I saw a man smoking a small brown joint that I knew at a glance was a drug—likely hashish. And I knew from his glazed and shiftless look, eyes darting around into nothing, that he was an addict of one kind or another. Often those men and boys loitered together, their faces lost in a sickly stupor that almost frightened me—under bridges, in the alleys, or just wandering half alive along the roads. This one was a solitary creature, large rolling headscarf and dark sun-bitten skin. I was sure that I'd seen him around before. As he leaned back and raised his arm to take a drag, a pistol poked out from his waistband. I would never have slowed down if it hadn't been for that pistol. The moment I saw the star emblazoned on the handle, I was back in the kitchen with my father in Darra Adam Khel—it was a Makarov, just like mine.

I risked a glimpse into his eyes as I slowed, and that's what did it, I think. With a swiftness and strength I could not have antici-pated, the man stepped forward, closing the gap. Then, as though catching prey, he reached out and took hold of my back wheel and lifted it off the ground. For a few seconds the wheel contin-ued to spin as I tried to pedal against nothing but air. For some reason, perhaps as a way to quell the shock, I thought of Newton's first law of motion—my feet moved fast to the ground.

I could feel my body start to shake, and I didn't know why.

Nothing had happened yet; the man hadn't so much as said a word as he came around to face me. It was around noon when most people took their midday naps. The whole city seemed deserted. The man was taking his time looking me over, head to toe. I pressed my palms against my sweat-slicked thighs. If I could have thought of a thing to say, I would have said it—but within a moment, he spoke. A metallic sourness tinged his hot breath, which hit me like a stream of exhaust. He was high on something—there was no question of that—but he was still solid and sure of himself.

"What are you?"

I had no idea what to say to him.

"Pashtun—Wazir."

My answer only irritated him, and he shook me on the bike.

"I know that. I've seen you coming and going out of that house over there. What are you—sister, brother, son, or daughter?"

The question itself told me that I was already damned, and I would not answer him. Before I could think of a way out, I saw him toss the smoldering joint to the ground. It crumbled but continued to burn and I glanced down at it for a second. It looked like it was full of searing dirt. The scent was strangely acrid and made my eyes water. Then he moved right next to me and his hands went to my arms, hauling me right off the seat. As we struggled my bike went to the pavement, scraping my calves. I didn't expect his strength or the pain that came with it, so I could barely take a breath as he grabbed me again and brought his face close to mine.

Against my cheeks, I could feel his breathing, which never quickened, and I fixed my wide eyes on his tossed stub, still burning by my feet. The scent was strange—hot and almost sweet—as the smoke snaked up my body to my flaring nostrils. I zeroed in on it, needing something to cast my attention on before I vomited. It wasn't hashish, which you could smell all over town. Hot stomach acid churned in my gut. I began to flail, and he held me harder. No matter how I maneuvered I could not break free of his grasp and he pushed his weight against me, I heard something fall from the folds of his clothes to the ground right at my feet. I looked down fast to a small clear sack, the strange contents spilling out. The things were peculiar: a collection of short brown stubs, curved and ribbed along their length and tapered at one end to a tiny fork—part insect. I knew instantly when I saw them—just like the pistol, they brought back memories of Darra—that the things in the bag were scorpion tails. Addicts who ran out of drugs often resorted to collecting venomous creatures and smoked the poison in tobacco as a last resort. Sometimes, smoking scorpions was the only way they could get high until they got their hands on more dope.

Then he asked his question again and the sliver of air between us seemed to go instantly hot. He looked at me then with red rimmed eyes, in whose perverse stare I read his full intent. His breath was rancid. If I stayed there, I was sure he would try to find the answer that I would not give. When I felt his hands twitch against my wrists, adrenaline took over. Hard and fast, my knee moved like a hammer, hitting him in the groin. As he stumbled back a pace, I stepped forward and kicked him again, but harder. I was screaming words like dog and bastard. He went to his knees and let out a groan. Moving away, I saw the broken end of a pipe on the ground and picked it up. Then I looked down at him as he peered up at me, squinting as I held it high over him.

"Yes—I'm a girl—sister, daughter, Wazir.

Then I tossed the pipe. I could see that he couldn't get up.

Finally I got on the bike, muscles pulsing, and every part of me ignited in terror. As I raced off, my head screaming, I heard him holler after me that I was a sin—and that my time was coming. When I got home, I went to the side of the house and was sick to my stomach.

Over the following few days, I saw that man again all around Bara Gate, smoking his scorpion tails. He lurked along the neighboring roads, waiting for me. Once or twice he was right outside our door, just watching as I came and went. In the end, I had to tell my father what had happened, or I believed eventually the man would do far worse. When I told him, I cried as never before. I knew that he was not the type of tribal man who punished his daughter for being violated—but for reasons I didn't understand, I was still ashamed.

He wouldn't summon the police—that's not how things were done in Peshawar at that time. The police would expect a bribe just to open a case, and plenty more to keep it open. Even then, we'd be lucky if they did anything, and we'd have even less money than before. When I saw the darkness fall over my father's face as I let the details unravel, I expected the pistol to come out, and for him to get up and leave, find the man, and mete out justice. But my father just listened stone-faced in his fury, asked a few questions, and was quiet. Then he made tea and sat for hours, doing nothing, just thinking. I was sure he was looking for a way to kill my assailant and get away with it—it would be hard in a city with so many people around—or to beat him senseless so that he never came back.

When the time came, I followed my father out and we walked the one block it took to find the offender. The man who'd been harassing me was standing around as usual, smoking another poison-laced reefer. During our talk, my father had explained that while scorpion venom made people high, it also made them angry. Baba had noticed the man around our neighborhood, knew who he was, and had wondered why he'd been watching our house.

We stood in the street, the men faced each other, no more than a foot between them. I waited defiantly behind my father. For a long time, they just stood there deep in a conversation that never showed a moment of hostility. They spoke about my family, who we were and where we came from—my father calm and tall in his pressed clothes. I heard Baba tell the man to stay well away from his children, or that he would not be as kind on their next meeting. The man nodded and looked around, smoking. After my father was done speaking, the man offered to take us for tea, but we did not accept. Then he shrugged and offered my father, who he now knew came from a prestigious family, an apology. After a time, the Afghan addict wandered off down the road into the haze, and my father and I walked slowly back home. As we approached our house, I could feel my own anger rise like another kind of venom. My father had done nothing, just talked. When he walked through the door, he assured me, hands on my shoulders, that I would never see that man again.

For the first and last time, I was angry with my father, and I showed it. I thought he was a coward. He should have beaten or killed the man for coming near me. It was how things were done. My father walked away from me just as I unleashed a tirade of tears and accusations. I stopped talking, followed him into the living room, sputtering. We sat on mats over the floor, me shaking as he quietly explained things, about the war going on and the Taliban and the other militant groups hell-bent on jihad, and what they wanted—what most of the legions of jihadists who'd infiltrated our country wanted—their version of Islam, that targeted women—freedom—girls just like my mother and sister . . . and me.

"The scorpion venom that man smokes is not nearly as dangerous as the poison in his mind. If I had done what I wanted to, what you expected of me, many more men like him—soldiers of jihad—might have come here. This thing he did to you is much bigger than you or I or what we think is right. It's part of a holy war."

The truth was that I didn't really understand what he was telling me. I'd been robbed of my dignity and then of the justice I thought a Pashtun father owed his violated daughter. It would take me years to untangle the knots of that anger and to figure out that he had been wise. What my father had done out there on the roadside, sweet-talking a crazed militant, kept his family—kept me—alive.

14. Rupees for My Mother

After my expulsion from school, alone in the empty house, I was lost in idleness. My second-hand racquet bag, tucked away in a corner, called. Sometimes I spent a whole hour just looking at it leaning against the wall like a rifle. In the end, I didn't ask for permission. I still wanted to play, just not among that abusive gang of boys; my father didn't want me to either. The entire family would be gone all afternoon—teaching, learning, and improving themselves, making the wages on which we survived. I finally went to the bag, got down on my knees, and unzipped it. When I took out the racquet and held it in my hand, it felt like a third arm. I twirled the handle, and a thousand shots screamed to come out. I sat there a long while, toying, thinking, wishing.

Instead of putting the equipment back in the bag, I took it with me into the kitchen. The far wall in there was long and painted bone white. At a glance, I knew there was enough space to hammer out a good shot. That was all I had in mind, one clean hit—maybe two. There was nothing to do but let the hours rot. Several times each week, I rode the bike on routine errands. Cleaned house. Cooked meals. Slept the dullness away. Sometimes I asked Allah for just one colorful dream of the open plains, of the rushing rivers—of my mother's smile, which I hadn't seen for weeks, as though she'd lost it on the long road between home and FATA. Those dreams never càme.

I pushed a small table all the way across the room to the other end; moved a stool; took down a map of the world. Then I raised a flat hand to the high, unblemished wall. It was perfect. All quiet in the kitchen, I stood with legs and arms poised. I could hear the dull drone of cars moving along Bara Road; sirens; squawking birds and wails of children. The ball warmed, smooth and so familiar in the cradle of my palm. I readied the racquet. Steady as a pump, my lungs filled with air, my mind shed everything but the moment at hand. Then I made my hit—the ball shot across the kitchen, smacking the whitewash. A thunderclap of sound ricocheted all through the vacant house and all through my body. A forgotten switch turned on, and every neglected muscle along my limbs suddenly awakened. When the ball came back fast, I slammed it, again and again, splitting the air. A long, uninterrupted drill ensued, cutting through time like tearing out a dull chapter from a book. When I finally missed the ball, I had to stop a moment and put down the racquet. I just stood in the dim kitchen, letting the ball drop to the cement ground. Bent over, hands on my once-pummeled knees, I closed my eyes and laughed out loud. Not a soul there to hear me. Then I stood up again and went back to it—harder. After that, I didn't stop for anything—food or drink or the long nap I'd been taking to wipe away each afternoon. I fired off shots for hours. The racquet had possessed me.

After days of covert kitchen drills, my only ball split down the middle. I might have thought those kitchen games were over for the time being, if I hadn't passed the broken lamp in the living room. I stared at the silver cast covering the joint and went to the cabinet where we kept things like hammers, nails, gun oil, thumbtacks, a broken abacus—and my father's prized duct tape. Finding the roll, I cut a small piece and put the tape back just as I'd found it. I wrapped the ball along the crack, and then I went back to the game. For a while, the fix held fast. When it finally gave way and the ball was ruined beyond repair, I had no choice: in the high heat of mid-afternoon, I hopped on the Sohrab. There was no thought of going inside the building. I had sworn I never would again. But along the outside courtyard and walkways, players often tossed their old, battered balls to the ground, scattered as litter. Foraging for squash balls became routine. Sometimes, if I was lucky, I'd find a new one lost in a hedge or in the gutter. Though my activities were still clandestine, I took great pride in filling up my days—and without costing my parents a rupee. We simply didn't have enough money for frivolities like squash balls, and I didn't want to tell them what I was doing. My father knew that I had suffered at the courts and he was concerned about my even considering going back there. He had yet to think of what to do with his peculiar daughter, and I was angry with myself for placing such a burden upon him. I didn't know how to tell him the simple truth: leaving the squash academy had been a mistake. Idleness was a far worse enemy than the boys and their taunts. Lately, when my father looked at me, all I saw was worry. While my siblings walked clear-cut paths—Ayesha elected proctor at school; Taimur studying with friends; the twins starting at a grade school up the road—I seemed only to drift around them on a lonesome current.

I must have gone on for weeks playing games against imaginary opponents in our kitchen—palms rebuilding calluses; limbs refashioning muscle; heart rediscovering its passion. It never occurred to me to simply ask to go back to the courts. When my father raised a concern you always considered it. So I lost myself in those hours of secret tournaments, drilling the ball until my body simply gave up and collapsed to the floor, sprawled over the cold cement like a dripping rag. What my parents couldn't know was that squash was saving me. When the racquet slipped into my hand, all self-doubt evaporated. When I hit the ball, there was nothing else, and maybe that's why, when my father came home early one day and stood watching me in the doorway, I didn't see him.

Eventually, he made a noise—coughed, shuffled his feet, something—and I stopped in my tracks. The ball pattered once or twice over the floor and fell dead. Standing there, panting and wide-eyed, I held the racquet out, body immobilized in mid-shot, skin drenched, chest pumping. At last, I had been caught. We looked at each other and then my father nodded, scanning a room in complete disarray—the table pushed haphazardly to the other end; a mess of plates waiting for me in the bucket; stale tears of bread my brothers had left on the counter in their haste—then back to me, to my still-frozen racquet hovering, and finally to the ball at my feet. He put down his overstuffed satchel, stood up straight, put a hand on the doorframe as though to steady himself from what he knew was coming. Then he laughed so hard I thought he'd made the lights flicker.

"Do you think we are blind, Maria? We all know what you've been doing. I just waited for you to tell me. But knowing and seeing are two different things—two different things by far. You realize this is the first time I've seen you play."

Bewildered, I just stood there, panting like an animal, the racquet hanging from my hands like a broken limb. Then my father walked across the floor and held his arms out to the battered white wall as though in reverence to a masterpiece. The full white surface was covered in a faint constellation of black and gray smudges. I'd scoured that wall each afternoon with a cleaning brush and then put back the table. I believed I'd done a good job—until then. Sitting on the cold cement, I realized the absurdity of what I'd been doing. Leaning down, my father took my racquet from me. He practiced a few empty swings, and then he held it up and looked at me through the mesh.

"Albert Einstein once said: 'A table, a chair, a bowl of fruit, and a violin; what else does a man need to be happy?' You are fortunate, Maria, because you only need one thing—a squash racquet."

"Are you telling me to go back to the courts, Baba?"

"I'm not telling you anything—I made that mistake already. All I will say is that if you do decide to go back . . . this time, be strong about it."

Then he handed me my racquet.

*

My timing was way off. The group had just finished a set of matches, and pairs were packing up, some already filing out of the courts. All those useless weeks behind me like a canyon, my father's laughter in my mind, I cut a straight line through the crowd of boys in long, determined strides. I could feel stares on me like a single hot sun. Racquet bag slung over my shoulder, I had a brand-new ball in my hand, a gift from the Wing Commander to welcome me back. One or two of the boys pulled a grimace, let out a laugh, but I just kept going. By then, I'd suffered much worse. I asked a boy if he was done with the first court. When he nodded, I thanked him eye to eye and went in.

Racquet unleashed, I got straight to it, never turning to see if any of the boys had lined up behind me, though I was sure they were there. From the first merciless hit, I drilled the way I had in the kitchen—for myself, for the sheer joy of the game. My only focus was on increasing my intensity and speed. When I fell, I grunted and got right up. Slammed harder. Ran faster. At some point, I lost all sense of anything but taming that wild sphere. Hours—who knows how many—evaporated. Those gawking boys had already seen me play until my knees bled. From then on, they would see me play to another level of insanity—from the time the complex opened until it closed. Any time they were there, I would be there too.

How long they lingered at my back, watching that first unbroken set of hits, I'll never know. Whatever their taunts were that day, they no longer meant anything. And as far as bullies went, my recent experience with the scorpion-smoking assailant just around the corner from home reduced their efforts to the antics of circus animals. There was a far greater evil waiting for me outside the academy walls. Not even one hundred miles away, men were shooting holes in each other in the name of God; just up the street, addicts and fanatics lurked in the markets; and back in Bara Gate there was an empty desk at a school that could put me to sleep for eternity. All in all, I was in a safe place, doing the only thing I knew how to do. Sweat flew off my soaked hair. The rubber on my shoes disintegrated. I pursued the ball like a crazed hunter.

I played that way for months, proving my point to them and to myself, and taking my rightful place. One night, as I packed up to leave the court, someone rose from the bench in the empty corridor and moved up to the glass. When I caught sight of his dark figure, I knew it in an instant—even his shape seemed surly. Our eyes met in the glass as though across a chasm. He'd been the first to come after me—the well-heeled, well-fed, immaculately dressed ringleader, the one whose whites, after a full afternoon of playing, never had a mark on them. We just stood there, his arms folded across his chest, the transparent wall between us. I could see from his face that he was holding something back, a card player afraid to give away his hand. I'd seen that look before, on the boys running the valleys and backstreets, and now I saw it on the smooth, scrubbed face of an elite player with every privilege, including insolence, to use at his leisure.

I wasn't leaving the academy—ever—and he knew it. One of us had to give in, and it wasn't going to be me. The smile I put up was more powerful than any punch I'd ever thrown. It hit him harder too, right through the clear wall, right between the eyes, and I knew he understood me at last. All I wanted to do was what I'd been doing—play the game like any other kid my age. Then I shrugged—*take it or leave it*—and I picked up my bag. A grin fought its way across his face, and he nodded. He raised a hand, put it up against the glass before turning and walking up the corridor. The next time I saw him in the crowded lobby, he said hello.

*

Within days, the Wing Commander slipped through the door into my court, a sheet of white paper in his hand. He'd been coming by more and more to watch my fanatical drills. Often we'd play a few rounds and he'd teach me new shots. In the end, he always made the same promise, as flimsy as the paper he was brandishing—to find me girls to play among. To build a female team. Despite recruiting efforts all over the city, and even past its limits, not a single girl had stepped forward to join the academy. Peshawar stood as a gateway to the tribal belt, whose conservative culture bled like an open artery into the largely

Pashtun population. Girls might attend school until they married, but playing sports crossed an indelible line. I was more than a maverick—I was a freak of nature. The Wing Commander waved the paper at me like a flag; I could smell the ink from the fax machine. His teeth flashed when he grinned at me.

"Your time has come, Maria Toorpakai. We are sending you to a tournament. You'll play girls from all over Pakistan."

*

Wah Cantonment—also known as Wah Cantt—is a city in the province of Punjab. Prosperous and civilized, it had the highest literacy rate in the country and housed the largest and most sophisticated ordnance factories in the nation. A military center into which government funds poured on a river of rupees, the clean city stood in a long, wide valley. Streams cut paths over the fertile bowl in winding ribbons; fruit trees grew in abundance. According to legend, a visiting Mughal emperor took one sweeping look from the hillside down over the lush landscape and exclaimed—*wah!*—in a reverent echo meaning "wow," and gave the valley its breathless name. Eighty miles southeast of Peshawar, it took us just two hours by bus to get there. My mind wasn't on the geography, though my father had sat me down to pinpoint the city on a map. It was on the event at hand, my unexpected chance to compete against actual people—against other girls. I took no small measure of pride from the fact that, win or lose, I was the only girl in Wah Cantt representing my city.

The squash club on the eastern rim of town was sandwiched between vibrant blocks of degree colleges and campuses on one side and a long span of ordnance factories on the other. Right off the bus, I was ready with my squash bag and the small duffel I'd borrowed from Taimur. I'd had to use a special glue to fix a tear in my shoes, and I'd scrubbed the dull white as best I could. It was either the tournament or a new pair of shoes—the tournament had won hands down.

No member of my family had traveled with me; the rupees it took to get me as far as Wah Cantt had been a monumental sacrifice. If I thought about winning, which I did every minute of the day, I thought about it first in the context of making good on the expense it took to send me there in those torn clothes and castaway shoes.

As I saw the other girls disembark from their buses and move toward the registration building, I felt those careworn clothes on me like a layer of dirt. Most of the girls wore bright uniforms that matched their full white smiles. Silky ribbons adorned their hair, and bangles glinted on their narrow wrists. Lean athletic limbs. Tiny waists. The Wing Commander looked over and smiled as though reading my mind. All around us, girls chattered in a way that made me think of birds, or of the front of the school bus before I walked to the back.

No question, I stood out. As I walked in and moved into a line, I thought I heard whispers. Heads turned over shoulders; quick glances shot like darts in my direction. I could see that familiar uncertainty flicker over faces. They were all trying hard to place my gender and coming up short. By then, questioning stares were routine. I'd already been attacked by a madman; a perplexed glance was nothing. I was too absorbed in what I was there to do, and the price my parents had paid to send me. The tournament had cost my mother several days' pay. When I did the math for myself, I nearly backed out, but the family sat down and insisted—without that sport, they told me, I seemed to die from the outside in. I didn't go to school, so there was no tuition or supplies to pay for; I never wore expensive dresses, oiled my hair, or asked for silk ribbons—overall, they said, I came cheap. In the lineup, I stood quietly, considering my best shots and picking out the strongest-looking players. None of them came close to me in terms of pure muscle. My biceps were as wide as many of their thighs. Two of any one of those girls could have hidden side by side behind me. For a moment, I thought back to the weight-lifting tournament in Lahore, which hadn't cost my family anything, but could have cost me everything. There was no way of knowing what would have happened if I'd been caught in that Genghis Khan masquerade. I squinted up into the bright ranks of electric lights overhead, relieved. It would be so much easier to play in a tournament without having to live a lie.

At the top of the line, I stared over the heads of the girls to a formation of desks. The girl in front of me took her identity badge, gathered up her paperwork, and moved off to one side. In her pretty long-haired wake, I stepped forward. I stood alone before the PAF official. I don't remember why, but the Wing Commander had left for a few minutes that turned out to be crucial. The man looked up. He took in the single earring studded to my lobe, and then the squash bag slung over my shoulder. Slowly, he replaced the cap on his pen. I remember that he yawned.

"Yes?"

I put down my racquet bag and the duffel, said my name and city. The man shrugged, took a long index finger, and slid it down a typed-out list, lifting pages silently and then tapping once against the typeface when he found me under T—*Toorpakai*. I remember that his fingertip was tinged orange—a saffron stain. Smiling, he scanned the vacancy around me and frowned. Right away, I understood that he thought I was a boy—perhaps the dutiful brother accompanying his sister, who was the only player from Peshawar. I wasn't offended. It was a routine error. I'd never felt any embarrassment about my appearance; if I had, I would have changed it long before. I laughed, shook my head, and told him who I was. The man simply refused to listen. Several times he said no, each time louder than the last. I could feel the few girls behind me who were within earshot go quiet. A smattering of quick whispers rippled along the front line like a small wave curling up a shoreline.

Perhaps sensing the confusion, the man's colleague in the next chair looked over. The men talked together quietly and then marched their eyes over me. Finally, one of them got up and conferred with the other PAF officials. Soon they were all at the same table. Now the auditorium was at a standstill while my sex was debated in hushed tones around the table in front of me. I felt the absence of my coach like losing hold of a life ring. The irony was not lost on me that, just a moment before, I'd felt such relief at playing as myself, as Maria. Now, the truth was my enemy, not the lie. When the man came back, he was grave and barely met my eyes. My registration was refused. I watched him sit down, take his pen, remove the cap, and summarily scratch my name from the list.

There was nothing else for me to do. My coach was nowhere in sight. Finally, the official put down the pen, pushed aside the papers as though they'd offended him, and delivered a long, quiet tirade that might as well have sucked the blood from my veins. When he was done, I could still hear single words ricochet in my brain like fired bullets—"fraudulent," "deception," "disgrace." In the midst of it all, I remembered how carefully my mother had placed my registration fee into a big envelope. She handed it to me as I packed my duffel. Her face was full of pride, but I saw then the circles that framed her once-vibrant eyes. In those eyes I saw long days in the poverty- and war-ravaged tribal belt. My mother could have requested a transfer to a safe school in Peshawar or further into Pakistan proper, but the idea never would have occurred to her. She endured so that illiterate children of our cousin tribes could learn to read and write. After all, she had told me, we were all fruit born from different branches on the same tribal tree. Standing there, my name scratched out on a registration sheet, cast out of the tournament in Wah Cantt all because of peculiarities that were cherished at home—I had squandered it all. Tears swelled and stung in my eyes. Then, as though out of the sky, a firm hand rested on my shoulder. I turned to see the amber-eyed Wing Commander looking down at me.

He shook his head and walked around me with an air of authority that seemed to double his height. A word or two into the ear of the official and then he handed over his military identification. Loud and clear, I heard him say my name. He found the scratched-out evidence on the roster and pointed to it, asked who was in charge. Then, before them all, he vouched for my identity. An argument ensued that drew in every official in the room and then, within minutes, more from elsewhere. By now the auditorium had gone silent. The back of my neck was hot; all of the eyes on me seemed to be drilling holes through my skin. From the ceiling, I could hear the whir of the ventilation system and the electric drone from the long banks of overhead lights. Still they all continued to debate my gender, voices low. I heard them say I looked nothing like a girl, dressed nothing like a girl, and therefore could not be one. I heard the Wing Commander laugh.

He began rummaging through his own duffel, pulling out files and envelopes from the depth of athletic clothes folded neatly inside—until he found what he was looking for. He looked up, gave me a calming glance, and I knew. The sheet of paper that had let me play the game in the first place was in his hand. When he handed over my birth certificate, the man who first questioned me sat back, holding up the seal to the overhead lights. Then he made a sound as though he had been punched. One last time, he looked at me, his mouth so round he could have swallowed a *jamun* whole.

A few minutes later, it was all over. Without a word, they handed me my registration badge and a color-coded map of the complex. When I turned, I felt all the girls down the length of the room staring, more than one hundred of them, straight at me. Swinging my bags over my shoulder, I followed in the long footsteps of the Wing Commander as though he were lighting a path.

Outside, I needed to sit awhile. We found a tucked-away spot on a low wall in the trembling shade of a tree. Next to me, but a space away, the Wing Commander faced the sun, eyes closed.

"The moment I met you, Maria, and realized who you were, what you were doing, and then watched as you played all those hours alone, I have thought one thing and one thing only. If you think it too, it will see you through."

"What is that?"

"Simple—it is written."

And my mother's soft voice dovetailed in over his like an echo. She'd said the very same thing to me as I left our home in

Bara Gate. I saw her face as she stood in the doorway, my twin brothers grinning waist-high at her sides, watching me go.

In my room at the girls' hostel, I chose a bed by the door. Still alone, I took off my beaten-up shoes. My feet were hot, and sweat from my hairline dripped down my back. I lay down on the bed, looking around the empty room that I would share with five other girls from all over the country. The space was quiet except for a fat fly buzzing and tapping against the windowpane. Soon, I could hear girls walking up the hall like music rising. Footfalls stopped at the door and it opened. When they came into the room, I was ready—ready to say my name and become a girl among girls. I'd lived the life of a boy among boys so long that I wondered how I would do at behaving like one of them—whatever that meant. I remember hoping that it meant being kind.

The first girl who came in paused, saw my cinder-block feet. Her gaze journeyed up my frame, taking in the trunk of my neck and then my attempt at a smile, which more than any other part of me seemed to astonish her.

"Hello, I'm Maria Toorpakai."

I didn't let her suffer so much as a nanosecond of confusion.

After I said it, the others came in behind her, not looking at me yet, just choosing beds. One cranked open the window at the far end, another zipped open her bag and pulled out a sack of sugar-dusted Turkish delight, which she passed around for the others to share. The first girl was still standing as before, speechless. After a moment, she turned to the others, waiting for them to see what she had seen. I didn't move from the bed, just sat up still smiling, opened my bag, and got out my water bottle to take a drink. I closed my eyes as the cool water quenched my thirst. When I was done, all the girls in the room were looking at me.

Shock moved through my body as though I'd jumped into a cold pool on a hot day. Before me, all I saw were smiles—shy, curious, surprised—without so much as a flicker of disdain. Then, as though lured, they all crossed the long room and converged around me, looking down, asking questions all at once. I had on shorts and a T-shirt, and the first thing they wanted to know was where I'd come by them; then how I'd had the idea for the single stud earring; my short hair—how my family reacted. All of those questions swirling without end, like the ribbons in their hair, led me to a full recounting of my childhood in Waziristan. It was there, in that room, that I first told my story to anyone—born a girl; burned my dresses; lived as Genghis until I picked up a racquet. In the awed silence that hovered, I waited for their curiosity to splinter into hostility—but no such thing happened. I should have known that more than anyone, those athletic Pakistani girls, all of them pioneers in their own way, would accept me as no one else could. When the sack of candies came my way, I took one and passed it to the next girl, and settled right in.

If I remember anything about that first tournament, it's how quickly it ended. The Wing Commander had told me about the prize money just before my first match. As soon as I heard the amount—1,400 rupees—I was flat-out determined to take it all. It was more than the trip had cost, which meant I'd be taking home a profit—a dream so unfathomable I'd never dared to think it. I played a series of games, each lasting bare seconds. My raw, lumbering strength was too much for those small-framed girls. Every time I stepped into the box, I sent my opponent to the ground right behind a lightning-rod shot. If I didn't win a match through a hard serve, I won within a minute of it. None of them saw me coming. Some of them left the court in tears. Others asked again and again if I truly was a girl. I had great compassion for all of my opponents and didn't want to damage what might be the first genuine friendships I ever had. We were all so new to the game. The matches were no more enjoyable for me than for them, so quick you could barely call them matches at all—but I had no choice. I played to win.

On the way home, I had the envelope full of cash tucked into my shirt, arms folded over my chest. I must have checked that envelope a dozen times. Sitting next to me, the Wing Commander grinned. After the team bus dropped us off, he made sure to take me all the way home by rickshaw, watched me go up to the door as Taimur opened it. My tall brother swatted me on the arm, made a funny remark about me wearing his clothes again, looked over my shoulder, and waved. I remember reaching for the rumpled envelope and pulling it out of my shirt. I held it high as the Wing Commander called out a cheer. Then his rickshaw pulled out into the street toward Bara Road, insects swarming behind it in the descending dusk. I found my mother at the kitchen table, hunched over papers, marking math tests, her weariness softly amplified in the dim light. She looked up when I came in, squinting. I was one full day early.

"My Gulgatai, you're back."

She hadn't called me that—her rosebud —in a long while. I remember telling her so.

Before she could get up, I moved over her and looked down at the dozens of sheets of paper fanned out. She still had a red pen in her hand. The young and timid handwriting stood out from the papers as though it were a living thing—each sheet a girl out there in the tribal lands who simply wanted to learn. It struck me then that I was about to do what Pashtun daughters never got a chance to do—with the exception of my own mother, who was at that time an equal breadwinner in our family. It was because of her job teaching for the government education board that we had a nice home in a clean colony in Bara Gate. Looking at me, my mother asked me how I'd done in Wah Cantt, if I'd placed at the tournament. Saying nothing, I opened the envelope, pulled out the rupees, and let them fall like leaves over the papers she'd hauled in a satchel all the way from the tribal lands.

My mother gasped. Then she gathered the money into a small pile and counted. I already knew that she and my father would set aside a portion of my winnings for the poor in an act of charity called *zakat* that is the obligation of every Muslim. Her hands shook and she stared. Her eyes shone, shedding so much worry. She asked me how I'd done it and started laughing. Fourteen hundred rupees wasn't much—maybe thirty US dollars. To our family it was a whole week or more of food. To her it was serenity—she had done well by me, her wayward Gulgatai, after all. To me, it was the whole world.

"How, Maria? How did you do this when you've never even played in a proper tournament before?"

I sat down next to her and smiled. We were both looking at the rupees piled up under the lamplight.

"But you already told me many times, Aami—it is written."

15. The Giver of Treasure

At barely seven, my twin brothers were a force of nature. Born minutes apart—which twin came first was long forgotten—I used to say that one came as lighting and the other as accompanying thunder. When Sangeen and Babrak were home, dishes flew off counters, furniture capsized, doors slammed, and pounding feet seemed to loosen nails. What my small, unbridled brothers needed, at barely twelve years old myself, I could not offer: sweeping valleys, climbing trees, stepping-stone rooftops, the winding Indus from which they came. And so my patience was as boundless as the blue sky I wished to give them—until they broke the one thing I prized and seemed to set off a long spell of bad luck.

After I won the under-thirteen championship in Wah Cantt, I trained at the academy every morning and right through the afternoon. But the demands of home came first, and I was always back early when it was my turn to care for Sangeen and Babrak. On those afternoons, the boys came hurtling home from their public grade school up the road, crashing through the front door, rucksacks upended in cascades of papers and books, sandals strewn into the corridor, hats tossed. Demands for drink, for food, which I gave to them only after they'd washed their hands, said a prayer, and told me one thing they'd learned that day and one kindness they'd given. Taimur, Ayesha, and I took shifts tending to them; my older siblings often needed days to recuperate from whatever catastrophe had transpired on their watch. I understood the wildness of the twins in a way the others couldn't.

We spoke the same unspoken language, harbored the same rampant urge to move, to hit, to play—to win.

When I waited on the road in Bara Gate, I could see them coming home from school at a distance, in a billowing cloud of kicked-up dust, their jubilant shouts preceding them. Pedestrians moved out of the way as they careened down the lane, racing each other, pushing and shoving, always grinning ear to ear and calling out my name. The day I saw Sangeen skulking toward me, school bag weighing his body down to one side as though his shoulders were a scale, I knew right away there was trouble. Sangeen lifted one feeble hand to wave at me; in the other he held a folded slip of pink paper. Then he shrugged, looked to his shoes, the laces undone and dragging—whatever had happened to Babrak, it had nothing to do with him. I was in a rush that afternoon, packing for a trip to Lahore to compete in the Asian Junior Games trials. It was an important tournament, and I'd been training with a medal in my sights for weeks; making it through the first round would secure me a place on the national team and propel my fledgling career: free lodging, real training, transportation, and food. My father was coming with me, and we had to take a bus straight after dinner to make it to my first match the next morning. We couldn't afford a hotel. He still hadn't told me where we would spend the night after the six-hour journey. Maybe he didn't know. If there was one time I needed my twin brothers to cooperate, it was that afternoon. I'd told them so that very morning as I sliced up their boiled eggs and filled their cups with goat milk.

When Sangeen stood before me, he dropped the bag at his feet, face still low. In my cupped hand, I took his chin, which buckled when I lifted it.

"Where is your other half, Sangeen?"

"Babrak was taken to Madam's house as a punishment."

Then he handed me the note with the teacher's name and the address and little more.

"What did he do?"

"A simple game of leapfrog, Maria."

"It can't have been that simple."

And it wasn't. The leapfrog game, brainchild of Babrak, took place at the closing bell, when the teacher left the room. Eager to get out of school ahead of the others, he hopped onto the teacher's desk and scanned the crowd. The clearest way out was along the empty row of desks that stretched before him like a series of stepping-stones. Babrak leapt from one desktop to the next and to the next, all the way around the class—never once looking back at the mess of tossed papers, books, and upended chairs he left in his wake. Reaching the last desk before the door, he hurled his body off the surface and soared right across the threshold—slamming into his teacher, who was just coming back inside.

"You have to save him now, Maria. Our teacher tied him to a chair in her kitchen, and he's just sitting there."

"That is a crazy idea. How do you know?"

"She's done it before. I heard the story and she took him by the ear. I watched them go."

Sangeen turned and pointed.

My father came up the walkway just as I stepped on the Sohrab. Shaking his head as Sangeen repeated his story, not bothering to come into the house, he turned back up the road to fetch Babrak. While he was gone, my mother packed his bag and I folded my clothes for the tournament. Then we all waited. When my father came home, he was hauling a whimpering Babrak. Over his tea, he chuckled through a description of the peculiar scene at the teacher's house. Shown into the kitchen by a dutiful Pashtun son, my father stood in the threshold only to find his own boy red-faced on a stool against the wall, feet dangling—hands indeed tied behind his back. Staring straight ahead and blinking fast, Babrak was repeating multiplication tables, tears running down his cheeks. My father heard the teacher say, "When you know those tables like the back of your hands, only then will I set your hands free." She was sitting at the table right next to Babrak, grading papers. Shams checked the knots, which were so loose around Babrak's wrists they might as well have been oversized bangles. Then he spoke to the teacher, who was unfazed to see her errant pupil's father standing in her kitchen. She offered him a cool yogurt drink and gave a blow-by-blow description of Babrak's antics. When she was done, she untied the boy. My father only nodded and told his son to make amends to his madam. Free at last, Babrak apologized and offered to stay after school for a week to clean the classroom. Then he followed in our father's shadow, cap in one hand, the rope he'd taken a fancy to coiled up in the other. Within a day, he used it to tie his twin to their bed while he slept.

After our family meal, in which Sangeen and Babrak sat, for once, in abject silence, I went to finish loading my duffel. Babrak came into the room not long after me, walking as though the weight of Pakistan proper sat on his coat-hanger shoulders. Stopping before me, he sighed heavily, holding out the palm-sized squash trophy I'd won in Wah Cantt. Made of cut glass, it was a dainty version of the weightlifting cup, and we kept them together on a table in the living room. I often held it like a talisman, wishing for good luck before going to the courts. Cherubic and sullen, Babrak apologized for creating drama before a big tournament. Then he asked to bring the trophy to school to prove that he really did have a squash player for a sister. Within seconds, Sangeen walked in. Saying nothing, he scampered up to the bed I shared with Ayesha and started jumping. I explained to Babrak that the trophy was far too precious a thing for him to take, and offered the tournament certificate in its place. Listening in the background, Sangeen jumped higher, the coils inside the mattress squealing. Behind me, he asked to see the trophy and held up his hands. Just as I turned to tell him to get off the bed, Babrak tossed my prize in an arc right over my head. In the periphery of my vision, I saw the glinting orb pass under the light. High off the bed, Sangeen leapt sideways, but missed the catch by bare millimeters. He hit the floor just as the trophy hit the wall and splintered in two big chunks.

From the threshold, Ayesha saw it all and gasped. In a moment, we were side by side and picking up the pieces. I turned from the bed with an expression I'm sure my brothers did not know me capable of. Each one pointed at the other. I pointed at the door. Then Babrak, his face a knot of guilt and tears, turned and said the thing that seemed to curse me all the way to Lahore and beyond.

"Is it a sign, Ayesha—an omen—a bad one for Maria?"

*

I'd been asleep, head resting on my Baba's soft shoulder, for most of the three-hundred-mile journey to Lahore. As soon as we took our seats on the coach, every part of my body ached from within. My father told me to drink from my water bottle and he rubbed my tired, cracked hands—"Never trust the soft palmed or the loose tongued, Maria."

It was nearly midnight. All around, slumbering passengers sat motionless, sacks in their laps. I looked out at the city, past the market streets and minarets I hadn't seen since I lifted weights as Genghis. I felt him out there in the darkness, the crowd still cheering him on. I smiled; I had trained as hard as I ever had in my life to make the trials. If I made it onto the national team, I wouldn't be going back with my father. The idea didn't frighten me—it made me proud.

Bus journey over, I wobbled through the streets, bleary-eyed, next to my father. To save money, we took a rickshaw only part of the way, and the rest we ambled through the dark quiet, hauling our bags, everything closed. It was a long walk along the old, walled city and through the high archway of Bhati Gate. When I asked him where we were going, he breathed deeply and said one word—"Heaven." Then he pointed.

A huge dome of light up ahead cast hues of teal into the pitch darkness. It was like walking toward a fallen star. As my father and I stepped into the courtyard, acres of white marble met our tired feet like wet ice. I looked over the glistening expanse. Serenity itself—the center of a cloud. The shrine of Data Darbar, one of the most famous in Pakistan, South Asia, or the entire world, visited by thousands—Muslims and non-Muslims—felt holy without requiring any such designation. Everywhere, in mounds over the ground like stones in a lake, people bowed and prayed. Dead center at the far end, a white mausoleum rose majestic; to either side, towers built in the shape of brass bullets stood sentry. A jade-colored vault crowned the shrine as though a hand from the night sky had dropped an upended bowl on the roof. Underneath it, my father told me, were the remains of the saint for whom the shrine was made. Pilgrims were praying all around the tomb. Chanting, crying, and calling out to the dead man inside. Lights strung in the tens of thousands decorated pillars. We simply stood a long while. Eventually, it was the smell of food that lured us away—so hungry, I was already eating the air.

The adjacent mosque was open all hours and served food on festival days to the faithful—whatever their faith. My father found a quiet spot, unrolled a mat, and I waited until he came back with bread and rice and bits of fruit. Then we sat together, watching as though sharing a dream. Scores of people came and went past us like servants in a palace. When we were finished eating, I leaned back against my father's chest. He told me he would stay awake through the night, keeping watch and thinking, as that was the best place for it. I was so tired that my bones ached. In front of us, a group of men crossed the courtyard pounding drums, and all around them a crowd followed, dancing, twirling, and tossing blooms. As they reached the tomb at the far end, some grew wild in their fervor, bending down low and wailing. I felt my father shake his head over me.

"Look at those fools, praying to marble and bones."

"What do they want, Baba?"

"They come all the way here from all over the place to beg for blessings from the saint Ali Hajveri. He was known in his life as the Giver of Treasure, but he's been dead for almost a thousand years."

"Is it wrong we came here to eat and sleep and nothing else? Maybe we should pray."

"We came here to nourish the bodies and souls God gave us. Getting down on our knees over there, Maria, will not make us more pious. Your brightest temple exists within you."

"I will go inside myself then and pray to win my games and be Asian Junior champion."

He laughed and held me tight. "Good luck."

"You don't believe in luck."

"No. Believing in luck is a curse—I just believe. Besides, it is all already written."

A man whom my father would always describe with a single word—"good"—met us outside the squash hostel. Rahim Gul, the national team coach, had a tall, sure gait that brought to mind the Wing Commander. His deep, sonorous voice was like a musical instrument. When he talked with me outside, taking my father's bag and asking about our journey, I felt at home. From the start, he looked after us, sharing his hotel room and his food with Shams. He admired my biceps, my rough hands, which he could see I'd had to tape just that morning to stop the bleeding. He never once made me feel ashamed about my old clothes. I don't think he cared about anything but making sure I had what I needed, and he could see that I needed a great deal. Mostly my body thirsted for rest, but it was too late for that. The first game was in less than an hour.

When I glimpsed my opponent in the tank, I knew we were unevenly matched. At the far end of the court, she stood facing her coach. I watched as they took turns making dizzying hand gestures between them, lips moving in voiceless tandem with their talking fingers. I'd heard of sign language but had never seen it—had never met a deaf person in my life, or expected to on a squash court. Squash is a game of the senses. Tracking the ball starts with the eyes and continues with the ears. Often in the heat of a game you must gauge the position of the ball through sound alone. Right away, I felt at an unfair advantage. I thought then of Babrak splintering my trophy, which I would have caressed before leaving, had it been in one piece. It might have been a bad sign after all—that I would win without having earned it.

From her serve, which shocked me with its precision, we set against each other in a rally that lasted longer than I expected. Immediately I had to change gears in my mind. Whatever her impediment, the girl made up for it in dogged control. After a few minutes of back-and-forth, she tossed me into a race around the tank like a mouse in a cage. When I got the ball, I nailed it. Most of the time, I was a millisecond behind. Best out of five, she tore through the third match in no time. Sensing defeat, I let out shouts and cries that she couldn't hear. Somehow, she had me hog-tied in a full burnout of muscle and mind. The chance for a place on the team evaporated before me. In my growing panic, I played to new lows, diving and tripping over myself. I knew I'd lost long before I actually did.

After that, I lost every game—one after the other. In his patience and capacity as the national team coach, Rahim Gul gave me another chance to run through a series of matches, but I failed again. Despite every ambition, the fissure of doubt that started in my mind during that first match soon tore me right open and settled in. From then on, I was doomed. On the last day of the trials, when the official from the Punjab team federation came out to tell me it was over, my bag was already packed. My father had left after the first day, and I sat outside alone on a bench.

From the direction of the squash facility, I could hear a man calling out. As he moved up the long cement path through the dancing shade, the breeze brought me hints of him before I saw his face. The scent of the courts: hot rubber, sweat, and a sandalwood balm that would always announce Rahim Gul's presence long before he ever came into view.

"What are you doing out here? You're not going anywhere, Maria Toorpakai. In three weeks there is a set of trials for the Asian Games and you will try again."

"Why would you keep me? I do nothing but lose."

"If you say so. I see something else—I see a winner. You can't leave until you see it too."

He had a way of making me smile through tears, and I simply nodded—"Okay."

*

After another long bus ride, north and closer to home, we reached the capital of Pakistan in the rain. Built in the 1960s, Islamabad replaced Karachi as the nation's seat of government in 1966. It was just another big city sprawled out in a backdrop to my dreams, and I remember little of it—my father would surely have been disappointed. The military was on high alert, though I wouldn't have known it at the time. Military checkpoints and tanks had become the wallpaper of Pakistan; soldiers with machine guns at intersections and outside buildings were as common as trees. Their dark presence all over the city foreshadowed nothing to me. In the background, there was a constant chatter of Iraq and the United States. I heard it crackling away on the bus radio—talk of chemical weapons, ceasefires, and UN resolutions. Before long, one of the girls asked the driver to put on music. He balked and turned our speakers off. I remember that when the sound went dead, the thin-boned girl next to me rolled her eyes and said: "If the Americans invade Iraq, we are done for."

But I never asked her what she meant.

Traveling alongside the national team was a muted thrill. For the first time, I ranked lower than an underdog. I knew I was a dead weight. None of the team treated me that way, in part because of my size, which was an endless source of fascination to those lithe girls. At twelve, I was also the youngest. Older girls looked after me in motherly ways I wasn't accustomed to—making sure I bathed, ate well, and went to sleep on time. Part of me enjoyed the coddling, and another part enjoyed nothing at all, because I couldn't seem to win a single match to save my life. Whenever we went into the courts to practice, I got crushed. Still, I didn't give up, not yet. I simply trained longer. Harder than the other girls.

Even more than the Asian Junior championship, the biennial South Asian Games, being held in Islamabad, were steeped in prestige. All I could think about was replacing my broken trophy with something better, my bad luck with good. From the start, it wasn't to be. The moment I stepped into the tank and went up against elite opponents from all over Pakistan proper, they hammered me down like a nail in every single match. Long gone were the days when I sauntered Peshawar taking down boys. In matches of pure brawn, I had beaten thoroughbred street rats. Genghis still lurked under my skin, as he would for life, and I hated losing, not just the matches—but against girls. The irony was not lost on me, but not relevant either. Genghis had been with me far too long, and in the courts he came to life. Still, even he wasn't enough. I was on a losing streak, and every opponent sensed it like an odor coming off my skin. I remember thinking that Rocky Balboa had said that nothing knocked a person down harder than life. He was wrong. There was nothing worse than being a loser—especially after being a winner.

Sheer nerve bearing down, I just kept at it right until the final match, which I thought I might take at last. I'd caught up against a girl from Karachi, point for point and game for game. If I could take her out, I might take another out after her and slip onto the team. A win had been elusive for so long that when I saw just a glimmer of possibility, I chased after it, panting. Then, like an intruder, a single thought, fleeting and lethal, took a jab at me while I met her toe-to-toe—*losing*. And I was back in a tailspin. When the ball swept high overhead, I cranked my neck, springing up. As I reached, pain tore through the muscles along my spine like a meat cleaver, and I went down to the floor like a felled tree. Lying there, looking up at the lights, for several minutes I couldn't move. Coaches came in and cupped their hands to their mouths to warm them, then held their palms against my back, pushing to release the wound-up muscle. Then I sat up, head in my hands—the game was over.

On the bed in the hostel, lying over bags of ice, I believed my time had truly come. I didn't pray to God so much as plead with him—asking why. Alone in a heap, I wept as I never had before. Later, when my back loosened and the girls were all still out, I went downstairs and through the doors—bags already packed and waiting in the lobby. There was a phone in an adjacent house that we were allowed to use to call our families. Before I went there to place a call to Bara Gate, I sat awhile on a bench outside. For weeks I'd longed for anything of home, and shuffled through stills of memories: the front door open and my mother inside it, putting down her bags and opening her arms; twin brothers running down the road, kicking up dust to greet me; Taimur's shy grin; Ayesha's hand so pale, like a bird's wing over mine whenever I cried about anything. And my father, who was home itself. Once again under a tree, on a bench and weeping for my losses, Rahim Gul found me.

"Here we are again, Maria—you thinking you're leaving and me telling you to stay. It's my job to decide. It's your job to play. Stop crying now. Stop crying and get back inside. You're staying to train with the team."

And I did.

Soon after, March 20, 2003, the United States unleashed war against Iraq. Rumors of an invasion had swirled through the corridors like confetti for months. Iraq, two thousand miles away over mountain chains and across deserts, beyond Afghanistan and past Iran to the west, meant absolutely nothing to me. All that mattered was winning a medal—and I'd failed at the trials. When the invasion started, it was televised the world over. I still remember people huddled around small TV sets, watching. Explosions over Baghdad bloomed onscreen in huge clouds of debris that flashed as though they had swallowed lightning. I remember wondering, as I made my way to and from the courts, if they were swallowing people too. Hardly anyone spoke. People just wandered the hallways. Some had already packed up and left. All of that silent foreboding made no sense to me until my roommates filed into our room and started pulling clothes from drawers, all of them weeping. I just sat on the bed, a bag of pistachios in my hand, watching them until one turned and told me to arrange for my bus ticket home.

"The Americans have invaded Iraq, Maria."

"So?"

"The games have been postponed."

"Why?"

"I don't know. It's like World War Three—that's what everyone says. In a few months, we will have to come back and do it all over again."

"Do what over again—the trials?"

"Yes. It's a disaster."

Not for me. My child's mind truly believed for weeks afterward that Allah had intervened so that I could try again. He'd heard my wailing whys and realized that he didn't have a good answer. Rahim Gul had also been coaching me at every chance; sometimes we played a match just for the fun of the game and nothing else. He told me that winning is a process, not an event, and that as soon as I believed him, I would start to win. The moment I got that miracle second chance, I knew that I would—after all, Allah would only start a war for a winner.

*

Months later, after Saddam Hussein was caught in a rathole, the games were rescheduled and I was in my right mind again. There isn't much to say about the matches, apart from the fact that I beat nearly every opponent in my division and finally made the Pakistani team. For the first time since before burning the dresses, I had new clothes of my own. Even now, I remember everything about those clothes—the smell of the cotton pulled from the crinkling paper; the fabric so pristine I didn't dare unwrap all of it for days. Piles of shirts, sweatpants, and socks. The feel of the cotton touching my skin was like a soft kiss. I had been welcomed, clean and ready, to a new life, the filth from my past all gone. I belonged somewhere. More than anything, I felt like a champion.

And I was. A fanfare of parades, speeches, television crews, and cheering crowds opened the games. All I thought about was going home with a medal to replace the broken trophy that had started me on my losing streak in the first place. In razor-close matches against top-tier players from all over South Asia, I won two medals—a bronze for the individual matches, silver as a team. I didn't win just because I was a better player; I won because

I knew finally that I could, my coach cheering me on from the sidelines. When he came up to me, jumping and clapping his hands, I saw myself as he did—at last.

This time, it was my father I saw when I came in with my bags. I'd come back home to tell my family in person that I'd placed well. He was dozing in a chair in the front room, papers in his lap, open books strewn all over the floor, a cup of cold tea on the table next to him. The house was silent, as though it had been sleeping the entire time I was gone, stopping time and just waiting for me. It had been months since I'd been home, and I stood there a long time in my team clothes, relishing the feel of it. Before I'd left Islamabad, a man had dropped off a government letter at the hostel, announcing that a cash prize would be awarded with our medals. Reading it over many times, it took most of the bus ride home for me to believe it. I had won more money than I could fathom—three thousand five hundred US dollars. When I tried to imagine what that amount would look like in cash, I couldn't. The envelope was folded in my pocket, the paper already going soft and tearing along the seams from constant touching. This time, I wasn't paying just for a bit of food for the family—I was helping to pave a whole future.

As I crossed the room, my father stirred. When he saw me there, he just looked at me, blinking as though still halfway in a dream.

"I've come home with a surprise, Baba."

Opening the envelope I'd placed in his lap, he read the letter and nodded. I could have gone all the way to London and brought back the crown jewels in a carpet bag, and I doubt he would have even blinked. He asked me to bring fresh tea. I came back with two steaming cups and we sat together in the quiet house, waiting for the others.

"Rahim Gul is a good man, Maria. He called and told me that you asked him why he had you stay there when you had given nothing but losses."

"Yes."

"Do you remember what they called the saint buried at the shrine in Lahore?"

"The Giver of Treasure."

"Right."

"It's why we could eat and sleep in his house."

"Sometimes, a person has a pearl buried in their soul, and they need to find a giver—except the precious thing they give is a thing you already have. Until we encountered Rahim Gul, I thought that was my job alone. It was a strange thing, finding out that another man could do what I had always done. Then I realized what he'd done for you, he'd also done for me."

"It was actually very simple, Baba. He said I had a loser mentality. I just had to find my winning mentality."

"Exactly. And now you know the power of a thought. There is no bomb that can match it."

"It was bombs that gave me a second chance at the games."

"No. When you walked in here and I saw you, I thought just one word."

"What was that, Baba?"

"Treasure. And I had no idea about your prize money. You look like what you are at last—and we owe it to him."

Later, when Sangeen and Babrak gifted me my glued-up trophy, the crack bleeding dried gobs of glue, I thanked them and put it on the table next to my new medals. For years, until it was lost in a move, it sat there untouched. In fact, I never touched anything for luck again—just went out the door and got to my game.

16. Number One

Rahim Gul was right: winning was a process—a state of mind. Sometimes I secured it only after a nail-biting inner conflict; at other times, victory slipped into my palm like fallen fruit. It began as a mantra when I walked on court, feeling it braid into my body as I paced the walls—priming muscle and reflexes even before I spun my racquet. The same held true for becoming a champion, the ultimate player, a dream that first stirred when I put on my team colors—green blazer, white dress, polished black shoes—for a tea party at the home of the president of Pakistan. The president had invited my team to celebrate our South Asian victories. The elaborate invitation came on embossed paper so thick my father said he could use it to shave.

I'd buffed the leather of my elegant shoes, the smell of polish like gun oil, until the tips flashed. Long-sleeved, hem falling below the knees, the first dress I'd worn since my bonfire felt like wearing a bag. When my family, assembled in the kitchen going about their daily routines, saw me, they all froze. Taimur put down a screwdriver and pulled a hand from the gutted Philips radio in front of him. My father put down his pliers. My mother stepped away from the counter, hands rushing to her cheeks as though to keep her head from falling off. Ayesha dropped a pen, Babrak a slingshot. Sangeen just laughed out loud, doubled over, and pointed at me.

In the days leading up to the event, I heard stories about the presidential palace looking like a multi-tiered wedding cake sitting high on a hill at the end of a long four-lane drive. A thousand windows. A hundred rooms. Gold-plated faucets. Elevators. A house right out of a movie. I couldn't wait to see it. Instead, the team bus veered fourteen miles south of the capital and took us up a short, narrow drive to a humdrum two-story building in the sister city of Rawalpindi. President Pervez Musharraf, military dictator in power since 1999, lived at the austere Army House. Someone said he went to the palace only to sign papers and call superpowers. No matter, the venue was a letdown. Going up the walkway to the garden where the party was already underway, I looked up at the house. Snipers along the rooftop, machine gun nests on the ground. Barred windows, barbed wire, and a satellite dish. To me, a Pashtun who'd been raised under the codes of tribal law—and had made the national squash team by the skin of her teeth—the dictator was just a curiosity.

Huge white tents had been set up outside. Pots of flowers, blooms spilling over. Uniformed servants floated among the guests, offering colorful bites of this and that from trays like exotic islands—samosas, patties, cakes, and sweets. My father and I enjoyed ourselves in a style we had never known—nibbling luscious food from china plates, dressed in finery, the pleasant cacophony of idle chitchat playing all around us like foreign music. I remember watching my father in his starched clothes and handsome Pashtun waistcoat, the way his hands moved when he talked, fingers swimming through the twilight. Standing among the crowd in his high decorative turban he showed no sign of the starstruck nerves I watched distort the faces of everyone else around us when the president moved over the manicured lawn as though it were an inspection line—as though he were a king—dainty porcelain teacup in his hand.

When it was our turn in the lineup, I remember standing next to my Baba, studying Musharraf as they exchanged pleasantries like business cards. I'd seen that dark face in the newspaper, heard his voice on the radio. The perfectly groomed black hair, markings of white up his sideburns and just over his ears on either side, so like feathers. His position should have transmuted him from man to lion, but he wasn't much taller than I was. The brief encounter under a white tent, towers of fruit and vases of birds-of-paradise as a backdrop—it was all so casual. I wonder now if my father wasn't chewing off his own tongue as they bantered about my wins at the games in Islamabad. Just the day before, my father had slipped in and out of the cauldron of violence brewing in the tribal belt to get to a lecture hall whose occupants were diminishing by the hour. The man he was speaking to through a serene veil of late summer was more than just a witness to history; he was one of its masters, the man in charge— and already losing his grip. As we sipped and chatted, militants were swarming the region like hornets. If my father could have said anything, anything at all, I'm sure he would have started with—*I could have told you so.*

Musharraf spoke to me about my game. It was the same conversation, repeated over and over again as he walked the soft grass. All those wide-eyed athletes clung to the tip of his tongue, though I doubt he would remember a single name. He had a gleaming smile that appeared so genuine; for a few seconds, it enveloped me. My father had warned me of the politician's first weapon: the brighter the smile, he said, the sharper the knife. In many ways, President Musharraf seemed like an affable man without a care in the world, but under that crisp uniform he'd strapped himself into a ten-pound bulletproof vest. Guards front and back carried sub-machine guns. Rumor had it that he kept cyanide pills in a hidden pocket over his sidearm. Still, none of these measures would make a bit of difference against that one bullet or one bomb in the right place at the right time. Musharraf's enemies were relentless. They could afford to try and fail as many times as it took to finally kill—he could not afford to fail once. At that very moment, militants—hunkered down in the Abode of God, scattered over valleys, cloaked in camps outside remote villages—were thinking up dramatic ways to kill him. If they could, they'd just mete out his punishment the old-fashioned way and tear him limb from limb. Suicide recruits were lining up by the hundreds for the chance to stuff backpacks full of explosives and blow him to smithereens. His crimes were simple and abominable—a pawn of the infidels in the West, he'd let his army and theirs run roughshod over the region. What began as a security mission to rout out Al Qaeda and their Taliban hosts was brewing into a full-blown jihad. If history could choose a winner, it wouldn't be the man I heard asking a girl if she'd enjoyed the cake. Though I liked him enough, I saw him for what he was: flesh and blood, slightly pudgy, fingerprints smudging his frameless glasses. Within less than a minute, he looked past me, and with a shift in the breeze, President Musharraf was gone, clanking away in his green uniform, guards at his side. All evening I could see that flashing grin as he made his way from tent to tent, entourage following his every move like a gaggle of birds in military clothes. When I got home to Peshawar, all I told my mother about was the food.

*

Into the heart of a cloud, white as ice caps over the Suleiman Range, I held my breath. Tears of condensation streaked the oval window; maybe it was rain. At thirty thousand feet, it was hard to tell. I took in every detail: the movement of the flaps as we shed altitude, the slight tip of the long, gleaming wing out my window, the way the sky showed through every now and again in winks of pure blue. Far below us—an expanse of thousands of miles—nothing but ocean. The plane shook, tossed us about gently. I felt my ears pop and swallowed hard, looked to the girl next to me and we laughed. Then, in an exhilarating flash, the plane shot like a fist out of the vapor and into clean sunshine. I let out a small sound of exultation, whispered a *sura*, and offered a prayer miles above the earth—as close to heaven as I'd ever been.

First time on a plane. First time out of Pakistan. Traveling with my team—we all had seats together across several rows. Hurtling and rattling up the runway, I'd felt the takeoff in my belly and was unafraid. I thought of my mother in the doorway early that morning, shawl wrapped about her shoulders. Sleep still all over us like mist, she touched my face. The awe was already there, ideas she could not fathom—while she sat on a ramshackle bus, detouring skirmishes in a hotbed of holy war, the daughter before her would be airborne in a giant silver bird. Unfathomable heights. Spellbinding speeds. Different part of the planet entirely.

The night before, our entire family had gathered around a map of South Asia, my father on his knees, an index finger tracing my journey. It seemed like a stone's throw—down Pakistan, slicing across India, sweeping over the Bay of Bengal. Over mountain ranges and rivers, dictators and holy shrines, all the ills and graces of humanity reduced to pinpricks. A stop in the Philippines, and then over the South China Sea to Malaysia. Places, my mother whispered, she would only read about for the rest of her life. A hand still on my cheek, she looked past me to the open door, sounds of morning in Bara Gate just rising. She was letting me go—"I give you to God."

Silver wings dipping into a long glide over the Bay of Bengal, whose waters married into the Andaman Sea—the ancient trade route between India and China—my father's backyard laundry basin world came to life as it had only in my childhood imagination when we pretended to sail the ancient seas in avocado hulls. I peered out, forehead pressed against the glass. Small mounds of islands like dropped stones. Whitecaps lay scattered over the teal water like miniature boomerangs. A wave. I'd never seen one. Never once heard its storied roar. And yet there they were—scattered below me, silent and waiting as far as the eye could see.

Coastline ahead, a giant hand rising through mist. Boats on the water. Low enough now that I could discern individual things: palm trees, a long ribbon of white beach, people dotted over it like ants. Thatched rooftops hemmed the sand, dwellings borrowed from a fable. Lush greenery. I kept thinking, *People live down there*. Paradise. Everything I thought about the future changed in that instant; it was like finding out I was going to live for ten thousand years. I sat back as the landing gear cranked out of the carriage and waited to touch the earth.

My team was all around me—the best female players in

Pakistan. Malaysia was a first for all of us. In Pakistan, we were antagonists, fought huge battles in the court—shouting at each other and hurling balls to the ground. The girls could be just as hotheaded as the boys. When it was over, we barely looked at each other. In the court, opponents weren't people. Not to me, not to them. They were pieces in a game, like checkers on a board—the only true adversary I ever played against was myself. Out there, I harnessed Genghis, often receiving warnings from the referees for my theatrical tirades. Back in the hostel with those girls, I was Maria Toorpakai, teammate, and the thing I'd never truly been before to anyone—friend.

Up against top-tier teams from all over the world, we weren't expected to play well and didn't—it wouldn't have mattered if we had never got off that plane. But even more than winning together, losing together brought us closer as a team. At the end of another punishing set of matches, we would meet in our rooms and share the suffering of our humiliations. Malaysia brought us up against a stark new reality: female players in Pakistan were third-class athletes. We were staying in a hostel; the boys were in hotels. We scrounged to pay our expenses; the boys had precious few. For the first time, I recognized that playing well and winning accolades wasn't going to be enough. I had to make them see me—and I would.

*

Whenever I came home from a tournament anywhere, my family welcomed me as though I had left just the hour before. It was their way. In the absence of a telephone or reliable mail, I had to take care of logistics on my own. When I packed my bags and left the house, I was simply gone—no looking back—sometimes for months at a time. My mother always kissed me when I came back in. My father would look up from his chair, from a map, from a radio.

You been playing squash again? Get the atlas.

My parents had no idea how to play the game and were never able to come watch a match together. My father saw me play just once in Lahore. It was already a miracle that I wasn't out running amok in the streets or living in purdah in a mud hut. Years later, it amazed me to learn how Western parents obsessed over the athletic achievements of their children. Mine simply didn't have that luxury—they were dodging bullets and bombs just to get to work. To get to my games would also have cost money we simply didn't have in travel expenses alone. We were all too busy trying to survive day to day. Though I didn't know it yet, our circumstances were slipping over a cliff. In 2005, tensions in the tribal belt tightened a thousand notches—Talibanization was spreading like a brush fire.

When people think of the Taliban, they think only of Afghanistan, when in fact it is a monolithic term used to describe a group of factions with separate histories, ideologies, and agendas. As I was building a squash career, the still nameless Pakistani Taliban was just taking root, gathering armies. Leaders killed off rival tribal elders, increasing their reach and galvanizing their intent. They harvested soldiers from disgruntled tribal factions in the valleys and mountains I still called home. Enemy Number One was the Pakistani army and government, who were conducting military operations against pro-Al Qaeda and pro-Taliban forces. Whole contingents of government troops armed to the teeth had already swept into the Tirah Valley of the Khyber Agency. Over time they moved further into the beating heart of FATA, into the Shawal Valley of North Waziristan, and soon after crossed into South Waziristan. Paranoid subtribes saw those maneuvers as a veiled attempt to subjugate them. Then, in October of 2006, a missile blew up a Muslim religious seminary, in Chenagai village in the region of Bajaur. Boys as young as twelve perished in the attack. Many people pointed their fingers at a US drone, though the Pakistani military took responsibility at the time. No matter. Innocent children lay scattered in pieces. Villagers wanted revenge. They would get it. Within eight days, eighty-five miles northwest of Islamabad, a suicide bomber blew himself and forty-two Pakistani soldiers up in Dargai. After that, it was total war.

And in the midst of it all, my parents took the bus, and when the buses stopped going into the mountains, they took the pick up. In and out every day—my father to teach classes in colleges here and there and my mother still a principal on the outskirts of Darra Adam Khel. Walls rattled against the bombs exploding in the mountains as my father taught groups of wide-eyed students the mechanics of combustion; my mother read fairy tales aloud to a kindergarten class whose teacher simply stopped coming— and for a brief moment they all forgot there even was a war.

*

Riding home on my bike that day, I came upon my father sitting in the front doorway, halfway out and halfway in. He looked up at me, his face covered in dust, as though only just realizing where he was: at home, safe and sound, in Bara Gate, all of his children but me still in their schools up the road. We went inside and I saw his feet, one shoe missing, small cuts on his calf. He had a slight limp. Satchel nowhere to be seen. Slumped down in a chair, fingers traveling his legs as though to make sure they were still there—or to hide the tremble that I could just make out when I brought him his tea. He spoke in a grainy whisper.

"It's gone."

"What is, Baba?"

"The college. First they came and took all of my instruments. Then they set off explosives. All that's left is a crater. How was your day, Maria?"

I didn't answer.

Deliberately, he asked again and sat back.

So I droned on, taking in his filthy clothes, the tears in his shirt. How strange to see him without his bag full of books— his treasure—as though he'd lost a limb. I told him that I had just changed sponsors from the air force to the army squash academy and wasn't happy about it, but it would mean a bigger stipend. The Wing Commander had broken the news and said he was giving me an opportunity and them a gift. My father nodded, motioning with his hands for me to continue. I talked about the tournaments I was playing, that I was ranked third, sometimes second. He coughed a few times, dust coming off him, hands scratched as though he'd clawed his way out of the earth. I gasped.

"My hands still look better than yours do, Maria. Keep going, don't stop for what you see. I'll get to that later—a few decades from now."

Door flying open, my twin brothers came rolling in. Fighting. Exchanging insults. One had the other in a headlock. They scrapped over the floor. Not quite teenagers yet. Their voices still high and piercing. When they saw our father there, they stopped in their tracks. Sangeen opened his mouth to speak, but I raised a hand and signaled for them both to leave the room—letting them know I'd brought home samosas from the market. As they went out, I noticed how tall they were getting, how broad in the shoulders. Not so long ago, they were half my height, came at night to wake me, and sat in my lap. From his corner, my father also watched them go.

"What is it they do after school, Maria—when they come home?"

"They eat, Baba. Make noise. Make messes. That's about it."

"Do they go out?"

"Sometimes. I don't know where."

"Not good. Take them to play with you. You'll need them one day, and they will need you."

They had their own bicycles—rusted red—nearly as fast as mine under their eleven-year-old feet. Up the main street, lengths of rope keeping racquets strapped to their backs, we rode across town. Gliding in and out of the lanes of traffic as a trio, I held out my arms to signal turns. Along the boulevard, through the market. Past men leading donkeys hauling carts full of firewood, the kebab sellers, the cobbler's shop. Past men huddled under a bridge smoking hashish. Past pale addicts, and holy men shouting out verses. Past the rich in their silks and the poor in their tatters—all of Peshawar in beautiful blinks of color. Every few seconds, I looked back to see my brothers, racing each other, racing the wind, their laughter rising over the welter. Then I looked ahead again, into the sun, and for that one moment, a golden memory even before it was over, I loved my city as I loved those boys.

For weeks, we rode that way to the squash complex, and I showed them how to play the game, hoping it would take hold before something else did. In the courts, they fooled around behind me—dueling each other, their racquets clattering. Caged in the court, their savagery seemed amplified. They hit the ball into each other to settle scores, wild accusations of senseless cheating, mouths full of insults. Sometimes I just set them to running the tank, lap after lap around the perimeter, to keep them apart. By the end of the day, they were a savage mess on the ground, all kicks and slaps and groans, until I hauled them both by the scruff. I'd had enough. The next week, Sangeen went to play tennis; Babrak asked to stay with me.

Huddled in the court without distraction, Babrak took right away to the game. The day he served the ball and split it in two, I knew he and I were one and the same. Of the two twins, he was the smaller, the one the Indus almost took back. When my parents had put them side by side on the bed, we could see that Sangeen had robbed most of the food inside my mother's belly— one full head bigger, his lungs filled like balloons. And pathetic Babrak—in his twin's greedy shadow—all feeble wishbones, arms so thin I was afraid to lift him in case they snapped. Fast-forward over a decade to a squash court—and there he was before me, splitting balls.

Just as I was seeing the babe in the boy, the corridor was suddenly dark. A bulb in the ceiling flickered, went out, went back on. It was dark as a cave for a few seconds, and I heard Babrak make a sound like the cooing of a dove. The vents chugged air, games still pounding away in the other courts. Someone yelled out a score. I saw the janitor, almost spectral, skulk past like a shadow, bucket clanging, mop in one hand and a wave from the other— it's peculiar to me even now how minute details embedded themselves like shrapnel. From that day on, I would understand what westerners meant when they said they could recall every horrifying second of 9/11. Then, from above us, ripping into the flickering quiet, the earth let out a massive groan. The air seemed to heave. There and gone again. What was it? We heard a man shout out. Then another. Then dozens. People ran into the corridor. A voice in my head said: *Something is happening*. Then Babrak dropped his racquet. He looked at me and said "Thunder." I knew better.

Outside, nothing but sirens. I yelled at Babrak to move and get on his bike. He was on the walkway looking up. Immobilized. In the sky, a thick plume of dark smoke rushed up, blooming over us. I'd seen that very thing before—on television screens in Islamabad. Babrak was still gawking. I hollered one thing to him to make him wake from his stupor—*"BOMB!"*—and our world changed in the blink of an eye.

Amazing what you can get used to: human beings who were turned into living weapons and let loose among us like a plague— not every day or every week, but often enough at first that people lived on edge at all times. We never found out what happened that afternoon—just that a man had wandered toward a mosque and blown himself up. No one died, just him—as far as we knew. Babrak and I were pumping away from the black spout of smoke, mouths open, sucking down air in a panic, me shouting back to my brother—"Faster, faster, faster!" When we got home, the radio was on. Ayesha and my father were standing over the table in the kitchen, papers fanned out, map of FATA unfurled. They were staring at it as though for a clue to some profound mystery. Ayesha was always working on articles, making speeches in Islamabad, researching university papers. When they saw us soaked in fear in the threshold, we didn't have to say a word.

We got to know the signs and sounds: distant thunder, questioning faces. Was it the sky, or a combusting soldier of jihad? When it was thunder, people touched their hearts and laughed. When it wasn't, they spoke in whispers, spoke to God, and rushed home. War turned the streets into a rumor mill. I tried not to listen. My father was specific: come and go; never linger;

take the backstreets; stay away from hotels, bazaars, crowds. Some of the bombers were so doped up, they could barely walk in a straight line. In those cases, rumor had it, a remote detonator was used. The sober mastermind watching from a rooftop waited until his stoned game piece got close enough—into a crowded bazaar, a mosque, a bus—then dialed a number on his cell phone. Sometimes we went weeks and heard nothing, and I would think a bleak phase in the life of Peshawar was over. I was wrong. We were all in the middle of a jihad that was just getting warmed up.

*

Peace came with the game I played—and I was playing well, all over the country, all the time. In 2006, while the world around me seethed, I turned professional and continued to play tournaments throughout the continent; meeting my team at the training camps and then leaving together on a plane or a bus; winning medals; making money for the family; coming home to Peshawar and holding my breath. I was the best player on the team—hands down. Coaches from elite clubs called me Jahangir Khan, after the legendary Pakistani squash player and former world champion, for my nuclear hitting style.

Looking back now, it was a miracle that anyone did anything at all—played sports, went to school—but we did. The sun came up in the main street, shops and restaurants opened, banks and businesses unlocked their doors. We washed and prayed—a moat of hope between us and *them*, to make it through the day without carnage. We had to. I played squash; Ayesha studied for her bachelor's degree in international relations; Taimur and the boys still went to their local schools—and driving the dusty roads, my parents went right into the badlands of the tribal region, fearless, into the mouth of war every morning. They taught the young who were still willing in an act of bravery that bound them to their students more than any holy ceremony or their shared ancient ancestry ever could.

Under those circumstances, reaching the top of the rankings wasn't a glorious moment; in many ways it passed me by. For four years, I'd been winning in my divisions steadily, one tournament at a time, concentrating on the individual match, never looking beyond what was happening in the court, wherever it was: another town, another country, another world—Hong Kong, Singapore, Cairo, Kuala Lumpur. Sometimes I saw my name listed in the newspaper, the occasional picture of me holding a medal buried in the sports pages, and I remember feeling something—as proud as I dared. Think too much and you start to lose—I knew that already.

Since 2005, I'd been making several thousand rupees per month playing for the army, and later the WAPDA (Water and Power Development Authority). When I played in the National Games against the top players from all over Pakistan—army, navy, air force, banks, provinces—I won two gold medals: as an individual and as a member of my department team. On the board at those games, I was ranked first in the country. I saw that with some measure of awe, then pushed the thought aside. I was there to play a particular opponent and beat her, and I did. I was on a long, steep road. Squash was all I had—home was all I thought about.

But you didn't go home after winning a medal, only to find out your mother's school had been bombed to the ground, and think of telling her how well you did in your tournament. Or tell her you were number one. Or tell her anything at all.

Just like my father, she sat a long time, drinking tea and staring out. She waited as though contemplating a terminal diagnosis. Then she said another one was gone—matter-of-fact. Eventually, the education board would send her elsewhere. She knew FATA like the back of her hand, hardly needed a map. As long as there were girls—even just one in a room with a thirsty brain—she would be there.

Most of the schoolhouses left in FATA were small brick-and-mortar buildings with few rooms, flags hanging outside until it was too dangerous, girls inside—shades were drawn if they had them. Some girls came on buses from many miles away, until militants popped off the drivers as though it were sport. To be fair, they issued warnings first: anyone caught behind the wheel of a school bus would be killed. The militants made good on their promise, usually from a great distance with a shot to the head. Sometimes the assassins simply climbed aboard the vehicle and dragged the man out, beat him senseless, then shot him— small faces all watching the scene unfold at the side of a dirt road, every detail going home, better than a bloodcurdling edict. In Waziristan, dozens of schools had already closed without explosives in just that way: shooting the adults in front of them was a perfect way to keep the girls from coming back, keep them in *burqas*, behind four walls.

*

My mother and I were home within minutes of each other, from opposite ends of Pakistan, separate ends of the earth. She sat down, drained her teacup, put her elbows on the table, and let her *chador* fall away. None of it made much sense to me. I'd been living inside a brightly lit box for hours every day; I took a bus back, slept most of the way. From another room, we could hear my father fiddling with the radio—not music anymore, just the news. Lately, they'd been going to work in FATA together, my mother always in the rear bed while my father drove. There was no radio in the car, which surely must have driven my father mad. Music was *haram*—forbidden. "What's next?" my father said. "Air?" They'd shoot you if they heard a single note. To be safe, he'd pulled the whole contraption right out of the dashboard.

As she sat there, breaths of the valley came off her clothes as though a nostalgic wind had perfumed her in my childhood—pine and clean river, mountain and mimosa. I brought her more tea—it's all I felt good for.

"How do they do it, Aami? They just blow it up?"

"They left a note first. Some of the schools have chalkboards outside; the girls learn well under the sky. They found our chalk. The spelling was very bad."

"What did it say?"

She was living it again before me—I could see it: trudging up the hill to the stone schoolhouse anchored to the rocky plain; small children gathered all around the defaced board. One of the younger ones said they should make corrections before Madam arrived. Another muttered that they should leave it as it was for her to see.

"It said: 'We are going to bomb this school. If you go in and die, your death is your own to answer for.'"

"Did you go in?"

"No. The girls had a math exam the day before that hadn't been graded. We could see the pile on my desk from one of the windows. I thought of going in, only for a second, just for the tests. They'd worked hard. I'd promised candy."

"But you did not."

"I did correct the board—the spelling. I thought: *Let them see me do that*. I knew it's what Shams would have done. Then we went down the hill fast, fifty girls at least running around the rocks. When it came, it was fast. Like a giant wave. And all the girls fell."

"And the schoolhouse?"

"Gone—like the ground just swallowed it."

"What did you do?"

"We were all scattered all over the ground like seeds. What could we do? We saw the smoke. We all cried. The girls went home."

"Did you see who did it?"

"There is no who, Maria—there is just a *them*. No faces, no souls—they are bombs and bullets and cries to Allah in the mountains."

In a moment, she leaned down and rummaged in her bag. Fishing out a stack of papers, she asked me to fill her cup. I could see the rank equations from where I was sitting—the young handwriting like pleas in the dark. And then she took out her red pen.

17. In the Crosshairs

People said they carried long knives for skinning and slitting throats. Whole villages were at their mercy, entire territories trapped under the ruthless fist of full-blown jihad. Tiptoeing treacherous terrain as though it were a playground, they picked off Frontier Corps and Pakistan Army officers like grouse, lured whole contingents into booby-trapped towns, where oblivious soldiers spread out into a labyrinth of empty dwellings packed with TNT. While the soldiers searched for them in vain, the Talibs slithered into a crude network of tunnels, coming out into the camouflage of nearby hillsides. There they'd wait with their detonators, bellies low to the ground, coolly calculating as the army cleared house after empty house, useless weapons at the ready—and when they'd ensnared a good number, giving a signal and blowing them all up. Elder tribesmen who stood against them were quickly done away with, usually out in broad daylight, the methods involving high degrees of pain and enough blood on the ground to make an indelible point. Starting out as many cells fighting for the same cause, they married into a single cruel and unrelenting force—the Taliban in Pakistan—and whatever prize they sought, they were winning.

Frequently now, men stopped in to speak to my father in the living room—old neighbors from our long-lost valleys in South Waziristan, others from all over the war-ravaged region. By now my family were living in a different house—I had my own room—not far from the last, nestled in a colony full of carpet-bagger Pashtuns like ourselves. It was a better home, with more space and among our own people, a move that was made possible through my mother's continued work for the education board. We called the neighborhood Little FATA, and you would think just from the people all jabbering away in Pashto and sipping tea on jeweled mats that we were back there again. Rumors spiraled up from those mats and hovered in the room like motes of dust—girls dropped in acid vats, pilotless birds dropping bombs into schools. People went missing in the night; whole villages vanished.

Every time I passed the front room on my way out, I heard the clink of cups, sibilant sounds of men sipping, the rich bass of my father's voice rising above the rest; more often than not, I also heard the word "Taliban" and my mind cleaved—to men lurking in alleys smoking scorpion tails and to the war in Afghanistan. I didn't know there were many rings of Taliban, stretched over FATA in a linked chain of common hatreds and shared ideals, just as there were many strains of viruses. Once they fused into a single deadly hydra, they took the name Tehrik-i-Taliban Pakistan—Taliban Movement of Pakistan—and they weren't just at our back door anymore. On our streets, burrowed in houses, roaming the refugee camps collecting recruits, the Taliban had been with us for a while, hunkered down and armed to the teeth for a long, cut-throat battle. What all those contingents had in common was a bloodthirsty pursuit of holy ideals: ridding sacred land of invading infidels—Pakistani military, government, the heretic West—while imposing their own extreme interpretation of Islam on the population. People said Taliban combatants had infiltrated every corner of Peshawar. Even more deadly than the ineluctable lure of their hatred, their most effective weapon was their ability to blend in—as filthy vagrants and affable fruit sellers, cobblers, scholars, the young boy next door, the man loitering at a corner; one of them could be right there, sitting among us in our front room, just listening in, gathering up information and marking the names of people to pick off later. My father sat talking, sifting out loud from the wild tales of the Taliban's unimaginable cruelties what was true from what could not be. Some of it he'd seen for himself. What was true was that the Taliban had gained more than just pure ground—they'd consolidated while the government and army blundered, and were running the show not fifty miles away.

"They have a special bomb that kills only impure women. They shot it into a village near Bannu, and only one female survived. Her they gave to the mullah for his wife."

"Impossible"—my father scoffed.

"A girl was caught showing her face at a window and they took her into the market, held her down, and beat her to death."

"True," my father said. "It's why they paint the windows black."

*

Bombs every Friday without fail—our holiest day of the week, like Sunday to a Christian or every day to a Buddhist. Each time the roar and rumble came, everyone stopped, looked to the sky for the telltale plumes of acrid smoke. It got so the day arrived, the sun dragging terror behind it, and the populace braced itself for the inevitable attempts at slaughter. Soon, there were attacks on other days of the week, more frequent and more elaborate—car bombings, kidnappings, and suicide attacks in the markets where women shopped. Second-nature survival habits emerged, as though awakened from some vestigial part of the brain. We scanned crowds along the main streets, checking from the safety of their fringes for a suspect backpack, for anyone walking too deliberately, mouth muttering a vicious prayer, or for the doped-up vagrant, weapon concealed in layers of grime, who had no idea as he zigzagged down the vendors' stalls that he had a short-term job as a mass murderer. We had to go out to buy things. Going into the bazaars and along the market streets suddenly became acts of faith. Faith alone was what kept people going.

In high school, my brother Taimur grew as pious as Ayesha. Every morning, he rose and washed himself with soap and warm water filling the sink upstairs—Fridays especially. I could hear him on the other side of the door: muted splashing, furious lathering, hands foaming, the way he sometimes whispered to himself in the gray light as though already halfway into his prayers. When he emerged, he was dressed in his white *shalwar kameez* and a soft grin:

"You have your racquet, Maria, and I have my Quran."

We hadn't played squash together in years. Plunged into his teens, Taimur went to school, met up with friends, became my father's apprentice—fixing things with duct tape, rebuilding radios, reading maps, and losing himself in books. Immersed in my game, I traveled the country and was gone sometimes weeks at a time, training at the academy in Peshawar, playing matches, accumulating medals, getting to number one in the rankings, bringing home a check when there was one—doing my fair share in unfair times. Between us, things hadn't been as they were before—his reckless brother Genghis, my silent guardian shadow. No argument, just a distancing as he went about the business of becoming a man. Agile. Tall. Superior. He'd used the racquet like a broom, sweeping me right across the hard floor as I scuttled after the ball. The last time we played, I was still a beginner. It was only our second week in the courts together, and I lost three games in a row, not a single point in my favor. I stood there, racquet at my feet, as he drank from his can of Fanta; every rise and fall of his Adam's apple as he gulped was an insult, and I seethed. Lowering his head, he saw my pinched face and raised his arm, can proffered in consolation: "Why so angry? I'm a boy—of course I beat you. I always will."

On little more than impulse, I sauntered over and sledge-hammered a fist into his solar plexus, felt that familiar wishbone cracking of the knuckles that would leave me sore for days; heard him let out a quick shock of air, the *clink-clink* of the tin can denting. Taimur stepped back, shook his head to brush off the blow like a sudden chill. He coughed a little, reached out, and shoved me once, not hard. We looked at each other. Then he just laughed and got his racquet, left me the last of his drink.

Now we were alone together in the kitchen, a halo of soap surrounding his polished skin. Through the shy light of daybreak, he held out a small pomegranate to me, like a forgotten memory of a time and place lost to us forever. Childhood. Pomegranates were costly and hard to come by, and I hadn't tasted one of those ruby seeds in years. I sliced the fruit open, offered him his half, which he refused, and so I sat picking soft gems from the white hull. Every Friday now, he and my father went to the mosque to assemble and pray with the other brave men of Peshawar. I listened to the sounds of pipes tapping from upstairs, my father's footfalls. I looked up and saw the brown webs of a slow leak growing over the sagging ceiling. Outside, a hot wind whispered through the open window behind Taimur, buffeting his short black hair. Cooking smoke floated in; the map of the world tacked to the wall rippled. Savoring my last pomegranate seed, I looked over at Taimur, his face faraway as he gazed at the backs of his hands, as though amazed they were still there. I wondered if he was thinking what I was—would that perfect body he lived in be in pieces later? There was a long list of things you couldn't say in those days—"Don't go" was one of them. "Why?" was another. He and my father had already made a pact between themselves and with God. Submission did not run in our Wazir blood.

In a state of *wudu*, my father entered. Taimur got up. Saying little, we all went to the door—squash racquet strapped to my back, holy books hooked to their palms. We moved up the street together. They were off to the side, ambling; I was in the road on the Sohrab, feet moving against the ground, spokes ticking beside them like a stopwatch. Mind moving a mile a minute, I took them in as one in sideways glances. Years later, I would meet other people who'd lived in randomly terrorized cities—Tokyo, New York, London. Each morning, as you left your loved ones in doorways, to tail lights, lumbering buses, or train whistles, it was always with a single unspoken question. Releasing it to the air would break open a dam of monumental fear, and so you held it in for all you were worth, managed a smile, and merely thought the thing that wouldn't have an answer until dusk—*Will I see you again?*

I let them go at the corner, turning right in a slow glide as they continued on up the narrow street, a single minaret in the distance like a high mast drilling into the sky, a long strip of cloud forming a soft banner behind it. They appeared in miniature before the tower, dissolving into the surge of a steadily forming crowd. More men, all ages, went up behind them in a white stream, pushing slowly forward, toward a fate dispensed according to the will of God—or the Talibs hidden along the rooftops, nestled in the alleys, behind the smile of the fruit seller with his pyramid of mangoes, and a detonator in his pocket. I remember thinking, at least once a day, *We moved to Peshawar for a better life*. I couldn't tell you how or when we started living within a dark cloak of terror—we just did.

*

A man at the corner doing nothing much. Loitering. His shaven face, jawbone flexing, showed purpose, though he was just standing there leaning against a rail. Turban so elaborate, I imagined that, unraveled, the pale fabric would span a full block or more. From the corner of his eye, he clocked me and I saw the shift of his eyeball, barely discernible, but years chasing squash balls left me hypertuned to the subtlest movements. As I passed, smooth and steady along the beat-up road, feet still on the pedals, his head didn't move to follow me. In fact, he didn't move at all, not yet—in itself a chilling sign. Then, barely in my line of sight, I saw him raise a hand and hold it up. I glanced over my shoulder to be sure. Not a wave. Instinct told me to pedal faster, but not too much—not in a frenzy. Up ahead I spotted another man, standing just like the first, in mirror image, like a film rewound. My feet stopped, bike wobbling when I saw him, the familiar roar in my ears as I held my breath.

Blinking dust from my eyes, I watched him, but he stared dead ahead just like the other man. A statue, a zombie—a soldier of jihad. Imagination in high gear, I tried to talk myself out of the foreboding—I'd heard too much talk in the front room. Gripping the handlebars, I made up my mind to hold my breath until the end of the street. Like a passing photograph, I saw a jingle bus go by. Heard the baying of a lamb. Not far now; he was less than a hundred yards away. Purposely, I braked a little and went ticking by, feigning nonchalance. I was just passing him, like a figment from a nightmare, and then he did it—one hand went up, marking me with an invisible target as I moved by—and I knew. Pedaling wildly, I scrambled up those last yards, shooting out the street and careening left, then right, and at the next turn right again. Blood rushed through my head, so I could barely hear the sirens or the call of the muezzin. I was on the move now—backstreets, narrow alleys, behind shops, along apartment blocks, tearing through the market thoroughfares. Sourness of the sewers, sweet warmth of butcher's blood. Winds of terror chasing me. And then a distant rumble of thunder. I knew that it wasn't a bomb—too long a roll, too far away. I stopped only to get to the building in which I took refuge. It had taken an hour's sidetracking to get there.

At the squash academy, I jumped off the bike still in a glide and pushed it right through the front doors. I took the Sohrab with me, clattering and scraping against the walls all the way to the courts. One of the boys I knew was there on the bench. He looked over at the bike I'd left against the wall, then at me, said something before trailing off. The blood had left my face, I could feel it, and I asked him to play. He nodded, got up from the bench, and offered a towel. I was soaking wet—cold sweat, the kind that gives you chills right down to the bone.

Hours later, fear exorcised in a long, burning game, hypnotizing drills, and logistics for the next tournament, I hauled my bicycle out of the building. In the sanctuary of the court, I had convinced myself that I'd simply made myself believe things. On the way out, I swung the racquet bag over my back—nothing and no one had gotten to me before. Outside, I walked past a large group crowded around a car with a flat tire; boys cycled about like a flash from another time. Two empty jingle buses flew past, all their bells silent. I got on my bike, joined the patchy traffic. A woman in a *burqa* scuttled across the road, tripped at the curb, and cried out. A blind man clattered along with his cane, though I could have sworn his dead eyes moved over me. Even as I observed all those things, I was storing them away like stills from a movie. Looking back, I realize that heightened awareness itself was a warning. Taking a different route home, I kept looking behind me—quick glances over the shoulder—sideways down the side streets as I passed them. Pedaling past our old house, I slipped into Little FATA and through the empty blocks. Up ahead, I could see the roofline, the torn blue shade in an upstairs window, the dead tip of a juniper. I kept the roof in my sights, as though at any moment I might lose my way and never make it. Already I could see the front door in my mind, feel the cool quiet of the interior. Off the bike and walking the last few feet, I looked back one more time—nothing—and I wanted to laugh. I was thinking about the pomegranate from Taimur, how sometimes you could only know you'd missed a thing when it reappeared. I wondered if we would ever live in beautiful fruit-laden FATA again.

Then, up ahead, I saw movement. Beats of a bird's wings as it shot out of a canopy of leaves. My eyes shifted—a man just rounding the corner. Instantly, I traded every thought for reflex—barely one second before, there had been nothing but open street. The glimpse of a dark profile, the slow lift of one sandaled foot, the last flutter of his clothes, and he vanished round the bend. I told myself that he was just a man like any other, and hurried over the last steps to the house. I put the bike against the wall at the side. Immediately, the air seemed to thicken—warm and slightly sweet—an acrid whisper that hovered like a visitation. Key at the ready, I stepped around the corner toward the front door. From the crumbling cement slab, pale tendrils of smoke curled upward. My hand flew to my face. Unmistakable. I didn't have to see the source, but my panicked eyes went straight for it—the thing tossed to the ground like an afterthought. Still smoldering, it crackled and hissed as though the serpent's soul was still inside it. I put my foot down hard and crushed the scorpion reefer, and then I went inside. Father and Taimur were home ten minutes later. A car bomb ripped half a block out of the other end of the city, so far away we never heard a thing.

*

Once again, I was a guest at the Army House with my father. Same set up as before: tents outside, twilight chitchat, right down to men carrying trays—even a menu. I tried the cake. This time I wasn't there as a member of a medal-winning team, but to receive the Salam Pakistan award from President Musharraf, along with several other athletes in other sports. It was described as an award for excellence, and my father repeated the phrase to me many times, looking at my hands, which he so liked to touch—they were evidence, he told me, of a life of purpose. When the ceremony started, I walked onto a makeshift stage outside under the glaring lights, and took a seat behind the podium. The president made a speech about sports in Pakistan. I heard nothing of what he said, was too busy scanning the crowd, assembled on folding chairs, for my father. He was three rows back and looking at me, eyes twinkling. I noticed that there was more security than the last time—three times as many guards on the roof and manning the tents. Officers searched our bags several times, checked and rechecked our identity cards.

It was August. I sat on the stage, sweating, blazing hot in my blazer; Musharraf's shirt revealed the ridges of the armored vest underneath. I heard him say my name and look over; our eyes met and I knew to get up. While I was crossing the stage, it all came into focus that I wasn't getting a medal for a single match or a tournament—I'd been singled out as an athlete. I heard my father's voice say it again—*award for excellence*—and the ripple of applause swept over me, but I saw only my father there watching. Swimming inside his proud eyes, at that moment I felt more like a champion than I ever had —or ever would again.

My father had told me even before we got there that we would leave right after the award ceremony. In the bus on the way back, dead of night, he turned to me as I stared out the window. Passing headlights going the other way. And beyond those, nothing but night.

"You're the number one player, Maria?"

I looked over at him and laughed. "Yes, Baba. National champion."

"When did this happen?"

"I'm not sure. Maybe a year."

"You never said."

"You never asked."

A belly laugh. "And you were the first girl to play in shorts and a T-shirt."

"Yes—that I didn't know, Baba."

He nodded, caressed his new beard. In just a week it had grown half an inch. "Of everything I could be proud of—that's the thing I'm most proud of."

If I could go back, if there was one thing I would change, it would be having my picture taken—or being there at all—using my name. When my brother showed me the picture in the paper, I studied it for absurd imperfections: my eye looked small; nose too big; didn't like my hair. I didn't know it was a death sentence.

*

There was a man standing outside the complex when I entered. Then later, when I came back out—same man, same look: red-rimmed eyes staring right at me. I rode past him and kept going. The streets smelled of rain. Not a soul in them for several blocks. Up ahead a glut of traffic, pairs of tail lights. Police checks. Lately, they happened everywhere and all the time. I veered into a side street and took many more.

Living in Little FATA had suddenly come to mean living inside a bull's-eye. The Taliban had their sights on the Pashtun, on their own cousins, to make us pay for disloyalty—though they'd enjoyed our hospitality when they hid away, plotting in our villages. Scared and moving swiftly along my serpentine route, I felt that I needed to get home faster. A labyrinth of stops set up like an obstacle course. Sirens and horns blared. I asked myself what day it was. Not Friday. Nowhere near a mosque. Men were shouting. A car backfired and I swallowed a scream. I was on edge in a way that made me feel dizzy, but I told myself it was the heat and stopped to take a drink. Too many bad things had happened to me over too many years—and now bad things were happening to everyone all the time. The crowds on the streets were thick, hot, and angry.

People lined up outside the movie theater on the next block: all young men in their teens. They leaned back at angles that made it look as if they were holding up the walls. I wondered which movie was showing and tried to read the marquee, but it was still too far away. That's when the white hatchback cut me off. Two men inside it—one at the wheel, another in the back. Beads dangled from the rearview mirror. As the car went by, the driver looked at me—eyes glazed, teeth yellow, several missing; the other man was slumped over, head pushed against the front seat at a strange angle. Ahead of me, the car pulled up to the movie theater and stopped, slamming into the curb. The line moaned as one; a few people stepped out of it to get a better look. I was already passing, and something told me things were all wrong—the checkpoints, the crowds, the sirens. The white car sat there, the engine revving. I looked back, pumping hard, could see how badly he'd parked. A man came out of the theater, shouting and pointing at the tire still up on the sidewalk under the marquee. Somehow I knew I shouldn't linger so I turned the handle-bars and moved right across the thoroughfare, braving angry oncoming traffic. On the other side, I headed for the next turn and took it on a tear.

It wasn't long, maybe five seconds, before I heard it—a booming roar that made the ground under my feet quake. As though it had been making chase since the squash courts, a wallop of soot and wind rushed up behind me. Pulverized cement and metal rained down into the alley. There was the hot smell of fresh ash. Immediately, I thought of the young men lined up at the movie theater. I remembered a face, full of acne, thin mustache, the way he leaned against the wall in a stupor of heat. He looked to be about Taimur's age, standing with two dozen or more just like him lined up like dominoes. Maybe they all hoped it would be cool inside. Hot dust billowing out all around me, my lungs burned as I breathed. I pedaled furiously, thinking only of getting away and nothing else. In the immediate aftermath there seemed to be minutes—years—of a strange, eerie stillness, everything deaf and mute. Then a woman shrieked as though breaking a glass jar in which the world had been turning, and behind me on that street, chaos erupted like a second bomb.

Inside my house, I heard the static of the radio. Feet shuffling. The loud bangs of drawers opening and shutting. When I moved, my hair and body released flurries of dust. My legs twitched from the frenzied pedaling. Unable to stop, I rewound the last hour in flashes: people running toward me, every mouth open, every pair of eyes white with fear. Then to the car, sliding along the road, one front tire rising up against the curb. The driver, passing in a strange slowing of time. The way he stared right through me, already half dead—just one thing left to do. The man in the back, head cranked to the side, gaping holes where his eyes should have been. I knew, looking back to that surreal millisecond glimpse, that he must have been dead. And over and over again, the boys with their backs against the movie theater wall, in what I think of now as an execution line. I wondered if any made it out. I moved upstairs to the washroom and closed the door softly. Cold water. Lots of it. Downstairs, I could hear Taimur's voice twine into my father's, and one thought brought me to my knees—*I'm still alive and so are they*.

*

Time stopped in Peshawar. The population seemed to live within a long, interminable second. I don't remember that period of Taliban terror attacks as a series of days or weeks or months—it just was. All over the city, people mouthed prayers as they passed one another and up to the sky when it bled smoke. Wails of sirens were a death knell we felt in our bones—though more often than not, we heard nothing of casualties or even of incidents. Officials, mullahs, teachers, neighbors went missing, into a void of forgotten souls, and no one asked after them. The vanished became frantic whispers at the corner, in our living room, and in the sleepless dark. On the news, in the papers, we heard nothing. Men grew long, reverent beards, *burqas* proliferated, and only the brave hearts went to the movies anymore. Still, I played squash, rode the red Sohrab—avoiding the main streets, on the lookout for a lone car, driver hunched in a lethal narcosis. I thought I saw them everywhere. On the roadsides, like solitary lamp posts, there were always men watching—me or someone else, I couldn't be sure. Vagrants who stared out from their squalor like spiders in a web were suddenly suspects. And always the one man outside the squash complex, tucked under a tree by the wall. Sometimes it was the same figure for a solid week or more, then another, as though they took shifts in some factory of fear. I remember thinking the Taliban had found out about my win as Genghis Khan in Lahore.

In a corner, my father sat, shades drawn against the beating sun. The interior of the house felt like a catacomb, so little light coming in, full of the damp smells of a leak he couldn't seem to fix. Drops of water falling from the faucet upstairs were the only sound. When I saw him there, I knew he was waiting for me, just by the turn of his head. He motioned, hand rising and falling as I went in. Several days each week, he still braved the drive into FATA, taking great care to choose his route well ahead of time. He'd grown a bushy beard that concealed half his face, and wore a labyrinthine turban made of starched cotton, sacred beads garlanding his hands. Anyone looking into the windows as the pick up passed would think one thing—*a holy man*—and put down their gun. Whether he was teaching or not, he never said. We knew he worked at something, probably ways to get another college back on its feet. FATA occupied his life like a newborn. It was a time of long silences and few details in our family history. We all tried to continue our routines: kids at school, Ayesha in college, parents working, me playing squash—all of it in survival mode. Heavy lidded, my father sat with a piece of paper between his palms that had been folded over many times—and I knew.

"Sit down and talk, Maria. There is trouble." About serious matters, my father never minced words.

Turned out, neither did the Taliban.

Death threats are direct: the muzzle of a gun, a knife blade held against the throat, the rattle of a snake's tail, or a note left on the windshield of the pick up. My Pashtun name, as printed in the newspapers or read out in the sports news—Wazir—branded me as tribal, not a regular Pakistani female squash player. My picture standing with Musharraf—Enemy Number One—was what had tipped the scales. I remembered just then how my mother told me the Taliban always sent a written warning before they blew up a school. So far, they'd incinerated four in Darra Adam Khel, and scores more elsewhere. Sometimes my mother was able to salvage odd things—desks, whole blackboards, boxes of pencils—to bring to the next building the board assigned. She'd work there a few weeks or months and then the warning would come—a note tacked to the door or scrawled across a blackboard. As my father leaned over and unfolded the paper one crease at a time, I knew I was about to hear mine.

"In a nutshell, if I don't stop you from playing, you will suffer severe consequences."

"What do they mean by 'severe consequences'—not killing?"

He was folding up the paper again, methodically. When my father thought hard, it showed in every muscle of his face. Just then, he looked like a man in pain.

"Not right away, no. Unless there is no other choice."

"It's just squash."

My father let out a sound, not quite a laugh. I've never heard it since. "The Quran is just a book. You are just a girl. FATA is just rock and soil."

"Do I stop?"

He looked at me then, eyes squared, and crushed the paper in his fist. "Will I stop going to the mosque Fridays? Will I throw out your mother's jean jacket? Will I take Ayesha out of university, place her in purdah, and marry her off to an old man? Will we never listen to music again?"

I had my answer.

*

Taimur came with me on his bike—both pickup and drop-off—on his way to and from the markets. We took a different route each day. Up and down the side streets, past the black craters where buildings used to be—remnants of another mosque, roof on the ground in pieces like a dropped porcelain bowl. We avoided landmarks and hospitals, schools, and the vendors who catered to women. When he dropped me off, I glanced over my shoulder. He was always still right there, standing over his bike, arms folded and looking around. I remember thinking the note was a ruse—a competing player with an ax to grind—not the Taliban. Why would they bother with me?

When I came back out, Taimur was still there, off to one side, his bicycle leaning on a bench, a sack of rice next to him, his face against the bark of a poplar tree, white and tired looking. We walked our bikes together up the shaded walkway, past two men standing where the paving forked. They were clean shaven and had on squash gear, tracksuits that looked brand-new, leather racquet bags, Ray-Bans. So well kitted out they might as well have been professional players, but I'd never seen them before. One of them looked right at me and grinned. For all the well-heeled newness about him, he was missing a tooth, right up front.

"Hello, Maria Wazir. How are you?"

I should not have looked, but I did—saw the eyes, all pupils, black as onyx, and the square hole in his mouth that reduced every handsome thing about him to a lie—should not have held my breath, and almost choked on it. I could see that his hands and the hands of the other man were empty, clean. Safe. They were just standing there, standing sentry to my fate, letting me know it belonged to them.

We got to about ten feet away, already on our seats and about to pedal, when I heard it, voice low, swimming under the breeze and the din of traffic so that I had to strain to make out words.

"Is that the older brother?"

"Yes."

"No matter."

My father was reading to Sangeen in the kitchen when we got home—about the Trojan War—and I sat awhile, listening. He was only at the very beginning of the ancient Greek story, when the goddess of discord, Eris, tossed a golden apple on which she'd inscribed "to the fairest" into a wedding feast of the Gods. Taimur put away the sack of rice, put on water to boil, and busied his hands. I looked over at my father; his beard had grown past his neck and had spread out in an unruly shape. Half his face was hidden, except for the eyes, which on him were the whole man. The electricity was off again, so a kerosene lamp sat flickering on the table, wick coiled like a snake inside the glass base, sucking up fuel. Watching him read to his sleepy son in that weak light, his mouth burrowed in that wild nest, I saw it—the purple gash to his bottom lip. Blood scabbed over it, and I noticed that when he touched his lip slightly as he turned a page, he winced. Barely. Taimur had his back to me still, making our tea, the spoon clinking as he stirred.

Sangeen went off up the stairs, down the hall. I sat between my father and Taimur, both tall as pillars next to me. It was a Thursday night. What I remember most is the heavyweight silence, unsaid things that had more power than any utterance. When my brother sat down, he looked at our father, a whole afternoon related in a blink. My father nodded, took a sip from his cup, blew steam from the top, thinking.

I waited to be told it was over, and I was ready. There were worse things than home, the kitchen, laundry. My boys. My bicycle. The wall in my room was perfect for practicing hits. All I'd have to do was push the mattress off to one side; it was the only thing in there. Things would be different this time—better than failing school, than never having had the chance to be a champion. Than being blown up.

"We have to make a few changes, Maria, in light of recent events."

"Yes, I know, Baba. I'm ready. What happened to your lip?"

"A minor disagreement over the meaning of life—turns out I was right."

"Baba, you won't admit to what I already know."

"Good, then we are on the same page, as always. The problem is the bicycle." He held up an index finger, twirled it, sending the lamplight into a minor frenzy.

"No, it's not the bike, it's my squash racquet."

"Put it in the trunk."

"What trunk?"

"Baba has traded the pick up for a hatchback, Maria. You can sit in the backseat while I drive. Lie down even. It's in the garage at the neighbor's house. No one expects it."

"What? How will you get to work?"

My father's hands went up with his shoulders. Then: "You'll go at random times and by random routes—but you will go.

"Yes, Maria. If we get to keep our Qurans, you get to keep your racquet."

*

When I went to bed that night, I could not sleep. I heard my father moving through the house along the narrow corridor, checking our rooms. We all knew he caught sleep only here and there, like morsels of food. His feet stopped outside the door. I could see them through licks of flickering light in the sliver underneath. The window was open next to the bed, all of Peshawar asleep but as restless as the rustling leaves when a breeze pushes between the emptying branches. My father stood at our door a long time. I imagined him placing a hand flat against the wood planking, as though checking for a heartbeat. Finally, my eyelids grew heavy. All around me the air of the city stirred, three million living breaths. How many fewer after tomorrow—no one knew.

18. Purdah

I woke early from fitful sleep, untangled my limbs from the single pale-blue sheet. I pulled open the shade next to me, releasing all at once the darkness from the room. Out the window, garbage littered the street. At the center of the asphalt, a crow picked bits of food out of a torn plastic bag. I watched him for a few minutes, chin on the sill, and got up. Inside, the house was still quiet. I slid into my clothes, the day ahead already taking shape in my mind—Taimur driving me on a meandering route, windows up all the way, to the academy. It wasn't Friday, but that no longer seemed to matter. There were random bombings all the time—hospitals, doctors' offices, theaters, police stations, bazaars, the homes of government officials; once or twice, a Christian church. Between attacks there were threats, and those were almost as bad: buildings evacuated, people racing out the doors in an explosion of panic. Once children were trampled. Before six, I was already in the kitchen slicing mangoes. The glistening juice running all over my hands always brought me back to the valleys, sitting on rocks with my old crew in the sunshine. They might all be die-hard Talibs by now—might be after me for all I knew.

My mother hadn't come home yet. I looked for her telltale satchel by the door—the one with all the pens and maps in it. Somehow, she always had a small bag of candy and a dwindling roll of happy-face stickers. I bit my lip, holding back a familiar dam of emotion that always threatened to break. My father was asleep like a dead man in a chair by the front door, waiting. When I touched his arm, he stiffened and shot up. Together we went to the kitchen, where I gave him a plate of fruit and nuts. He looked at the offering bleary-eyed, as though he didn't know what to do with it. Cups of tea—our shared elixir. We sipped and said nothing, though we'd expected her home twelve hours before. While we didn't think the other was looking, we each glanced at the door.

Then, in that tense morning stillness, the sudden shifting of door locks changed everything. In a moment she was there, satchel thumping to the floor, *chador* falling from her head to her shoulders. As though she'd been holding her breath all night with us, she exhaled—"Well!" We stood together, all talking at once. Usually, when people didn't come back for hours, they never came back at all. My father dropped his head into his hands and I thought for a moment that he might collapse. Then he looked up at her, shook his head and took a long deep breath as though to hold back a high tide of emotion. In my entire life, I've never seen my father cry and I doubt I ever will—it simply isn't his way. Then we followed my mother across the front room and my father signaled for me to help her. For several minutes he was still too overcome to speak. I went to her as she sat down on the mats in the living room. One after the other, and as though they were precious things, I removed her worn out shoes. In a moment, my father moved close to me on the floor watching, but somehow unable to touch her. Aami looked over at him, smiling, and held out a hand as though caressing his stunned face through the air. "Come now, Solomon. Get up from your knees."

We didn't have to ask what had happened; she was already telling us as she removed her *burqa* from a sack and placed it over a cushion next to her. I looked over at the empty fabric draped like a deflated thing, pictured my mother staring out from behind it and wondered what she'd seen through that tight mesh. Then she peeled off the *chador*. A few small grains fell to the floor— maize. In them I saw undulating fields, churning from green to silver in the wind. Underneath those coverings, she had on a *kameez* with flowers embroidered all over it. I rarely saw her that way, without a shawl, hair in a long black braid down her spine. She leaned back and sighed.

"Two Taliban leaders were in a shoot-out in the village—rival leaders. It had nothing to do with the school, but of course when the gunfire got going, we had to stay in there hiding. It went on and on through the night. They blew out windows. We were all on the floor under desks while they went at killing each other. It didn't stop until dawn."

My father was next to her now, as she was undoing her tight braid, pulling the soft lengths of curls from her long hair. He sat transfixed as her fingers ran through the strands. His gaze alone was an intimate act I rarely saw between them. I was thinking about how minutes before he'd taken her shoes from me and put them away, and then brought a damp towel for her tired feet. When she let her hair fall, I could see in his eyes that he was somewhere else, swimming into the past—maybe to the young girl he married, her bird-wing hands caressing the new jean jacket folded in her lap. In his eyes, my mother was still Queen of the House.

"Who won, Yasrab?" He watched her shaking the dust of war from her hair.

She laughed, reached back, and took his hand. "No one, of course. I must sleep."

Gratitude shed years from my father. He put a piece of mango in his mouth and ate it, sighing as though he'd never tasted anything more luscious. For the first time that morning, he looked at me, all the grimness peeled away from his face. The thick hair around his mouth glistened. He asked me for more and I gave it to him.

"Baba, what is it they want?"

"Who?"

"The Taliban. They want me to stop playing squash, for you and Aami to stop teaching. But what is the thing they want for all this blowing up and shooting they do?"

My father didn't miss a beat. He pushed aside the empty plate, wiped off the untamable beard I knew he hated. "They want the government to get rid of our constitution and impose their version of Islam on everyone—I've told you about it before —that's the whole thing in one sentence. If I go on, we will be here for years."

"You never told me exactly what it is—their version of Islam."

"It isn't Islam—that's the thing you must know above all. First they took the word 'taliban' from our language for themselves and murdered it."

"It is why everyone has started to use the English word 'student.'"

"Yes. And now they have adducted our faith."

"They have their own laws."

"Yes. Many. Women must not work outside the home, attend school, see a doctor when they are sick, play sports, or go anywhere without a male accompanying her. In public, they must be covered head to toe in a *burqa* with only a mesh covering at the front to see through. They must not wear shoes that make noise while they walk. No music is permitted, no entertainment. Windows of buildings housing women should be painted black, so there is no possibility of a woman's face being seen even by accident . . ."

He went on, but as he spoke, every word weighed me down. I saw everything I was doing in a new, harsh light—the gross insult of the white T-shirt and shorts I so often wore, my uncovered face, the single large earring looped to one lobe, my short spiked hair—my ways. The game I played—all over the country and continent—ranked number one. The bicycle I hardly ever rode anymore. And the target over me seemed to darken like a stain. I looked around the kitchen as he came to the end of a long, memorized list—the last edict something about polio vaccinations.

"The Taliban believe the vaccinations are a Western plot to sterilize Muslims. They banned those too."

"How long until they stop?" I wanted to hear a general timeline—months, weeks, anything but what he gave me.

"I don't know." Eye to eye, he looked at me.

"I understand something that I didn't before now, Baba."

"I thought you might."

"They won't stop until I do. Stop playing squash."

"No. It's more than that. That's just the beginning of what they're after. You're a tribal girl. They want you in purdah as an example to all the others."

"What does that really mean?"

His gaze moved all over kitchen—kettle coming to a boil, cutting board soaked in sweet juice—and then came to rest on the *burqa* my mother had left over the chair. "Between four walls"—he held up the dust-covered garment—"in this."

After that, I shifted into survival mode. I did everything to the letter: tracksuits with a hood, backseat of the car, head down. We never took the same route twice in a row, never stepped out the front door without someone checking. I adopted an erratic training schedule; I came and went to and from the academy at all hours, telling no one when I would be there or when I planned to leave. My whole life was reconfigured—eating, sleeping, breathing—because of a letter tacked to my father's hatchback. Every night, desperate for sleep, I heard my father's voice go down the list of the Taliban edicts. We, and everyone in Peshawar who lived in a constant state of terror, wondered as they kneeled and prayed five times a day to Allah, what kind of Islam the Taliban were following. It bore no resemblance whatsoever to our peaceful faith. Fifty miles away and closing in fast, that was daily life. The note on the windshield was just the first step in a long campaign. I lived in a constant state of agitation—living without living, breathing like an animal, walking fast, eyes darting like prey. The Taliban were terrorizing me in the coolest manner possible—a little bit at a time.

When the air marshal in charge of the squash academy came into the court, two cans of Fanta in his hands, I put down my racquet. A military badge emblazoned his green tracksuit, under which you could see the sheer cut of his shoulders. To look at him, I had to crank my neck, and when I did, I could see the pulse beating in his. Beads of sweat gathered at his sideburns. It was hot in the tank—the ventilation system kept going out. A long, serrated scar cut across his cheek; a thin mustache sat over his top lip. People conjectured about the scar, said he'd been in a plane crash or been wounded as a youth in the days when brave young boys went into the hills to fight with the mujahideen—he looked like a man who'd survived horrors he'd never talk about. I wondered why he was there, sharing a soda, knowing as I sipped the saccharine drink that it couldn't be good news.

"People talk, Maria. See you come and go. See your face."

I didn't deny the thing that anyone could see. I was pale from fear, no hiding it.

He told me about the threats the academy had received, telephone calls. The first call was specific—*Get rid of her*. After that, just the crackle of dead air on the end of the line at least once every single day. Other players reported sightings of strange men standing around outside, watching the entrance, studying the building, and taking notes. Each morning, he told me, the staff expected to find a letter tacked to the door. It was only a matter of time. In my mind, I turned over the reality the air marshal presented me with, as I turned my racquet in my hand. What had begun as a single threat against me had multiplied to involve many other souls.

"I can't play here, can I?"

"Maria, you are the national champion. If you stop playing here, we all do. I've made a few calls."

*

At the first knock, my father let the men in—four officers, none of them in uniform. They sat in our front room on mats, legs crossed, notepads in their laps. Question after question. I answered each matter-of-factly, told them about riding past the two men in the alley, about the pair outside the squash facility dressed to the nines in professional sports gear. As I spoke, one man looked at me intently, as though searching my face for something he'd lost. Another man scrawled notes in a strange staccato handwriting my father told me later was called shorthand. The other two simply stood by the door, one inside and one out, watching. Every now and then we could hear the lone figure outside the front door pacing the cement ground and letting out a quick cough. Taimur told me afterward that there were many more positioned up and down the road. As the night transpired, we learned that the threats to my life had reached the local government offices, where members of Parliament discussed the logistics of my security needs. Funds had been allocated to secure around-the-clock protection for me. It was all surreal.

It started at first light when I pulled up the shade. Standing in the sunshine, a man outside looked over—one of the officers from the night before. We didn't wave; I was under strict instructions not to. Most of the time, they told me, I wouldn't even know they were there. Just like the Taliban, undercover officers used disguises—vendors, students, addicts, holy men, squash players. Two boiled eggs for breakfast and I was right back upstairs. Checked the window. The man was gone, but as I was about to turn away, another man stepped into position across the street.

In the car, Taimur and I took turns spotting them. I was in the backseat, peering over his shoulder. One was driving behind us in a rust bucket almost identical to our own, wearing shades, gloved hands on the wheel. When Taimur turned, he turned; when Taimur doubled back, he followed suit. Others weren't so easy to pick out: the vagrant sitting at the curb at the end of our block, rolling cigarettes—my brother slowed the car, told me to take a careful took at the man's clean, dead-giveaway hands—the kebab vendor in the street outside the complex—"Did you notice all the kebabs are burned black, Maria?"

I took a long drink from my water bottle before getting out of the car. The water tasted clean and cool, and I let myself savor it. Overnight, everything had transformed—we'd laughed all morning in the car. I'd slept without stirring through Technicolor dreams of the ocean—boomerang waves and thatched houses on the crystalline beach. Those men formed a net around me; they were experts at protecting people. And for a while, I thought I was safe.

On the roof of the academy, I saw men dressed in full black

gear, sitting like giant bugs. They had guns on bipods fixed to each corner, scopes flashing as they scanned the walkways all around me while I made my way across the quad. A window washer, bucket at his side and rags in his hand, looked over as I went in. He'd be there until lunchtime, when his replacement took over.

In the courts, I trained well. For the most part, the undercover officers stayed outside and, over the weeks, started to blend in like wallpaper. I wondered how long they would keep going, following me, watching my back. The first night, the man in charge had told me that when the threats stopped, they would leave. So far, that hadn't happened. As soon as I started to believe the threats would never materialize, I'd get a stark reminder—the sound of another car bomb detonating at the market; murdered bodies dumped in the street like trash; more people going missing. At that time, many prominent Pakistanis were abducted and killed.

I didn't think anyone would get past my protectors. The day that certainty disintegrated, something was off from the start. An oversized tracksuit consumed me; it was all I had to wear, and the fabric baked my limbs like an oven. My body seemed to have a life of its own, changing size all the time. Shorts that fit fine the week before were suddenly tight rubber bands about my waist. Already perspiring, I stood in the court alone. Sore knees, especially the left one, which had been giving me trouble. All around, the sounds of other games in full swing reverberated—the laughter of children. The academy had just opened registration to new players in the under-thirteen category, some as young as five. Maybe it was all the noise coming from the other courts and the constant high chatter of the children, but I couldn't tamp down the pulsing of my nerves. I was on edge, and nothing was falling into place—my swing; my focus; all my hits were dull.

I stood in the court, heating the ball up in my hands. Thinking. A whistle blew and the air quieted down. I was still standing at the T, and I felt something stir behind me. I shot around, but there was nothing in the glass. I shook the feeling off, laughed at myself, and got into a slow drill. Ten hits in and I felt it again, behind me: a shifting of shadows and a slight bend in the light. This time, I saw a figure slip fast past the glass in the corridor. I waited a moment—nothing seemed unusual except for the tingling creeping over my skin. *Could have been anyone.* Just a few minutes before, I'd seen my guard pretending to be a window cleaner in the lobby. I recognized him as the man who'd taken all the shorthand notes. I told myself over and over that I was safe.

Still, I couldn't drill my nerves into submission. My skin was hot inside all that fabric, and I finally went out into the corridor and paced slowly to the lavatory. The fluorescent lights in there were always half out, casting a sickly glow over the eggshell walls. I washed my face many times in the sink with cold water, as cold as I could get it. Just then, I heard footsteps in the corridor, tapping against tiles, growing louder, slowing on approach, stopping. In the half-inch gap under the door, I could see a shadow flicker. I told myself it was the guard checking, waited awhile, seconds maybe, and then the feet moved and the tapping started up again and receded. The light overhead dimmed, and I went to the door—put my hand on the handle, held my breath, and opened it. Left to right, the hall was empty.

In the corridor on the way back to the courts, all the tanks were lit up and full of new recruits. The Wing Commander had them all lined up against the walls. The children seemed so small, though some were the same size I had been when I started. When he saw me, he waved and pointed. Even though the air force no longer sponsored me, we maintained a good relationship and often played matches when we had the chance. All of the children looked over at me in tandem, mouths breaking into smiles that took up half their faces.

Immediately, I thought it was my mistake—it's hard to trust your instincts when it seems that there is always something or someone waiting to kill you—but as I returned to my court, my eyes darted to the empty water bottle, right where I'd left it, then to the strange bag in the corner. Leaving unattended parcels anywhere, inside or outside buildings, was strictly forbidden. Pushing back a tsunami of panic, I searched for an explanation or an owner of the abandoned bag. Mouth instantly parched, breath quickening, I didn't go near the black duffel, just stared at it for a long time. Too long. Frozen. It was just like one I owned but brand-new, tags still on it. The zipper had buckled from the pressure of the packed contents. I kept hoping for someone to rush in and claim it, apologizing. Then a child's squeal of pain in an adjacent court snapped me out of my lethal confusion, and I sprinted down the corridor, turning my head just enough to see the Wing Commander, small bare foot in his hand, a young boy wailing before him. I slowed, our eyes locked, he took in my face and rushed out of the court. I told him about the bag. We looked all around ourselves—nothing but glass, wall after wall of it. In a moment, everyone was running, and he was right behind me, shouting.

In three minutes flat, everyone was out of the building, hustled into the daylight, frantic and quiet. The entire sports center shut down, blocks were cordoned off, snipers in position at their scopes. I kept moving down the walkway in the thick, tense crowd, wondered how I would get home, what had happened to my guards. Military everywhere; helicopter overhead. Then I saw Taimur across the street, holding a bag of flour, just standing there stunned on the pavement in front of the car while chaos erupted all around him. I could see he was looking for me and rushed over the jammed lanes. He'd gone to work out in the next building, run on the treadmill, lifted a few weights, and then he'd left to shop for food. Only he and my father went to the market in those days. People were still hurrying all around us in a strange, quiet melee, like a fast river parting around two stones.

Taimur passed me his sacks as I slid into the backseat "What was that all about?"

I heaved the bags to the floor and lay down flat across the seat. The sweat on my cheek glued the side of my face to the warm plastic upholstery. I closed my eyes. Behind the lids all I could see were the children lined up against the white walls, just like the young men at the movie theater. I saw the black duffel, like a body bag for an infant, sitting in the court. Then I thought of the thing that scared me more than what might be inside it—all that glass. The engine sputtered several times, Taimur's foot lightly pumping the gas pedal. I heard him ask the question again, his voice slightly frantic—"What's going on? What was that all about?" Taking a page from my father's book, I didn't mince words. I sat up for a second and met his eyes in the rear-view mirror.

"I don't know, Taimur—but I think it's because of me."

*

Living with such fear finally sucked the life out of everything. Rain fell daily for a time, cleaning away the dust and soot of the bombed-out buildings. Peshawar was grim, its death toll climbing. We were all living in a nightmare. The constant human perimeter of plainclothes officers surrounded me, and around them the Taliban watched and waited for a breach. The duffel taught me they would easily find one. The military bomb squad had checked the bag, sent in a German shepherd trained to scent explosives. The technicians, dressed like astronauts in heavy protective gear, took it away in a specially designed hold. Turned out it wasn't a bomb, just an ordinary bag stuffed with brand-new white towels, as many as would fit before the zipper gave way—a cunning ploy that served its purpose. I was terrified—we all were.

Holding court in the living room, my father explained the mechanics of a bomb, how it worked, how it killed in several lethal phases. Men were all assembled, quiet and attentive, just like the students I'd seen in his lab. On sheets of paper, which he would later incinerate in the cooking stove, he drew basic diagrams, used cool scientific jargon, eyes bright though the subject was grim. Standing there, I was transported to his warehouse lecture hall in Dera Ismail Khan, the open back doors as big as a movie screen showing a sun-swept panorama of dry foothills. I'd watched him build a four-cylinder engine from nuts and bolts and intricate pieces of metal covered in thick grease, young students circling him, gutted cars surrounding me while I played.

They had all looked at my father the way those men did now—spellbound.

"Depending on the point of impact, a bomb does its job in several ways. The initial blast wave: highly compressed air particles go out from the source at rates faster than the speed of sound, causing structural damage to whatever lies in its path—human or material. A series of supersonic stress waves follow. We haven't found a way to protect people from stress waves. These carry more energy than sound waves and pass invisibly right through the body, tearing up tissues and organs. After that, we see fragmentation from materials packed into the bomb—ball bearings, nails, and razors—that travel at high velocity. Makes a machine gun look like a slingshot. Then you have secondary fragmentation from the buildings themselves—glass, concrete, metal. There's fire, of course, smoke and intense heat, which kills those trapped inside the wreckage. Finally the blast wind, a great vacuum of smoke and debris that sucks the polluted atmosphere right back into the initial explosion."

On the periphery, racquet bag still hanging from my shoulder, I made calculations. A blast wave from the white car had ripped all those boys outside the movie theater to pieces; others not killed by the first impact succumbed to the echoing stress waves, which explained the visibly untouched bodies littering the ground, looking as though they had just lain down and fallen fast asleep. Others were sprawled in sickening positions.

Standing there, my father before us all, drawing pictures of clouds and buildings and stick-figure human beings, I realized I had seen the real thing. I was remembering it all, like opening a box full of macabre photographs. Suddenly I knew that I had in fact gone back to check, back to the movie theater, my mind not wanting to believe what it already knew. It wasn't just a nightmare I kept having night after night; it was a real thing I'd done—ridden my bike past the raging black hole where the theater had been, looking for a face, even just one, to know that one had made it. I saw people maimed from the first fragmentation of projectiles, skin peeled right off, eyes gouged out, limbs obliterated. Inside what was left of the building, I heard the screams of those in the middle of dying from the bomb's last bites—secondary fragmentation of the structure littering their bodies with gruesome oddities, like a light switch cover in the neck or a door handle through the abdomen. Some fell victim to the fire that left their eyes bloodshot as it sucked out all the oxygen—their very last breaths. The flames still raged as I drifted through the block of horrors.

When I got to the court the next day, I looked all around me and worked through the raw mechanics—walls of glass, secondary fragmentation. From the lobby, I heard the next group assembling for sessions in the courts. Giggling down the hall, high-fiving me as they passed along the corridor of clean windows, one after the other they dovetailed into their chambers. I felt every muscle in my body suddenly go lax. My protective officer was still hard at work making the surface shine and watching out for Talibs, but I was on my knees. I might as well be a ticking bomb wrapped in flesh and bone. No one was safe around me. I had to leave, and never come back.

*

I counted the days I'd been in my room. Thirty-nine—as if the number meant anything at all. The days all seemed to slip away—seconds, minutes, and hours all falling over a cliff. Sometimes I took a break and went outside, sat on the stoop. The men were still out there watching, taking shifts. We never acknowledged one another. There were fewer of them now that I was locked away at home.

It was the same routine every morning. Make breakfast for the others—small jug of watered-down yogurt, slices of fruit, nuts; laid out in bowls like the offerings Hindus leave at their shrines. Not much, just whatever I could find and turn into more than it was. Lots of bread. I stayed in the background, busying myself with dishes, with the boys—their hair, their manners, a stubborn stain on a white shirt. I watched them eat and washed the dishes afterward. Then I cleaned the whole house. I mopped the floors, remembering all the while my childhood days of carrying buckets of water down from the clear stream, the gateway of dead acacias opening to verdant fields that I might never see again except from the oval window of an airplane—if I was lucky. Then to my room and my new routine, mattress heaved onto its side against the wall. My racquet, my ball, making myself find angles that would send me all over a confined room not quite the size of a real court. The men outside could hear me. The first day, they'd come racing through the front door, breaking it right off the hinges, flying up the stairs with all their weapons drawn, four pistols out. Then they saw what I was doing, nodded, and left. After that, they just stood out there listening to my pounding through the hours and into the night. Sometimes I wondered if they went home and told their wives and children: "You should see this girl—crazy. She hits the ball in her room ten hours a day. It's true. We actually counted. Nothing else to do."

One hundred days—a milestone. Still in my room, in the timeless void. I'd started falling, regularly. One injury to the knees or a hamstring overlapped another, and then another. I didn't have medical care or a coach or trainer anymore. No one—just the wall in my room to keep me going. As an act of defiance and survival, I still played in tournaments. Taimur found out the schedules for me, memorized the information, and we got in the car to go to the bus station or the airport, depending on the venue. I'd arrange my travel itinerary at the last minute, never buying tickets in advance of my trip, often showing up to register unannounced. Every time I was in the newspaper, a new threat followed. Once, my father was stopped in the street. Two men shoved him around, hacked off his beard—he always gave me the usual tongue-in-cheek explanation: "A minor scuffle."

Over the weeks, I found myself weakening, a steady ebbing away like a slow leak. The bruises on my knees from so many falls against the concrete floor in my room built up into mounds of immovable flesh like hard shells. Silent witnesses to the deterioration, my family never tried to stop me. Following my steps, Babrak watched silently inside my slow shadow as I crawled up the stairs before bed. My father just took my hands in his rubbed them with ointment, tapped the cracks, and said a small prayer.

If I went back to the academy, the Taliban would bomb it—that was a certainty. Staying in my room meant saving lives. They were beating me the way they beat everyone. First they terrorized me, then they just burrowed in—into my city, into my sanctuary, into my psyche. They wore me down. Those weren't boys at the end of an alley; they were soldiers of an angry god. For the first time, I couldn't find a way to win.

I started to lose tournaments—not all at once, just here and there—against players who'd once been easy marks. And I knew my future was slipping away. Despite the hours of grinding training in my room, my mind and body were on a downward slide, along with everything else. Strange things were happening to me. My bones seemed to stiffen and my mind started to close in. I heard things over the dull pounding—voices muttering. Sometimes I fell to the ground and just went to sleep, waking up hours later in a pool of sweat.

One hundred and twenty-seven days—when my father found me, both my knees were bleeding. He called down to my brother, who came running. Then I heard them drag the mattress down from the wall. He opened the window and brought cool rags to my limbs, washing me down the way the women in the villages washed down the sick and the dead. I couldn't move. He and Taimur picked me up at each end and put me on the bed. I lay there staring out as though from a pit in the ground. They were gazing down at me and talking quietly to each other. I reached up, and then realized that my hands and arms were just dead weights. A tear fell. My eyes burned. I didn't have to try to cry; I just did. It was a relentless pouring out of my soul, an involuntary weeping that had no end. When I wailed, they later told me, it went on for hours, all breath and no voice, like piano keys playing without strings.

Not knowing how to stop me, Taimur brought some of my medals up. Babrak followed suit, carrying a trophy in each of his hands. Then came my mother and Ayesha, who was home on a break from her university studies. One after the other, they quietly brought trophies to my room as I lay there, feet swollen and wrapped in cold towels. They lined them up all around my bed, which was lying at the center of the floor like a raft out at sea. And last came Sangeen, a small ornament in his hand. He sat down next to me and held out the glued-up trophy he'd broken all those years before, when I was just getting started. First time I'd ever won. I reached out then, let my fingers touch it, and fell asleep.

*

I woke to a laptop computer glowing in my room. It was Ayesha's, and in a dream I'd seen her white veil shifting over my floor. She kneeled down to leave it there, touched my face, and went out. Blank page; cursor flashing. I could hear voices murmuring like ghosts all through the house. I looked over at the racquet in the corner, waiting for me. The wrapping on the handle was tearing away, just like the fabric of my mind. Lately, I had difficulty just arranging my thoughts—get up, cook, clean, sleep. All over the floor, balls lay scattered, some in better shape than others. I'd glued several back together. The new ones I kept in a bag hanging from the door handle.

Then that door handle turned slowly and my father was there with me. Shortened beard; he'd taken care in repairing the hack job. Clean feet crossed the floor. I heard a soft voice behind him and knew my sister was waiting in the corridor. In a moment, he was on his knees like another figment, and his invisible perfume of rich soaps and oils fell all over me—state of *wudu*—it was Friday. I turned my face to the window and saw the sun going down. I'd slept all day. I looked at my father; he was still alive. From another part of the house, Taimur called to my mother—him too.

Delicately, my father pulled back the thin blue sheet and checked me over. Unraveled the towels from my feet. Turned my hands over his and touched the palms. Kissed one, then the other.

"This room is ruining you, Maria."

"I must play, Baba."

"You will play. I swear it. Just not here. Not this way—not in purdah."

"Purdah." I breathed the word out loud, looked around at the four walls, all of them closing in. I saw what he did—I was no better off than a lost girl out there in the tribal lands.

Ayesha moved behind him. She had a piece of paper in her hands and held it out to me.

"I've made a list of over fifty colleges around the world with squash programs, Maria. I'll help you write an email. You can try each one. You are a national champion—someone will help you."

Past the row of medals surrounding me, I saw that screen again, glowing white like an empty ocean. My father stood up. "You will play far away from here—in peace." Then he left the room and nodded to my sister. Ayesha was on the floor, clacking away as though I wasn't lying there wasted on the mattress in a squalid room in Peshawar, a bull's-eye over my tired heart.

"I'll help you get started and then, in a few days, when you're better, you can keep sending the letter until someone answers."

"Okay." It was all I could manage to say.

"I wonder how it should start."

Slowly, I rolled onto my side, bone and muscle screaming, saw the bruises on my wall, heard men shouting outside. Dogs barked. The sun slipped below the tree line, and I hadn't even asked yet if there had been a bomb that day. I didn't have to. There always was.

I took a deep breath—I didn't know a thing about letters, had never written one in my life.

Dear Madam/Sir, I am Maria Toorpakai . . .

19. Breakbone Fever

Dear Madam/Sir,

I am Maria Toorpakai Wazir. I belong to the South Waziristan Agency of Pakistan's Tribal areas on the Pak–Afghan border. South Waziristan, one of Pakistan's most turbulent Tribal Agencies and the home of the Taliban, is also my home. In this war-ravaged and mountainous area my people reside but without any ray of hope.

Here, young girls are passing their lives in such miserable conditions. They have no facilities in education, health; and no recreational activities. They are restricted to four walls despite a desire to come out of the Stone Age and get assimilated with the rest of the world. Things have only worsened since the Taliban took over. They have barred girls' education and blown up girls' schools, barber shops and music centers. You should be well aware of the suicide bomb blasts emanating from these areas. My father, despite being severely opposed by the tribe and threatened by the Taliban, seeing my aptitude, not only permitted but encouraged me to play squash.

Now I am the sole and first ever Pakistani and tribal Pashtun girl to represent Pakistan in international squash tournaments, reaching the rank of number 58 while securing the World Junior number 3 title. I am training

hard to achieve the world number 1 position; but as
you see, I come from a highly conservative area. I was
threatened to stop playing sports, which has totally
disturbed my squash for the last three years, as I couldn't
move for training and with peace of mind . . .

I will be waiting for your positive response.

Regards,

Maria Toorpakai Wazir,

Professional squash player

One email multiplied more than a thousand times in more
than two years; sent out into the ether across millions of miles;
landing at universities and colleges, squash camps and academies;
illuminating the inboxes of international champions and coaches
all over Europe, Australia, and North America—only to be
ignored. During that time, my parents scrimped to pay for a
third-hand laptop so that I could keep sending and checking,
sending and checking, morning and night. By the summer of
2010, I was running out of places and people—I was also running out of stamina. Taliban threats loomed like a guillotine, and
I was still training alone in my small room, pummeling the same
dirty wall, which had gone from bone white to black, end to end.

I'd made up my mind not to fall apart again and just managed
to keep my psyche from unraveling. The trick was not to think
too hard about how I was living and continue day to day, sometimes hour to hour. Steadfast as ever, my family had picked me
up off the floor, tended to my wounds, and watched me go at it
again—no questions asked. The fact was, so many other people
had seen worse—like the girls confined to squalid huts in the
hills, forming a ring of despair in the desolate miles outside
Peshawar. For a time, ambition and hope sustained me. Every
separate email going out was like a message tucked in a bottle
and tossed into an ocean current. While I snapped the ball and

shuffled around my room, I ran down my list of emails; the rou-
lette wheel of pleas continued despite ever-lengthening odds. Just
like the region I lived in, no one outside Pakistan wanted to
touch me.

*

Taimur brought me the news, feet flying up the stairs two at a
time. Soaring into my room, he all but fell straight across it,
clutching a sheet of paper in his hand. Then he stood to attention, almost swaying from the delight that swirled in his eyes.
Leaning against the wall, catching my breath, I looked around
the room. Whenever I was interrupted in the midst of hours of
drills, it was like climbing a ladder out of another place and time.
When I played in that room, I wasn't there at all: I was at the
British Open in London, the Malaysian Open in Kuala Lumpur,
in the United States up against the best players in the world—
and I won every time.

I took the paper from Taimur, and from the first sentence the
words seemed to rise right off the page and land all over me. As if
by some preordained miracle, the 2010 National Games of Pakistan would be held in Peshawar—a stone's throw from our house
in Little FATA. Hosting the games while the Taliban prowled the
full periphery of the city was an act of monumental bravery—
some said it was just plain stupid. The Taliban had declared
sports as *haram*—forbidden. Taimur watched me go to the
window and gaze out in the direction of the stadium. At night,
when the electricity was out in our neighborhood, I sometimes
thought I could see the light of the arena punching through the
darkness. I wondered who was playing whom and at what.

I already knew I was going. Holding on to the top rank in
the under-seventeen and -nineteen divisions was no small feat.
Just to make it to tournaments and hold my own, I had to conduct covert operations that risked my life. I believed that, given
the right environment to play in—a real court for a start, and a
good coach—I could be world champion. All I wanted was a fair
chance, like everyone else. The games were just what my battered

psyche and the whole of demoralized Peshawar needed. Twenty-one sports, top-ranked athletes from all over the country invited to compete while the rest of Pakistan watched, casting a bright light over the shadow of tyranny looming all around us. Suicide bombers had already gone racing through volleyball courts and cricket pitches uttering homicidal prayers—my father said they'd dynamite a hopscotch game if they came across one.

When at last I snapped out of the sudden daydream Taimur had handed me, I looked at my smiling brother. What I loved most about him was that while he watched my joy, he made it his own, right down to his toes, on which he rose as though filling with air. He didn't have to say a thing. I nodded, letting him know I was going. Then he came over and picked me up, threw me over his shoulder, and lugged me around the four corners of the room. I shouted and laughed.

"Why are you so happy about this, Taimur? I play at other tournaments."

He lowered me to the floor, hands still on my shoulders. "Don't you know what this means, Maria? Finally, we will all get to come see you play."

*

Just a six-minute drive from our house was one of the biggest sports arenas in Pakistan, Qayyum Stadium, with a capacity of 15,000—all packed into a bowl of bright bucket seats. From a mile away, you could hear the din of the assembling crowd, the beat of drums. As we made our approach down the cordoned-off thoroughfare, the arena floodlights pressed up into the sky in a great teal-colored arch that we all pointed to. In the absence of his beloved radio, my father was singing out loud—an Elvis Presley tune. They might take his precious machines and gadgets, but they could not take his booming voice. He belted it out—"Blue Suede Shoes"—as we all made our way down Mall Road in the glut of traffic. There were ten police and military checkpoints: we all kept our provincial ID's at the ready. Five of us were jammed into a car borrowed from a friend of my father's: my mother,

Ayesha, and I in the backseat, the men up front. My security detail for the night were in unmarked cars front and back. Now that I was under a self-imposed house arrest, the protection officers only made random checks, or called on us if there was a new threat.

Peering out the window, I felt the warmth of my family pressed like a soft fortress all around me. How many years since we'd all traveled together in the same vehicle? So many moves— chasing freedom along the Khyber Pass, following steady jobs and good schools with my father at the wheel and the rest of us jostled in the back among the oranges and chickens and the pelting dust. Outside, in the lit-up night, the city of Peshawar awakened. In droves, the population poured out from cramped apartments and dingy houses and closed-up shops, flooding the streets in a great tide of defiant hope. On behalf of the squash federation, I was asked to carry the national flag, spotlights blazing across the full length of the playing field. Being there was a triumph—for the first time in years, I was outside in the open. No hoodie. No rushing—on the way to the arena, we never changed license plates once, as we often did in those days. Despite the multitude of threats to us all, not one athlete turned down the invitation to compete.

But one was turned away at the gates.

When we pulled up, a uniformed man approached and ushered me aside. Dressed in my full team kit, I presented my identification cards and invitation. Barely looking at them, he talked into his phone and looked me over. I stared up to the great white rim of the stadium; the glow and the fanfare poured out over the lip. All around me, the air pulsed. I could not believe that I had gone from playing in my bedroom to this. It was a great day—for Pakistan, for Peshawar, for our frayed ideals of freedom . . . for me.

The threat had come in only that afternoon, in a disturbing series of calls to the event officials. If there was one person the Taliban didn't want at the National Games, it was me—the first Pashtun girl to play professional sports and win a national ranking. One thing singled me out from the rest—my tribal blood. I was an example to those they'd already enslaved and to those still tearing their way out of the Taliban's nets. Outside the tall iron gates, I heard only the gist of what was said to me, the other athletes filing in holding flags and banners. All I knew was that I wasn't going inside. *Too many lives at risk.* I was devastated, but I walked away.

Taimur told me later they'd put my picture up on the jumbo screen, my name in flashing lights. When the crowd jumped up and cheered, he said the thunder went up his legs and out his arms. My mother wiped away a tear, my father shook his fists—and I saw none of it. I was back in my room—just a twenty-minute walk down straight-as-a-blade streets; sliver of moon, not a single star; every window shuttered for the night. For once, I wasn't afraid of being kidnapped or shot on the way home. The Taliban were too busy trying to get a bomb or a shooter into the games or plotting future acts of revenge.

The fact was, as long as I played, they'd come after me. As long as I lived in Pakistan, they could reach me. They could stuff me in a car, take me up into the barren hillsides, *do things*—that's how people put it. It was widely known how they violated the girls they took before killing them. They'd done as much to female doctors and writers, artists and musicians—plucked from the streets and never seen again. In our living room, over the warm perfume of black tea, I'd often heard the stories of how they treated girls who had sinned. After I heard the first one, I secretly researched how to buy cyanide pills to keep in my bag when I went out to compete. Several times I asked my father for a gun. We weren't living in the wild west of Darra Adam Khel anymore. I might have held my own with a Makarov while picking off cans of Fanta, or needed a pistol to fend off a lone intruder out to teach my family a lesson. In a time of unbridled jihad I was no match against a contingent of well-trained Talibs sent to kidnap and kill me. My father refused, knowing they would just turn it on me, or that I would be forced by some violent act of perversion to turn it on myself.

The street outside was submerged in darkness, all the electricity out except for the lights of the stadium. Moving along the empty road, the packed arena behind me, I knew I was doing exactly what the Taliban wanted—vanishing into the dark.

*

Days later, Taimur found the outdoor courts. Riding a bike or driving the car, he never said how. It didn't matter. Out in the middle of a desolate park, two side-by-side squash courts sat abandoned like ancient monuments. Standing very still, you could hear birds sleeping among the reeds of a nearby pond. Taimur took me there under the cover of night, hand on my shoulder, hoodie tight over my head, blindfolded.

"Open your eyes, Maria."

Then he let the flashlight dance over the ground, moths and insects drawn into the beam like flurries of snow. Gasping, I ran ahead, fast—faster than I'd moved my legs in a straight line in years. On my back, I stared up, those forsaken walls like a frame to a clear starry night. Grass knee-high in the long-forgotten park, the courts might as well have been in purdah with me, waiting. I felt the ground—still smooth enough. Taimur got our racquets out and started hitting. I stood up. Together, we danced around the court, the ball darting back and forth between us— pure joy. Mid-match, I turned to him, panting.

"Taimur, I will never punch you again."

As soon as it was dark, we always found a way there, crossing the damp, wild grass that caressed my calves on the way to the lonely courts, the sounds of the night insects pulsing low to the ground. It was like sharing in a forbidden dream. Several times each week, Taimur gave me his hours like a gift and expected nothing in return but that I play well. And try my best to win.

Somehow, I did win—third at the World Juniors, and better at tournaments across South Asia—often by the skin of my teeth, and just to spite the enemy at my heels. Each time there was any publicity in the local papers, we'd hear from the Taliban. Warnings were usually leveled against my father, who still slipped in and out of the tribal areas, finding ways to teach like a Robin Hood of knowledge. There were still young minds out there, and somehow he uncovered them. When the Taliban seized one region, he moved with his bags of books and mind full of ideas to another, just like my mother changing schoolhouses. I think he secretly enjoyed what he was doing—teaching against dire odds. I know I enjoyed what I was doing—winning against them.

Every time I left the house to compete, it was the same frenetic routine: borrowing cars, switching license plates, hunkering down in the backseat under a hoodie. I began using my computer for more than just emails. I was conducting research and following the news. My father always said: *Know thy enemy*. In 2010, the Taliban was on a tear, overrunning FATA: North Waziristan, South Waziristan, Kurram, Orakzai, Bajaur, Mohmand, and Khyber. Once those regions fell under their dark curtain, the Taliban's cloak settled over districts of the North-West Frontier Province, where the government had all but lost control: Tank, Dera Ismail Khan, Lakki Marwat, Bannu, Hangu, Karak, Swat. In the territories over which the Taliban held dominion, they imposed their barbaric version of Islam, complete with their own courts. Noose around its neck now, the city of Peshawar was under constant siege. What I learned about my enemy, more than anything else, was that they were indomitable. I would know—I shared their warrior blood.

I was up late at night, computer screen aglow, when a three-line ad caught my eye. My inbox remained empty, and my faith was splintering. For a time, I simply gave up sending out the letters. Sometimes I sat looking out into the night, imagined the person who might answer me one day, living in a distant country—free from end to end. The ad was simple and faraway, like a diamond shining at the bottom of a deep well—*Academy seeking a full-time squash coach*. Several times, like focusing on a blurred line, I read the name of the academy and the man who ran it. Already I knew his face, had tried to copy his magical trick shots, and dreamed often of doing what he did—just once.

Fingers hovering over the keys, I hesitated a moment and then started to type:

> To: Jonathon Power
>
> From: Maria Toorpakai
>
> Subject: want to coach squash

Anyone who knew anything about squash in Pakistan, or anywhere, knew the name and the auburn-haired legend behind it. Jonathon Power—double world champion—needed a coach for his new academy in Toronto, Canada. Across the Atlantic, on the other side of the world. I pressed SEND and turned off my computer. Got my racquet.

*

In the dead of night, moonless and warm, Taimur shone his flashlight over the court ground, illuminating our feet as though in knee-deep water. Sometimes we could barely see the ball until it came shooting out through the dark. Already we talked about me becoming world champion. Once I found that belief, I wrapped it up in my mind like treasure and put it away for later—for when I was free.

Mist rose, insects buzzed all around us; I could hear their pulsing chorus as we played. After a long match, we lay on the court, flat on our backs, staring up into the night and talking in whispers, the way we had as small children in the unspoiled river plains. Talking like two kids anywhere. When I was down, which happened often, it was Taimur who took charge like a coach, made sure I never went under. In those days, I don't think he let us go more than a week without taking me out to play.

"You must go to the training camp in Malaysia, Maria. Get out of here. Ayesha checked your travel permit. You played in the tournament in Kuala Lumpur, and the visa is still good. If you leave now, they will extend it by a whole month."

"No chance."

"We'll find the money to get you there."

"Where will you find it? I need a plane ticket, food, a room. It's impossible."

"Let us worry about that."

On the way back in the car—middle hours between waking and sleeping—I lowered the back window. As I'd so often seen my father do in traffic jams along the mountain passes, I let my hand rest along the warped frame. Cool wind blew the sweat off my forearm. Streetlights all out, I felt the heat rise and leave my skin. Taimur glanced back at me, said nothing. It was a brazen act, but I ignored him, ignored reality. On the cool, steady gusts, I could smell rain, saw flashes of summer lightning heat up the blackness. All day, a sea of roiling cloud overhead had churned to deepening grays, and I said something to Taimur about how there wouldn't be a bomb if there was a good storm. Hands gripping the wheel, knuckles all bone, he simply nodded. I looked out again and then down. A mosquito sat on my arm. Sitting back, I just watched it for a moment, tiny tentacle boring into my skin, drinking. Finally, I reached over and swatted. When I pulled my hand away, my forearm was streaked with blood.

Days later, Taimur took the bus with me to the airport in Islamabad, with an envelope marked "Kuala Lumpur," full of rupees, tucked inside the pocket along my waistband. It was just enough to get me there and home again. After coming back from those secret courts with Taimur, I'd found the money sitting on my mattress wrapped in paper, a happy-face sticker holding down the seam. Between them, my parents had been scraping for weeks to come up with the money in time. I couldn't say no. I'd purchase the ticket on standby at the very last moment. My father had found a room for me in the home of a Hindu family who had an apartment across the street from the training facility. Next to me on the bus, Taimur kept his attention up the aisle while I slept the journey away, head against the window, asphalt rushing under the wheels in a dizzying blur. Hood halfway over my face, I cocooned myself in a tracksuit, felt my own breath beat against my tired skin. There was a steady pain behind my tired eyes. Every inch of me felt bruised. The traffic was slow, and I chugged water whenever I woke up, usually with a start. Then I'd look around, see the domes of slumbering heads propped against the seats in front of us; rain hitting the glass; wipers at the front beating back and forth slowly. Several times, Taimur turned and asked if I was all right. I told him I just needed sleep and would get plenty on the plane.

We bought my ticket in cash—next available flight, in case anyone was watching. The Taliban had a network of spies at the airports. Within hours, they'd know which plane I was on, even which seat—everything but when I was coming back. Taimur counted up the money, and I watched him slapping the bills down on the counter like playing cards, realizing that my father hadn't come home from the market with meat in over a month. It was the third day of Eid, when Muslims the world over finally broke their month-long dawn-to-sunset Ramadan fast. It was my sacred duty to show happiness, to give thanks, even just to smile, but I couldn't feel a thing. Over the past few weeks, I'd steadily slipped down a well of depression. During the first day of feasting, I'd come back from our prayers morose and hadn't shared in the celebratory meal of sweet, fragrant food. Every morsel that crossed my blistered lips tasted bitter. It was that night that my family enlisted Taimur to convince me to leave for the camp. If the Taliban didn't kill me, they believed my purdah would.

Kuala Lumpur, the capital of Malaysia, is the glittering crown jewel of South Asia. Not even there yet, I already felt the distant lure of that majestic city, which I'd visited on several occasions with my team. When I'd come home the first time and Ayesha asked, "What was it like?" I said simply: "Another planet—beautiful."

When I left Taimur at the gate, he held me a long time, whispering things in my ear that I don't remember now. He told me I was too warm and pulled down my hood, saying I couldn't dress that way at an airport. Then he handed me the laptop and my racquet bag and ushered me to the security line. He stood way back. My brother had never been on a plane—been anywhere—and I could see the wonder in his face as he watched me feeding my bags into the mouth of the X-ray machine, taking off my shoes, handing over my computer. Over the loudspeaker, my flight was called, and I hauled my belongings off the conveyor belt. My throat was sore and dry. Water bottle long empty, I was dizzy with thirst and asked a man if there was somewhere I could get water. As though in a trance, I watched his mouth form words; I was so tired I could hardly speak anymore. He pointed down the hall and I simply followed his finger. Once, I looked back at Taimur and raised a hand; he waved back at me, stepped forward a pace, and stopped. I remember his smile slipping into a frown before I turned away and hauled my gear down to the gate. I stopped once to take a long drink of the sour water coming out of the drinking fountain—it tasted just the way parts of Peshawar smelled, and I thought it might make me sick.

The grinding of landing gear, the rush of wind, a stream of cloud racing over the flaps; I awoke from a long, cold sleep. Through spires of white cumulus cloud, I could see the two rivers my father had showed me years before in the atlas, Klang and Gombak, which converged down there into the brown water that gave the city its name: Kuala Lumpur—meaning muddy confluence. Around those watercourses, the city spread out in a wide mass of towering structures, like a child's dream of the future made manifest. In the background, the Titiwangsa Mountains ranged. I let go of my breath slowly, my heart laboring from exhaustion. I thought I'd feel better when the plane touched the ground.

Curving highways wove through the heart of the city like asphalt ribbons leading into a giant jewelry box. Rain falling lightly on the cab, the sun still peeking through, streets glistened. Hundreds of towering buildings, glass faces all blazing, rose into a thin canopy of mist. I remember telling Babrak once: *They are called skyscrapers because they really do scrape the sky*—and in Kuala Lumpur it was true. But I wasn't paying attention to any of it. The pain behind my eyes made them twitch. When I blinked, it felt as though my lids were made of sandpaper. Every now and then my limbs erupted in strange aches and twinges. I kept drinking water from my water bottle. The driver kept look-ing at me in the rearview mirror. I remember his turban—white and wrapped tight around his scalp. My father told me they never take it off in public, but I couldn't remember why. Hindi music playing low, he asked me questions, and I know I answered him, though I'm not sure how.

The apartment building towered into a polluted haze, and as I went toward the entrance, I looked up into that rough yellow veil, felt myself falling, and held out a hand against the front door to steady myself. Tobacco smoke stained the air of the lobby in which I met the man who was renting me a room. In the eleva-tor, he gave me a key. Then, inside the apartment, he showed me to a room with a foam mattress and sleeping bag on the floor. I barely recall him or the hour that passed like heavy water between us. I told my landlord that the flight had made me tired and light-headed, and he left me alone.

Wallpaper swimming around me in strange patterns like snakes, I found a glass next to the sink in the bathroom and took a long drink. Moving through an eerie pain in my bones, I did everything in slow methodical movements, thinking only of the thin mattress waiting for me like a raft at the other end of the room. I had the laptop open—I'd promised to email when I got in. Ayesha would relay the message; she and I used the same address. I just made my fingers hit the keys. The inbox flashed blue and I stared at it, seeing blurred words that I couldn't read. I typed out a single word—*here*—pressed SEND, and went to sleep.

Twelve hours later I awoke and reached for my laptop. I kept thinking I should tell someone I was sick; Taimur might have guessed it already. Even as my body heaved and trembled, I thought it was a combination of raw nerves and overexertion. In training, I often took things too far. I stared at the white screen a long time, at the lit-up blue line in my inbox, read the name through the inertia of my steadily rising fever—*Jonathon Power*. For several minutes, it meant nothing. Then its full meaning rose into my consciousness like a massive bright balloon. I might have read the message two or three times, not quite believing it. All I could think of after that was that I would wake up any minute, and how cold it was in the room. Somehow I typed out an answer that I would later forget even having written in the drama of my unfolding agony.

Sometime after, I slogged to the door, took the elevator down. I felt like I was drowning inside that small box. Then, as I heaved against the elevator walls, I slowly lifted up my squalid sweatshirt to reveal a sea of red patches covering every inch of my skin. So hard to focus, eyes and head pulsing like the inside of a struck bell—where was I going? I didn't know. The lobby spread before me in a forest of people and potted palms. My feet dragged across it as though through sand. People walked past me in bright, flowing clothes that made me think of tropical birds, or the streaks of sunset I'd seen the last time I was in the city.

Crossing the street in the damp heat outside was like wading through water. Twice I fell across the road. I cried out but made no sound—it felt as though every bone in my body was breaking into pieces, like a tapped eggshell. In the quick space between my falls, the air of the city breathed over my blazing skin. I kept thinking, *What's wrong with me?* People milled all around as I lay there; I could see their moving feet. Some stopped, glanced down briefly, and shuffled past. I was only one hundred feet from the sports center, but it might as well have been a thousand miles. Eventually, a few people came out and led me into the shade of a tree. Spine against the hard bark, I stretched out my legs and winced. After conferring around me, several other squash players from the camp helped me to the medical center. I heard myself mutter that I must have gotten injured playing in the bedroom.

At the doctor's office, a nurse took vials of blood and I watched them filling fast. The deep color brought to mind the purple *jamun* fruit of home, and I asked her if it was true that inside veins, blood ran blue. If she gave an answer, I don't remember it. The only thing I do recall is the calm face of the doctor explaining what platelets were, how crucial to life, and that mine were dwindling. It wasn't the first time I'd heard the words "dengue fever," and I knew well what that meant. In the month of

Ramadan that had just passed, a cataclysmic flood had ravaged parts of Pakistan, swallowing whole villages and washing away the inhabitants. In its aftermath, deadly illnesses erupted, many born of the stagnant, polluted waters and the insects they harbored. At the golden hours of dawn and sunset, insects swarmed in such numbers that the air seemed to vibrate, and people who lived near the swollen river banks often stayed indoors. It wasn't a sports injury that caused the throbbing tearing in my limbs but a mosquito of the genus *Aedes*, carrying a lethal virus. Mosquito bites and their scars stippled my arms and legs perhaps from those late-night squash matches in the abandoned park with Taimur. As the doctor explained my diagnosis, I remembered that last drive home, car window down, watching the mosquito coolly sucking at my blood.

Dengue was also known as breakbone fever—and I knew why. When I moved, I thought parts of me were snapping away like twigs. When I was given a phone to call our neighbors back home, they rushed to find my mother and brought her to meet my shaken voice. As the name of my illness crossed the receiver, she let out a high-pitched cry I'd never heard before. People told me later she had fallen straight to the floor, where she sat bent over herself, phone cradled. Then for several minutes she spoke in a whirlwind, horror and fear fraying her words. She assured me several times that they would find help by nightfall, and hung up. It took three men to get her to her feet to go find Shams.

While I was sent back to the apartment with a bottleful of pills and instructions to rest and drink fluids, my mother was flying out into the street, a half-dozen neighbors behind her and my twin brothers at her side, to look for my father. The doctor was hoping my youth would overwhelm the pathogens waging war over my blood, but my mother knew better. When she found my father, he was coming up the walk with a satchel full of fruit he'd bartered for—with what, no one knew. Sometimes he left the house carting nothing more than a grin and an empty stomach, strolling back home with delectable gems—a box of honeyed dates, squares of Turkish delight, a ripe pomegranate, a handful of *jamun*. When he looked up and saw my mother rushing toward him, they say he dropped the bag, oranges and mangoes, plums and lemons hitting the sidewalk and rolling into the gutter. The book he held on to tight.

One of our neighbors in Little FATA knew a Shia doctor from Para-Chinaar in the Kurram Agency who now lived with his wife in Kuala Lumpur. When the man heard that there was a Pashtun girl lying sick in an apartment in the city, he came for me. Dr. Saadat and his wife, Umehani, both dark-haired angels, brought me to their home, and helped me into a clean bed. Having crossed into their forties without the blessing of a single longed-for child, they embraced me as their own. It didn't matter to either one of them that I was a Sunni Muslim and that our people often existed in opposition to one another—we were Muslims, and one way or the other that made us family. I, in turn, came to think of them as a mother and father, while I was so sick and so far from home. Over the next four or five days, they took shifts administering medicine, brought spoonfuls of soft, warm custard to my lips, telling me again and again to eat, to drink a lot, a little at a time. We all kept thinking that eventually I would get better; but as hard as my body fought, the virus was ransacking my blood, cell by cell—fast.

In the predawn hours, I woke, shirt covered in vomit. A gulp of water seemed to slice down my throat like a serrated blade. My mouth was coated in a strange slick paste of saliva and blood—so much, I thought I was losing all my teeth. Pulling back the sheets, I lay there and looked up at the ceiling, where fan blades rotated. Stirred air that should have been soft seemed to pelt my hot skin. I could see myself as though from above, saw my red eyes, the rash creeping up my neck, blooming over my cheeks, making them look as though they'd been slapped. I could feel my pulse slow until it barely registered at all. Then a numb weightlessness ran down me like a shaman's dancing hands, lifting away every possible sensation, and one by one the waking world shut its doors.

Later, Umehani found me and called the ambulance in which I woke up howling. Somewhere within, a moving carousel of razor blades was shredding my body. In that blinding fog of agony, I saw my father standing at the end of the stretcher, holding up a sheet of paper on which he'd drawn a diagram of a detonating cloud and a stick figure on the ground—*stress waves enter the body invisibly, and rip apart tissue*. A paramedic was trying to put the oxygen mask over my face and yelling my name, but I heard him only as though from some deep underground cavern. I grabbed his hand and squeezed, the ambulance siren clanging, until be brought his face to my lips. I said the only thing I could say—"Taliban. Bomb."

After that, there was nothing, a void of people moving over me as though casting a spell, voices like tiny flashes of light beaming randomly through the dark: *gastrointestinal bleeding, fluid accumulation in the abdominal cavity, blood pressure dropping, shock.* I woke up wrapped in white sheets. I had been dreaming of the Americans and their colorful candies, pulled from a white sack. Opening my eyes, I smelled the faint sweetness of sugar, heard one of them laugh, felt myself holding out a hand as he dropped a yellow gumdrop into my smooth palm, like a tiny sun. I raised an arm and tried to rub my face, and a tangle of rubber lines came with it, as though half of me had been tied down. The painful tugging in my forearms made my eyes flutter open. It was that dull ache that told me I was still there, still anywhere—wherever that was. At the foot of the bed, a man was standing, something in his hands, and speaking softly to a figure in a corner chair. Drawing back my sheet, I tried to sit up, squinting. The sheet felt as though it was made of lead.

The man came closer, said my name, and felt my forehead. He brought a cold disk to my chest and held it there. When I tried to speak, the words wouldn't come, as though they were trapped deep down in my throat and I had to tug hard against a rope to pull each one out:

"Taliban. They have a bomb that only kills impure women."

"Sit back now, sit back."

And I did. Closed my eyes and was gone again.

*

Umehani was there, sitting by the window, wrapped in the soft tulle of early morning. Even as I stared, she vanished. Then, what seemed like a minute later, she was standing near me, touching my face. Dr. Saadat was there too, and I could hear their low murmurs. They knew something I didn't—what was happening, whether I would live or die. The doctors at the hospital said the odds were fifty-fifty and were calling my family back in Little FATA. I remember the cold phone against my ear and the voices of home, listening with a strange detachment, telling them not to worry, as though I was embarking on a long journey. After that, time peeled away and I stayed still, just went back down into some primal cave in my mind, in which I nestled like a hibernating animal. Sleep. I wanted nothing else for a while. Forever even. I checked one last time to see if Umehani was there, and the chair sat empty. Then my eyes shifted to the other side of the room. From the corner, nestled high up like a spider in its web, a man watched and waited. Just there, staring out from tight rolls of silk turban and mottled skin, he drew a smoldering reefer to his lips. The acrid smell of smoke, warm and venomous—I knew the scent with a horror that made my soul fall back into itself, before I drifted off.

While I traced the thin line between life and death, my body making up its mind like tossing a coin, my mother was counting out rupees. On the outskirts of Peshawar, she went with Taimur and found a man who sold her a black goat for a good price, and somehow they got it home. The farmer wished her Allah's grace; her request for a dark beast meant she had suffered a misfortune. By the time she came home, my father had brought back a mullah to conduct the sacrifice. With a red autumnal moon already hanging, the mullah led the animal into our street, long blade in his hand. Just behind him, her head bowed, my mother carried a white cloth in the crook of her arm. The animal bucked and whimpered—it knew. People watched my mother, her face pale with panic, her expression wild; she was muttering senseless things, her eyes darting. No one dared go near her. Lips forming a breathless prayer, she clutched the animal by the fur along its head, which jerked between herself and the mullah. In a moment, the mullah forced its chin up exposing the full smooth neck. For a few seconds the animal resisted, the whites of its eyes bulging, as you could see the whites of my mother's knuckles while she held fast to the beast. For the moment, the hind legs scraping over the pavement was the only sound. But then Aami spoke softly, her face close to a twitching ear, her tears dripping into the black fur. As though her words were a lulling drug, the animal's full body gradually gave way, its head drooping to one side. Just then the mullah held up the blade. In the end, it let him do the thing my mother believed would save me. My calm, beautiful mother watched as he slit the neck of the gasping animal in one quick movement. As red liquid poured from the fissure and over the ground, she invoked the name of Allah and stared up silently, eyes begging the darkening sky. Slowly drained of its blood, the animal struggled to stand. It went down on its forelegs before collapsing, the last breaths coming out in slow labored beats. When the animal was dead, my mother handed the white cloth to the mullah in which to wipe his hands and wrap his blade. Then in a final act of charity known as *sadaqah*, she cut up and gave the fresh meat to feed the poor. That night, my fever finally broke.

The next time I waded up to wakefulness, Umehani was back in the chair. Darkness behind her, her pale face glowed blue as though she was gazing into a pool. Fingers tapping on her cell phone, she made small movements with her mouth, and I thought somehow that she was swallowing words instead of speaking. I struggled to sit up.

"Umehani."

Then she was right there, clutching my hand. I could feel her pulse in the space between our palms. I was making an inventory of things—my feet, legs, arms, and hands—all of me still there and moving. Twitching. A burning itch flared over every inch of my skin, and I winced. It would take a thousand hands to quell it.

"Umehani."

Bending to push me down, arranging things all around me—IV lines and pillows—she was shaking her head. "Maria, Maria, the fever has passed."

And I looked up into the corner of the ceiling for the man who'd been sitting there on and off, watching me, for days. He was gone.

"He was here. He left."

"Who left?"

She was frantically pressing a button next to my head.

I heard an alarm in the hallway and then the man with the clipboard was back. He sat down next to the bed and talked to me awhile, told me just to listen. The doctor who saved me had quite a story to tell. I lay there taking in everything that had gone wrong with my body: internal bleeding, build-up of fluid around the lungs and in the abdomen, severe hypotension, decreased blood supply to vital organs. When I got to the hospital, I was hours from death.

I'd been in intensive care for over a week. Umehani had been sleeping in the chair in the corner for days, though her clean *chador* showed no sign of it. Three times, she'd been told I might not survive the night. Doctor gone, the nurse stood next to me. Umehani held my head while she brought a phone to my ear. My sister's voice came through, and I let out a feeble cry. We spoke for a few minutes, and I remember telling her that I was better, only very tired. She told me about the goat my mother had slaughtered at nightfall, and how everyone believed it was the reason the fever had lifted. She had messages for me from each member of the family, and from others whose names meant little to me in the confused state I was in. Talking to her was like slipping in and out of wrinkles in time. When she asked a final question, I was barely there:

"Maria, who is Jonathon Power?"

I said nothing and lay there limp, phone hot against my ear. Maybe I didn't believe her. I'd already had my miracle—I was alive.

"Did you hear me, Maria? Jonathon Power . . ."

Ayesha said later that I never answered, and she wasn't sure if I'd even heard her. Long before the call ended, I was in the deep forest of another long dream.

20. Liberty Bell

Dengue fever had pushed me to the very edge. My platelets were hovering at just above the benchmark of death. I remember telling someone later that the agony was more than a physical sensation, it was a primordial pain. It yanked me right out of my own skin and into a void of hot light, like drowning in a star. When the fever was done tearing through my insides, it simply cast away the leftover shell, as though on a raft far out at sea, on which I lay in a languid stupor. Arms and legs, fingers and toes no longer had any form. I seemed to have dissolved. For a long time I couldn't feel anything. As the viral hurricane disbanded, I was no more substantial than the stillness in which I blended and fell asleep, a sleep so deep it came with the feeling of falling until there was nothing, and I floated in my own bottomless slumber. Several times, I wondered if I was still alive.

Buried under cold sheets, arms sprouting strange vines of tubes and wires, whenever I came to it was in an anguished torrent of confusion that made me flail and gasp. The room was so bright with electric light, the walls pure white, it was like waking up within a glacier. I remember the nurse coming in and speaking, and the hard feel of a telephone held to my ear. Members of my family had called several times, spoken to me softly, their voices chiming in my empty consciousness like tiny distant bells. At last, on her third try, my sister's voice, clear as a songbird through the crackling static, flooded my head. Somehow, I could not reach her; the air from my lungs came out in thin rasps, as though I was buried in gravel. Nothing she said seemed to make any sense; my mind struggled to understand simple sentences. When I heard Ayesha say my name, I know that I wept, my eyes burning, incapable of making a single tear. She said again and again how they had all prayed night and day, and that I would be going home soon.

Grief engulfed me in a new pain; I wanted home, but not Peshawar. Back to where it all started, our big house in the time-less valley . . . filling a metal bucket with cool water from the stream . . . the perfume of tamped clay floors. As she spoke, I felt my arms lifting that full bucket, upending the water down over me in the courtyard. The scent of the soap my father brought from the market, wrapped up in tissue like a precious gift. The taste of it forming on my tongue as I took the tiniest of secret bites. On hot days, when I plunged my full head into that cool water, the world outside was instantly muted—just as it was as I stared out from the curtain of my slowly lifting illness, unsure of what was real and what was not. Before Ayesha was done talking to me, I was back in the courtyard, my small head submerged in the full bucket, the cold dark water dulling all the pain. Then my father came and pulled me out, carried me wet and cold in his arms, stepping across the threshold of our home, and placed my ruined body in bed between himself and my mother.

When I woke again, he was gone and I was back in the hospital, wondering what had happened to Ayesha's voice. Trying to think was like trying to untangle a huge knot and pulling loose only a few strands at a time. My sister had called, asked me things I could not answer—that was all I knew. Under my skin, the flesh was soft and bruised in strange mottled patches. I stared down the length of my lifeless limbs, trying to imagine what they had once been capable of: running around courts—winning. I was the number one female player in Pakistan, and here I was, lying in a small room in Kuala Lumpur, hardly able to move. At no time did I recall the name Ayesha later said she had repeated many times—Jonathon Power. He was just a vague figment in a dream I had, and then let go of.

Seven days later, I was back on a plane. My family picked me up at the airport in Peshawar, and I recall the flurry of their arms and hands touching, so many voices speaking in a chorus. My mother said that she'd sent a whole daughter to Malaysia, but only half of her had come back.

The neighbors slaughtered a lamb, roasted the meat, and everyone ate outside in the street. I was in a chair, wrapped up, always cold. Every now and again someone came to sit with me, filled my cup with water, and held it to my lips. Later, from the quiet of my bedroom, I could hear my family gathered downstairs in the front room, talking. I heard my name repeated and sensed in the quick, breathless intonations the fullness of their fear. I wondered how bad I must look for people to stare at me and need to touch my skin softly and so often. My mother came in several times, sighing in the near darkness as she moved about, and rubbed a pink lotion over my body that smelled of roses and made me want to sleep. And I did, on and off, for days.

*

When my father came in with two cups of tea, I was sitting up. Squash racquet in my lap, I was taping the frayed handle. Outside the open window, a soft rain was falling, perfuming the warm pavement. Now that I was recuperating, my senses had sharpened. It was almost as though the fever had left a live wire running through me. I heard every murmur in the house, sensed every movement, smelled every layer of the outside world, from the asphalt and damp earth to the scent of coriander and butchered animals rolling in from the market street miles up the road. Even the distant mountains came to me in whispers, alive at that time of year with so many fragrant flowers, no one bothered to name them all. When my father sat down near me, we sipped in tandem. I knew what he would say before he said it. The Taliban had increased the intensity of their attacks in the city, bombing crowded markets and killing by the dozens, or sniping their enemies one bullet at a time. Even in my debilitated state, I was still firmly in their crosshairs. If I stopped playing squash altogether, I would still be me—half boy, half girl—a freak of nature in their narrow eyes. Without even thinking about it, a Talib with my name on his list would shoot me for riding a bicycle or wearing shorts. I no longer had the energy to continue living a life of self-imposed purdah. My father took my racquet from me and squeezed the handle, checked the wrapping before giving it back.

"There isn't any time left, Maria."

"I know, Baba

"Have you thought about what to do?"

"Yes. There is a tournament in Delaware. Taimur told me. All I have to do is register as a player. The Pakistan Squash Federation can help me obtain a travel visa to the United States. They give visas to professional athletes."

"Good. If you can go, you must go."

"But I won't play well."

"It's not about playing anymore, Maria. It's about staying alive."

At the end of all my options, it still never occurred to me to follow up on the emails from Jonathon Power—I simply had no recollection of their existence. As far as I was concerned, our brief exchange had never happened. In my stupor, I'd even deleted letters, so there was no way for me to check up on my failed memory.

During the weeks before the tournament, I was unable to train because I was too weak. Just once, and for what would turn out to be the last time, I went to the complex, huddled in the backseat of a neighbor's car. The administration at the academy had changed hands, and the new one wasn't keen on supporting the female team. Most of the new girls came from poor backgrounds, with few resources. The fact that they were playing a sport at all in their battered shoes and thin veils was a miracle. The academy gave them nothing more than the court on which they played for an hour here or there. No clothes. Broken racquets. Even balls were scarce. No coaching was made available. No training. Things had changed. The new order just wanted all of us to disappear, back into our homes, into hot kitchens, into suffocating *burqas*— where we belonged. As I walked the corridor between the courts, scanning the long line of young girls waiting for a turn in their tattered clothes, I looked across at the boys assembled on the other side. All whites. Their sneakers so new, I could smell the clean rubber. They were filing into a single court, where the secretary who ran the squash program was handing out new racquets. Members of the media were there taking pictures, scribbling. So many smiles, they could light up the box for a week. I watched it all through the clean sheet of glass, the girls behind me whispering in the darkened corridor. I was the number one player in the nation and I knew, as the secretary's eyes fell momentarily on me, that he had no idea who I was—and didn't care. When I was in the hospital in Malaysia, my family had to scrape together my airfare home. The squash academy had ignored their many entreaties. Thankfully, the hospital hadn't charged a rupee for saving my life.

Various teams were leaving for a tournament the next day, and I assumed that was the reason for the media attention. Soon everyone was crowded in the long hallway, and I listened to the federation secretary—whom I didn't recognize, but a well-fed man by the looks of him—make a short, impassioned speech in his tight-fitting green blazer. He spoke about his mandate as the head of the academy to foster the female team, and as I listened and camera shutters snapped, the girls stood quietly. I studied each one, but they were all the same—just a row of poor girls from all over the country in their scuffed shoes and old shirts, used-up racquets in their hands. Pathetic.

As the man droned on, my anger grew so vivid that it seemed to take on shades of red as it rose to a boil. My eyes pulsed in their sockets. Something had happened to my mind since I'd been ill. At any given time, an emotion or primal urge could overtake me like a rogue wave. When I was hungry, I gorged. When I was sad, I wailed. When I was tired, I slept all day. When I felt anguish, I raged. The secretary didn't see me charging for him up the hall and through the crowd, accusations spilling out, finger thrust at his face like a dagger. I gestured to the girls' shoes, might have pulled one off a hapless foot to show him the filthy, frayed laces, the fact the girl didn't have socks—none of them did. I grabbed and held up a broken racquet for all to see. Then I told them, in a voice that I didn't recognize as my own, that the Taliban was winning with their bombs and bullets. Still I wasn't finished. I pointed out the boys' team in their immaculate clothes, as they stood around gawking. A few of the journalists ushered me, half wild and still raging, into an office and brought towels and cups of water. The secretary came in after them, calling me names like "big mouth" and "troublemaker." He still didn't know who I was, as I sat breathing fast and wiping sweat from the back of my burning neck. When I told him my full name and rank, just like a soldier might, I remember that he blanched, as though someone had taken an eraser to his face and rubbed away all the high color. I don't remember what happened afterward, but I didn't get any help from him with my US visa application. Later that day, I was told that within an hour of my tirade, the girls were all having their feet measured for new shoes. Before nightfall, they were decked head to toe in brand-new Nike athletic gear. By the next day, I was standing in a long line at the US consulate, application in hand and waiting my turn. Ayesha, who was active and well-connected in regional politics, made several calls to influential friends and secured me a last-minute interview with an American visa officer. The rest, she told me, was up to Allah.

As I waited, I became anxious. My mother and brother were several blocks away, waiting for me in the car. In April of that year, a band of militants had swooped onto Hospital Road in two vehicles packed with explosives and attacked the consulate in Peshawar. The suicide bombers blew themselves up to become *shaheeds* or would-be martyrs, while others tried to storm the building from behind a furious hail of gunfire. In another part of town, a simultaneous and coordinated attack took place at the headquarters of the Pakistani intelligence service. Over fifty people died that day, and more than one hundred were critically wounded. Several months later, just gaining admittance into the heavily fortified consulate building in Islamabad was a serious undertaking, requiring several checks to my pockets and satchel. Steely-eyed Marines were everywhere, kitted out in combat fatigues and body armor, assault rifles at the ready. Every now and then, one of them would walk through with a German shepherd scenting the ground. Though packed with people, the building was eerily quiet. When a man coughed in front of me, everyone turned around fast and stared at him.

"What is the purpose of your travel to the United States?"

One look at me, all bones draped in wasted muscle hobbling to the wicket, and he didn't believe my answer. I'd entered in a veil but pulled it down over my shoulders as I stood before the bulletproof glass screen to reveal a track suit underneath, in a gesture that seemed to startle him. I remember that he had green eyes, and that when he blinked, his lashes were so long and pale that the light shone right through them. It wasn't often you saw a full-blooded Westerner. I looked at his hands as they sifted through my application, smooth and strong and all-American. Papers, jars of pencils, pens, a tray full of paper clips cluttered the counter. There was a small photograph of an old couple on a sailboat smiling broadly, the sun beaming over their faces—grandparents. A steaming coffee mug stood on the desk to his right; every few minutes he lifted it to his face and put it back down. I sat staring through the thick glass and across the cluttered expanse as though it were an ocean. Just two and a half feet wide, to me the air between us was the whole world separating Pakistan from America. When he looked up shaking his head, my panic was instant. I don't think he even knew his power over me—that with a single word, barely a fraction of breath, my future would be obliterated.

A little over a year before, CNN had posted a short article about me on their US website. My father had printed a copy to take along in case my documents and explanations weren't enough. I had that paper folded and tucked into my pocket, and my fingers trembling I pushed it fast through a small drawer cut into the partition. Decision made, red tape in place, I could see the officer wasn't interested. He glanced over my shoulder. The line behind me stretched down the hall. As he unfolded the thin sheet, he looked dubious and his shoulders rose and fell. Then, as he took in the headline—TEEN ATHLETE FLED TALIBAN STRONGHOLD TO PURSUE DREAM—I saw a perceptible change. He read for about a minute while I waited—never once touched his cup. When he looked up, I could see his surprise and told him quietly that I *had* to go to the United States to play. As an American embassy official in Islamabad, he was a bigger target than I was, working in the biggest target in the capital. I hoped he would understand. Nodding, he picked up his telephone, and within seconds, another man walked in and they conferred for a while. They checked my passport and read the article. The entire time, I was perfectly still, as though someone had glued me to the floor. When the other man left, I struggled to breathe. In the end, the visa officer nodded. The space between us clear as he handed me back the article.

"Okay, your visa is good to go. Good luck, Miss Toorpakai."

On a one-way ticket, I was twenty years old and boarding a plane in Peshawar bound for Philadelphia. Two stops in between—a total traveling time of thirty-seven hours. When the plane went up, cutting through the wash of morning light, I thought of my family. It would be a long time before I saw them again. Before leaving, they'd all found their way into my room to help me pack my bag—the single tattered duffel that had shuttled my few possessions across Pakistan and all over South Asia. No one was sure what I would need, but just about everything I owned fit inside that bag. My sister, Ayesha, gave me a small envelope of photographs, my brother his copy of the Quran, the pages soft as silk. The twins went out into the street and found a pebble, slipped it into my palm, saying I should take a small piece of Pakistan for luck. My parents gave the thing I needed most of all—their blessing.

On the plane, I held that little bit of Pakistan hard in my hand. I felt as though I had jumped off a cliff and was simply falling through the air, hoping someone down there had a plan to catch me. My father had once told me all I needed to be happy was a squash racquet, but I knew on the cusp of my departure that I would need more than that.

The night before, the entire family sat around a small television set and watched a Bruce Lee movie that my father had brought home from the market. I don't remember the movie, but I recall my father's passion for the iconic martial artist. If Rocky Balboa was my fighting hero, Bruce Lee was his. Before the film, my father had told us that Bruce Lee had developed his own form of fighting called *Jeet Kune Do*—the way of the intercepting fist. When he came into my room, he was still talking about it, as though he hadn't slept all night and was simply going person to person, finding ears for his lecture. I wasn't in a state to listen; I wanted to say a proper farewell and knew he was filling that dwindling space with anything but the vocabulary of goodbye. I stopped him in mid-sentence. I remember that he was telling me how Bruce Lee had taken a steamship from Hong Kong to San Francisco with just one hundred dollars in his pocket and an aptitude for kung fu.

"After the tournament, Baba, where will I go? What will I do?"

"I've been trying to explain it. This is the best day of your life, not the worst. It is only the worst if you see it through a lens of fear. Bruce Lee called it having no limitation as a limitation."

"I am afraid, Baba."

"You will find your way, Maria, the way you always have. At four years old, all you needed were your brother's old clothes and a new name. Now all you need is a racquet. If you work hard, America will give you everything else."

*

Wilmington, Delaware, the first week of February—when I stepped outside without a jacket, the bitter wind walloped me. I remember that I had to hobble to a minivan, the door sliding open against the driving gusts. The happy, chattering sounds of other girls swirled all around me. International players at the tournament were put up in the homes of local squash club members, and the family I would stay with for three days was generous and kind and gave me a nice clean room. Looking back on those strange seventy-two hours, I'm sure they found me oddly quiet compared to my bubbly counterparts. They heated up their car until everyone else was sweating and unzipping coats, and still I shivered in the back as though I was sitting on a block of ice. I remember the father staring into his rearview mirror and asking several times if I was well. I nodded and breathed out a yes, but no one could have believed it. Everyone around me went silent when I spoke. The sound of my voice was so hollow, my words were practically lost in the air that carried them. The truth was, I'd never been more terrified.

At the tournament I fared poorly and was beaten in the first round by a German girl with the raw drive of a great white zeroing in on a kill. Before we even spun our racquets, she had me beat with the cool look in her eye. Back in my prime, she was just the kind of opponent I liked to toy with, send racing around the court like a mouse, tire out before a final scalping. I'd do it with a shrug and a smile, but now I could barely catch my breath. I wasn't going to be a contender in that tournament and everyone knew it, so they paid me little attention. When I lost the third game after a humiliating dusting, it all seemed inevitable. Up in the stands, a loser chugging lukewarm water, I looked down and felt my body sway. I was angry with myself for ever believing that I could find a way to just stay there and live. All I kept thinking was—*how?*

Ayesha had printed copies of my résumé and told me to hand one to every coach there. I also had a long list of government offices I could go to for assistance. All around me, I heard the muffled beats of racquets hitting balls, the reactions of the crowd. The air seemed to thicken by the second. I closed my eyes and listened to a fast rally play out in rapid beats. When I opened them again, the lights seemed to flicker, and I felt the floor fall away. A loud sound like thunder crashed in my ears, but no one else even flinched. Suddenly, as though a hand had come down and plucked me right out of the stands, I was back at the squash academy, looking over at my brother Babrak. I saw the whites of his eyes, heard the strange birdlike sound he made. Somewhere a bomb had just gone off. When I came to, I was at the tournament again. I saw the court, but could still smell the dank streets of Peshawar. In a moment, I keeled over and retched. My gut heaved and acid rose up my throat, but nothing came out. I dripped saliva to the dark gray floor. Head between my knees, temples pulsing, my skin burned as though I was sitting over open flames.

Soon people were surrounding me, offering water, offering words that had no meaning. As though it were a lifeline, I grabbed a gym towel from a generous hand and buried my face in it. I remember feeling shocked at what was happening. And it would happen again and again over the next two days—like a switch going off, my feet would lose the ground, my breath catching, heart thumping. I would fall away, mind and body lost in a maelstrom. Sometimes a voice or a hand on my shoulder would bring me out of it for a while. I thought I was going mad.

On the last day in Wilmington, I was sitting in the back row, trying to calm my mind and stake out a desperate plan. Deon Saffery, an English girl, had just beaten the Canadian Samantha Cornett. At the winning point, the audience stood up and cheers whirred around me. Nothing registered. My bag, sitting at my feet, let me know I was still there, and I was still breathing. I clung to those moments of peace until something set me off again. It could be anything—flickering lights, a loud shout, someone asking if I was all right. People were hurrying to leave. I just sat, immobilized. There was a dinner afterward, but I knew that I couldn't sit at a table with white cloths and folded napkins. I wouldn't be able to lift up a fork, eat a meal, and pretend that I was all right. I felt people moving and shifting all around. Part of me was desperate to call Pakistan. I had our neighbor's number and kept repeating it in my mind, knowing full well as I did that it was both a beacon and a bullet. Then, in the darkness of my closed eyes, a familiar scent rose like a specter: coriander, cumin, and a fine ribbon of sweet sandalwood—home. I looked up, expecting to find myself inside another dream. In a way, I did.

A gray-haired man in a dark woolen sweater was looking down at me. Right away, I knew him for what he was by his wide eyes and the sharp bones in his face. Then a smile, like a flare going up, and a Pashto greeting fell down into my pit of fear like a ladder back up into the safe world. Everyone called him Zia; but for the next two months, I would refer to him as Uncle. Someone in Wilmington had found a way to reach my parents back in Pakistan and had related the desperate state I was in. In no time, my father had the entire block at our house, looking for anyone who knew anyone in America. Suddenly, the man who did everything for everyone was calling in a favor. It turned out that one of our neighbors had an old Pashtun friend who lived in Charlotte, North Carolina. When the neighbor found a way to reach Zia and told him that there was a tribal girl stuck in Delaware needing help, he got straight into his car and drove more than four hundred miles to reach me. Uncle Zia was from our valley back in FATA, and he knew of my parents' good work in the region. He'd been living and working as a taxi driver in the United States for more than ten years. By the way he spoke to me about our home, as though reciting a cherished prayer, I knew I would find safe harbor in his.

Our Pashtunwali code is a wonderful living thing, a constitution by which my people have lived and thrived over generations and centuries. It has sheltered the good and the bad, but mostly it has kept the good alive. It was what made it possible for me to find family among my own, thousands of miles away from the ancient mountains where all of us were born. Uncle Zia helped me to pack up my few things in Delaware, and then we traveled more than ten hours back to his pleasant suburban house. Feeling protected under his wing, I slept most of the way in the passenger seat of his hatchback. Zia had five sons and two daughters, and they all lived in a large redbrick house in Charlotte. His wife made huge mounds of hot-spiced food for us, and we sat together on the floor over a big flowered sheet, eating.

Even there, tucked under the arm of my own people, uncertainty made chase. It woke me like a fist in the night, choked for breath, sheets coiled around my legs. Quietly, I wondered what I was going to do, how I'd ever find my way back to the squash circuit. I was trapped in a pleasant labyrinth with no way out.

What happened next doesn't seem quite real, even now. Uncle Zia showed me how to use his laptop so that I could check on the news back home and send emails. It had been weeks since I'd checked my mail. My family hardly ever used their shared account, but with me ensconced on the other side of the world, we had to change our ways. As soon as I logged in, my inbox flared. The latest message was simple: a phone number—the same one he has today. I remember turning to my uncle and calmly asking to use the telephone, though my heart was leaping. I don't know what I expected—dead air, laughter, or a busy signal that went on into oblivion. Standing by the kitchen window as a thin flurry of snow descended, I dialed and looked out. An upended deck chair on the patio made a bridge over the flagstones, under which a small bird sat huddled against the cold.

The ringtone at the other end stopped. Then I heard the voice and knew it was his. Back at the squash academy, I'd seen videos of his greatest matches—he often yelled at referees and later gave interviews, cool as a cucumber, to an admiring media. When Jonathon Power visited Pakistan, it was always national news— red carpets came out, dignitaries cleared their schedules, squash players everywhere held their racquets in reverence. Auburn-haired, hot-tempered, and tall, with a repertoire of trick shots that could fool lightning, he had a cocky curl to his lip when he spoke. I never thought a man like him would help a girl like me. But I was wrong.

"This is Maria Toorpakai Wazir. I apologize for my lateness."

I was holding on to the phone and holding on to myself as he talked. He sounded happy to hear from me; he sounded like he was in the next room. Based on that first email, exchanged before the dengue virus abducted my mind, Jonathon had gone to work on my behalf, making calls and hatching plans. I remember asking if he needed my résumé, not realizing he already had it.

Several times he broke out into a full laugh—it had been years since I'd heard anyone laugh with every part of themselves that way. Jonathon knew my country, understood its culture, understood the unfathomable miracle that a Pashtun girl was the national champion—was still alive in the dark time of the Taliban—and standing in a kitchen with nowhere to go in Charlotte, North Carolina. At the other end of the room, Uncle Zia leaned against the wall, listening. I could see his eyes jumping as he hushed the rest of the family. The children were skipping around the room, hands over their mouths, not knowing why, but trying not to laugh.

*

March 22, 2011. Another plane, another one-way ticket. Two hundred Canadian dollars that my parents sent via Western Union tucked into the envelope my mother had given me back in Peshawar, which I had used to keep Ayesha's gift of photographs. The envelope still had one of her old happy-face stickers stuck to it, the edges curling away. From time to time, I caressed it, reaching into my pocket with the other hand to touch the pebble. In my duffel bag was a small, smooth stone plucked from the cool stream right where I used to collect our daily water in FATA. All my talismans holding sentry, I thought of my mother's small chest of mementos—her own river stones, bangles, embroidered shoes, and a blue jean jacket frayed at the cuff—that she carted from place to place like a grail. Soon, a honey-voiced captain came over the intercom to announce our descent into Toronto, and I felt a light pull in my belly. Tightening my seat belt, I gazed out. Inclining through soft cloud, far below was a sheet of white without horizon. Patches of black lay scattered over the surface like giant puddles. Lake Ontario. I'd seen it on a map. As soon as Jonathon booked my ticket, I asked Uncle Zia for an atlas. Canada—a vast land nestled between oceans—was the second-largest country in the world. Somewhere down there was a small room that would be my own. Somewhere down there a world champion waited, and a nightmare spanning years started to lift as the plane touched down on the runway.

At every step after disembarking, I waited for someone to stop me. In line at customs, I was sure an official would pull me aside, send me back to Charlotte, and toss me back to Pakistan in shame like damaged goods. An officer stamped my visa and motioned as though it were nothing to a pair of frosted-glass double doors. I didn't have any baggage, just a racquet bag and the duffel, as I stepped out into the massive airport arcade. I remember that it was very bright, full of windows, and there were hordes of people waiting. Some held up signs, names written on them in black ink—Kaplan, Russo, Chang. I didn't see Toorpakai. All those people assembled outside the doors sent me into a whirlwind of panic—he might not be there; I might be in the wrong place. I followed the footsteps in front of me; the rolling suitcases; children lolling in strollers, their blankets dragging all the way down the gallery and outside into the cold. People were coming and going under the overhang—taxis and hotel shuttles—and I stood at the curb shivering.

Then I heard my name rise over the hum and turned to a smile coming toward me over a sea of heads. Feeling his eyes on me, eyes that I knew from pictures, I squinted, torrents of fear dissolving as though into a full sun.

The first thing Jonathon Power did was grab my bag and hoist it over his shoulder; he was talking the whole time, telling me where we were going—right to his squash academy, just as I'd asked. Walking barely a pace behind him, I had a quick chance to study the man—the icon. I could see the swells along his arm as he held my bag, which against his broad frame seemed diminished. My family pictures were in there, Taimur's Quran, my precious stone—all my simple treasures. Jonathon maneuvered through the crowd, lifted my old bag higher. His hand curled around the handles, the same way he held his racquet. Those very same appendages, moving less than a foot from me, had made that man the best in the world at our game—twice.

In the car, the air was warm, and Jonathon reached out and

turned the ignition. He was telling me about his academy, how I was precisely the kind of player they were looking for. Many weeks later, he would tell me that he was just as stunned as I was that I was actually there, sitting in his car. Out on the straight highway, snow fell and I thought of my father at home sitting in his chair, and then of everything that had led me there. I had my birth coin in my hands, tarnished on one side. Over the drone of the engine and the whistling wind, I heard my father say my three names in my ear—*Maria Gulgatai Toorpakai*. I remembered then what I was above all else: my father's daughter. I was a Wazir. Above all things, that meant not being afraid.

When we pulled into the National Squash Academy, snow was falling in heavy flakes and there weren't many other cars in the lot. Jonathon had built his state-of-the-art squash center out of an old aircraft hangar, and the massive structure loomed from the frozen ground. Trudging through drifts toward tall glass double doors, bits of ice melting into my eyes, I looked up and saw a towering ground to roof billboard in full color come to life. A man holding out a racquet in mid-shot, body electrified: a four-story giant leaping right out of the wall. I stopped and gazed at it, then looked over as the man in the flesh, dressed in a black parka, opened the door and waited for me.

Right away, we were inside a court, sitting on the polished floor, backs against the wall. We talked awhile inside his temple, our voices echoing, sharing a bag of chips back and forth between us. He told me that he'd spent years raising the money to build the academy. It was the fulfillment of a long-held ambition: to teach the next generation the game, find and coach new champions, help underprivileged kids get off the streets. When he talked to me, I thought of what my father had always said—"Give those drug-addicted Talibs a racquet, and they won't ever want a gun."

After we got to know each other a little, Jonathon tossed me a ball. If I was nervous, I labored not to show it. It was already obvious to him from the way I walked, with a slight hesitation, that I'd been through an ordeal. He already knew that I could play. Taking a good breath, I whispered a quick *sura* and sent the ball out. It kissed the back wall, and then I returned it again. Jonathon was poised at my side, a miracle I tried not to let distract me. From the get-go, he was giving out clear directions and coaching on the move.

"Shuffle, shuffle and snap. Go back. Now snap the ball, Maria. Go back. Shuffle. Snap the ball. Hit it hard. Show me what you've got in there."

And just like that, we were in a rhythm, like two people playing music. It was all so natural and so surreal. I was in a court in Canada. I was in a kitchen in Peshawar. I was holed up in a bedroom afraid to go out. I was in an overgrown field in the dead of night with my brother, playing the game I loved. I was with Jonathon Power. I was free.

When we'd played awhile, Jonathon caught the ball in his fist and told me he didn't want to tire me out the first day in. Right then, heart galloping, my limbs hot and pulsing from the exertions of those few exhilarating minutes, I asked the thing I'd wanted to know from my first hit—the one thing every professional athlete wants to know.

"How did you become a world champion?"

Jonathon shrugged and took a drink, his mouth rising to one side into the nonchalant grin that was his trademark. "One game and one country at a time."

"Do you think I can do it?"

Jonathon frowned. "When I saw you standing outside at the airport, I was a little concerned. Then I saw you hit just now, and I said to myself: *This girl has soft hands, soft hands and a hard hit.* That's really all you need. It's gotten you this far, right? From the sounds of it, you've gotten halfway around the world that way already."

I didn't know what he meant by the term "soft hands," and I asked him to clarify. Putting down his racquet, he came up to me, held open my palm, and pushed a ball into its warm center.

"You don't just take hits, you absorb them in your fist, suck up the power, make it yours, and shoot it right back. That's what we call having soft hands."

"Soft hands. I never knew that."

And I looked at the ball in my hand and gripped, feeling it against my skin. I thought back to everything that had gotten me to that moment, standing in a lit-up court across continents and oceans, winning against impossible odds, absorbing one hit after the other.

*

Ten months later, in January 2012, I was in Philadelphia for the Liberty Bell Open. After nearly a year of grueling training under Jonathon, it was my maiden tournament. I'd found my old body again, limber and strong, able to tiptoe around the courts, bewitching the ball. When Jonathon told me I was ready—I believed him.

From the start of the tournament, I was a curiosity and an underdog. I'd been there before, nearly everywhere I'd lived—in the valleys running wild as Genghis, in the alleys taking down enemies, in the weight room stacking up the plates with Taimur, and on the courts those first few weeks in Peshawar when I was Maria again. Even with Jonathon at my side, stopping to sign autographs, shake hands, and pose for pictures, they all thought I was going to lose—and maybe that's why I didn't.

In the qualifying rounds, I stampeded through four seeded players—from France, Japan, Canada, and the United States. I didn't stop there. There wasn't any choice: I had to make my mark, or it would all have been for nothing. Game after game, I tore right through my opponents, not giving them even a square inch of wiggle room. I went in and yanked out every hit, took it into my racquet, hurling the ball back in a wild zigzag, with Jonathon shouting to me over the frenzied crossfire, the squeal of my shoes, and the roar of the blood rushing through my veins. Later, the press would refer to it as a giant-killing spree—I took the title, winning every single game.

My trophy, which I accepted with so much joy I could hardly

speak, had the Liberty Bell engraved on it. Over and over again, his hand on my shoulder, Jonathon had to tell me to stop holding my breath. Back in my hotel room, I Skyped with my family back in Peshawar on the computer Jonathon had given me the week I arrived. I can still see how my father squinted forward when I held the trophy up to the screen, his face momentarily filling the frame and obscuring everyone behind him.

"Maria, just a twenty-minute walk across downtown Philadelphia from the Liberty Bell is the Rocky statue. Imagine that. I had Ayesha google it."

Then he held up an opened book that I recognized from the stacks he kept on the floor in our living room. The old American history tome had followed us from house to house and town to town, through the hellfire of Darra, whose dust still hid in its spine. An image hovered over the screen, and I was looking at a sepia-toned photograph of the cracked Liberty Bell, the tips of my father's fingers holding back the page. Then his voice boomed behind it. My father didn't need to read the words, he'd long had each one memorized—and I was sitting there living them.

"Listen to this, all of you. Don't make a sound: 'Proclaim liberty throughout all the land unto all the inhabitants thereof.'"

The trophy was still in my hands. I couldn't let go of it. "I don't know how I got to this land, Baba, but those words came true."

My father let the book fall, and a tiny plume of dust went up against the screen. Through it I could see his big smile and, through the darkness of another blackout, the joined forms of my family silhouetted behind him. Their battery was running low. I reached out then and caressed the screen.

When he spoke, my father had no idea I was touching his face, or that I might not see him in the flesh again for years. I might not see him at all if the Taliban got hold of him—or any of them.

"It was simple combustion, Maria. You found that bottle of kerosene and struck a match."

Epilogue: One Thousand Marias

When my hard-won liberty was still new, I kept track of it in simple everyday acts—each one a marvel: taking the subway, buying T-shirts, trying on a pair of designer jeans, learning to play guitar, riding a bike through snow. For the first time, I had roommates of all races and creeds that I came to know as friends. We shared meals, a bathroom, utility bills, practical jokes, and a pet cat. We shared dreams, both small and lofty—I wanted to get a driver's license, go to high school, take acting classes, star one day in a Hollywood movie. On weekends, I often went to the movies, perused bookstores, ate fast food. In October, I carved my first pumpkin, dressed up as a witch for Halloween. On one of many explorations of Toronto, I discovered an art supply store, bought an easel, brushes, blocks of canvas, and started to paint. Whenever I wanted, I listened to music—loud—watched television, danced, thumbed through a magazine, rolled out my mother's silk mat and prayed. In those early days, I prayed a lot: *Alhamdulillah*, to thank my God for writing the word freedom into my fate. When I was finished, I thought of my family and of every person who had helped me along the way and I just bowed to the ground saying one thing—*merabani*, thank you—again and again and to them all. Every morning, I took the public bus, stood among the bleary-eyed commuters, all of us one and the same. Most days, I met Jonathon Power at the National Squash Academy, where he always greeted me with a high five before we went together into a court.

When I first came to Jonathon, I was but half a person, a

dying champion whose destiny was slipping away in tandem with her mind. He worked me hard and, in less than half a year, made me whole again. When I needed something, he knew it and quietly gave—a cell phone, a computer to reach home, words of encouragement, a hand on my back. Most of all, the space and time to heal, then the chance to win again against all conceivable odds. He provided doctors and therapists, a clean place to live, and a job—a second life. Over time, as we sat in the courts between drills, he learned about my first life in Pakistan, never prodding. Uncertain, I doled details out to him in small morsels. We talked about our mutual drive to win, what it really meant, and found our common ground. At first it had been about the accolades and later, when there had been more than enough of those, it grew into something greater than any accumulation of spellbinding wins, or even ourselves. At some point, we looked at each other across that polished court floor and realized the magnitude of what had happened between us. All the way back in Peshawar, I'd jumped off that cliff with nothing more than my racquet in hand, and he'd reached out and caught me. There was no trophy in the world that could compare to the miracle of that simple act—replying to one desperate email and binding us together, win or lose, in friendship for life.

*

Nearly two years after I landed in North America, The Economic Club of Canada secured a visa for my sister to fly to Toronto for a two-week visit. Months before her trip, on May 11, 2013, Ayesha had been elected to the National Assembly, representing the Pakistan Movement for Justice, and became the first female parliamentarian ever elected from the tribal regions. Right away, she was the target of extremists. It was only when I walked the city streets with Ayesha that I saw my freedom again, in all its glory, through the timidity of her white veil and wide eyes. Often, we just went out for no reason at all, so she could feel what for me had become so casual—the power to just go where I wanted, without a male companion, dressed however I pleased, five earrings in one ear—not a single sniper in sight. It took her days to break the habit of always looking over her shoulder, checking passers-by for the extra padding of a suicide vest. Before leaving for the airport, she told me that the experience of full autonomy, more than any other, despite all she'd accomplished at school with her degrees and political career, had changed her. Upon her return to Pakistan, the glow from our visit still all over her, she called me on Skype.

"Our time together gave me the one thing I needed to do my job well, Maria, more than any other. Even now, when I look at you, I see it. You have actually become that thing."

"What was it?"

"*Hila*—hope—that's you."

*

After Ayesha took the reins of office, my father gave up teaching to further her mandate of building a modern state based on the rights and welfare of each and every individual. In the morning he drives himself into FATA to find out what the region most desperately needs—everything from medical doctors to sewing machines or seeds—and brings back lists for his daughter to fulfill. Not long after, Taimur started doing his part and joined a non-governmental organization (NGO) providing charitable services across the country. The twins are studying at university. Babrak continues to play squash and has started competing in international tournaments, and Sangeen plays varsity tennis. My mother, the bravest of us all, wakes up each dawn with more threats against her now than any of us ever had. She continues to run schools, though most have been bombed to rubble, and her *burqa*-cloaked trips into the tribal belt are now few and far between. With two tribal daughters out in the public domain, defying the Taliban—one in government on their doorstep, the other playing squash and making speeches in the infidel West—she is considered a malignancy. On any given day, she can be found at the kitchen table, grading papers or going over maps, scouting new locations for schools. Even colleagues at the education board have begged her to seek a transfer into a safer district, fearing that a gunman will walk up to her any day and open fire. She says she isn't afraid. Girls out there still need schools. They need sports fields. They need her. "This is my life's work, Maria. I am not afraid. It is written."

*

Not long after I arrived in Toronto, still somewhat disheveled, Jonathon settled into my seat and took a turn on Skype with my father. They spoke for a long while, laughing together in no time as though they were long-lost friends meeting again in the ether—6,700 miles of Earth between them. Before saying good-bye and closing his screen, my father looked out through the darkness, a single light shining over his tired face, and told Jonathon: "My precious daughter is now your daughter. Our job here is done." I thought my new coach, mercurial legend that he was, would be taken aback by the statement. It was a heightened responsibility he might not want. After all, he and I were just squash players—a master and a protégé.

Unflinching, Jonathon only smiled. I could see him in the periphery, his skin tinged blue before the screen, and he lowered his head, nodding.

"*Merabani*—thank you."

Right then, more than at any other time, I knew I was all right. And I was overcome with gratitude.

After that, becoming world champion meant more than winning at a game—that ambition transmuted into a new way of life and purpose. Soon, I started making speeches, getting my feet wet in small local venues. At first, standing up onstage under the hot glare of spotlights was terrifying, and I wasn't sure that what I had to say would matter to a soul. Then, the more I met with people from around North America, and saw my story unfold through their eyes, I began to realize that my journey, and all its minute details, wasn't singular at all. I was only one girl with a racquet—and a lot of luck.

The night I won the Liberty Bell tournament, the last thing my father said to me before we signed out of Skype has become the mantra through which I map every day and my entire future.

"Behind you, waiting alone in the dark, are one thousand Marias."

My dreams are for them.

Acknowledgments

Maria Toorpakai:

I am grateful first and foremost to my whole family, who have always accepted me for who I am. My parents risked everything so that their children could receive a genuine education and reach their dreams. I am privileged to have a father who not only respected my individuality as a girl, but also gave me the courage to express myself and relentlessly pursue my own freedom; and a mother, who in giving hope to thousands of oppressed girls across the tribal regions, is my great inspiration. My wise and beautiful sister, Ayesha, is not far behind her. Above all, I am nothing without my parents.

So many people have made my long journey to freedom possible. I am fortunate to have the steadfast support of my coach, mentor and friend, double world champion, Jonathon Power, who makes every single day a living miracle.

I would also like to thank everyone at the National Squash Academy (NSA) in Toronto, Canada, for their daily encouragement. You have all become my second family. In particular, Karen Knowles, Jamie Nicholls, Gary Slaight and the Gary Waite family. You all have my heartfelt gratitude. Thanks also to my fitness trainers Bob Bowers and Hajnal Laszlo. And a great thanks to S. Kristin Kim, Rhiannon Trail, Julie Mitchell, and to Cathy Eu who has worked selflessly supporting my dream to empower other young women to follow their dreams.

The coaches and individuals who have enriched my life and game deserve particular mention: Air Vice Marshal Inamullah

Khan (Pakistan), and Wing Commander Pervaiz Syed Mir (Pakistan). Rahim Gul (National coach for the women's team of Pakistan, 2003), who my father always refers to as "good", will never be forgotten for his many acts of kindness. The generous and in many ways life-saving Zia-ur-Rehman family (North Carolina), as well as Tanveer Khan and Meher Khan (Philadelphia), Sami Kureishy and Romeena Kureishy (Philadelphia).

I am also appreciative of every squash player from around the world whom I have ever competed against. Win or lose, our shared passion for sport unites us all. If more people picked up a racquet as we do, fewer would reach for a gun. And a thank you to the many who tried relentlessly to stop me from playing and living as I am, for making me stronger and giving me a louder voice with which to reach all the girls I left behind.

Many thanks also go to my people in FATA, across Pakistan and the entire globe for their unwavering support and encouragement.

The staff and doctors at the hospital in Kuala Lumpur whose names I never learned were extraordinary. You brought me back from the brink of death and never charged my family a single rupee. Also in Malaysia, I am grateful for the kindness and generosity of Umehani and Dr. Saadat Ullah Khan.

I'd like to give Cassandra Sanford-Rosenthal a heartfelt thanks for helping me share my journey with others and managing the full spectrum of my career outside of squash. I am also fortunate to have Meg Thompson as a literary agent, along with her colleagues, Elizabeth Levin and Sandy Hodgman (foreign rights), at the Thompson Literary Agency. Because of their attention and commitment to this project and others, I have been able to concentrate fully on my sport. Also to a team of champion editors who believed in this story: Libby Burton at (TWELVE/Hachette), who was there right at the start. Thanks as well to Carole Tonkinson (Bluebird/Pan Macmillan, U.K.) for her great insight. And to Nick Garrison, Associate Publisher at Penguin Canada, who was wonderfully enthusiastic.

Also on the book, a very special thank you to Katharine, for making my dreams her own and somehow turning them into these beautiful pages. You brought such patience, tireless skill and positive energy to your work. It simply amazed us. Above all, you understood.

More than anything, I would like to thank the peace-loving people of Canada, for welcoming me into their beautiful nation and making it a safe home away from home.

Katharine Holstein:

First, I'm grateful to Alexander Holstein, fellow scribe and an unfathomable genius, for calling Jonathon Power and saying: you need to talk to Kate right now about writing the book—and then for encouraging me all those months when the toil took over. It worked! And I thank Jonathon for saying: OK.

The team at Twelve/Hachette have been amazing, especially my exceptional editor, Libby Burton, who led me to huge rooms in my own brain that I didn't even know were there. And to Rick Ball whose copyediting skills are simply spellbinding. And across the ocean, thank you to editor, Carole Tonkinson, at Bluebird/Pan Macmillan for adding her own extraordinary brand of magic. I must also acknowledge Nick Garrison, associate publisher at Penguin, Canada, who was among the very first to get behind the book.

Thank you, to my agent, Marcy Posner, at Folio Literary Management. You take care of the good, bad and ugly with amazing charisma so that I can just hunker down and write. I must acknowledge the assistance of Scott Hoffman, also at Folio.

I am profoundly grateful for the generous love and support of my mother and father, who contributed to my work in innumerable ways, and made so much possible. And thank you to my fine big brother, John, who has always been my rock.

Many thanks to the families and people who enrich my life and career; Trevor and Hilary, Cristiano and Jane, Eddie and Maggie, Jasmin and Julian, Lesley and Ian; also to the Fyalls, Hayeks, Greens, and Boyles; Alex Van Wey, Mike Williams, Eli Campbell, Dr. P. Thibault, Dr. A.E. Brown, and "Nana".

I could never have finished this project without the boundless generosity of Matthew, Avery, and Eden. A particular thank you to Kalen Kennedy at whose IKEA desk these pages came to life. You always made me welcome.

My heartfelt gratitude to the people of Pakistan, a country that I have come to love. So many of you helped me to find my way to the end. My gratitude goes especially to Maria's father, Shams, and her sister, Ayesha, for the time we spent together. In an instant, your warmth bridged the world between us.

Above all others, to my treasure—my children. Thank you for enduring my many long absences with such love and patience. Your smiles alone make me the richest woman on earth.

And finally, *merabani*, lovely Maria, for giving me the thread from which to weave the tapestry of your life. Our time together was a gift.

About the Authors

Maria Toorpakai is a professional squash player, currently ranked as Pakistan's top female player and in the top fifty in the world. As a child growing up in a highly conservative tribal area of Pakistan, where girls' involvement in sport was forbidden by the local Islamic culture, Toorpakai trained and competed as a boy. Toorpakai currently resides and trains in Toronto, Canada, under former two-time world champion squash player Jonathon Power. Toorpakai is the sister of Ayesha Gulalai, who is a member of the National Assembly representing Pakistan Tehreek-e-Insaf on a reserved seat for women.

Katharine Holstein has lived throughout Europe and North America. Working with actors, personalities and producers, she develops and creates original material for both print and screen. Her writing has sold around the world.

A Letter about the Maria Toorpakai Fund

Dear reader,

The book that you hold in your hands is more than the story of my struggle to live life and play my sport in peace. Through it, I am raising my voice on behalf of the millions of "Marias" I left behind, who remain the hostages of regimes and ideologies that have stripped them of their most basic human rights. My own fight for freedom has made me feel the distress of so many— men, women, and children alike, all ravaged by war and unimaginable cruelty. Lighting their dark path to peace has become my purpose. When I fled the Taliban with no more than a squash racquet and my every worldly possession stuffed into a small duffel bag, I made a promise to one day ignite hope in the hearts of the forgotten. Now I pledge to provide the tools that foster freedom and build a lasting peace.

I founded the Maria Toorpakai Fund to empower those oppressed citizens of inhumanity, because I was once one of them. If I went back home tomorrow, I would be again. Every person, regardless of gender, race or creed, once given the right opportunity, has the power to reach their maximum potential, transform their communities and become an agent for peace—but they can't possibly do it alone

The Maria Toorpakai Fund invests in state-of-the-art schools that provide quality education; provides funding for up-to-date technology and skill development, as well as resources for local businesses to bolster employment; and will be a driving force in the development of modern athletic facilities. All of our work will begin in local communities where support is most urgently needed.

We seek innovative solutions to the age-old problem of rebuilding human lives after the ravages of warfare and brutality have made scarce simple resources like paper, pencils, books—and sports equipment. To create real opportunity requires real investment that empowers individuals—this is our mandate. My father, Shams, once said: "Give more people a racquet or a pen, and they won't pick up a gun." I know for a fact that this is true.

I hope you will join my team and shine a bright light on freedom. Serving humanity is the noblest cause of all.

Become a Maria teammate and find out more at
MariaToorpakai.org

Thank you,

Maria Toorpakai Wazir

Professional Squash Player